Frankfurter
and
Due Process

Richard G. Stevens

UNIVERSITY
PRESS OF
AMERICA

LANHAM • NEW YORK • LONDON

Copyright © 1987 by

University Press of America,® Inc.

4720 Boston Way
Lanham, MD 20706

3 Henrietta Street
London WC2E 8LU England

Printed in the United States of America

British Cataloging in Publication Information Available

Library of Congress Cataloging-in-Publication Data

Stevens, Richard G., 1925-
   Frankfurter and due process.

   Bibliography: p.
   Includes index.
   1. Due process of law—United States.   2. Frankfurter,
Felix, 1882-1965.   I. Title.
KF4765.S74   1987   374.73   87-10881
ISBN 0-8191-5615-9 (alk. paper)   347.307
ISBN 0-8191-5616-7 (pbk. : alk. paper)

To my wife.

Table of Contents

Acknowledgments

This was a doctoral dissertation and had the doctorally ponderous title of "Reason and History in Judicial Judgment: Mr. Justice Frankfurter's Treatment of Due Process." The work was done under the supervision of the late Leo Strauss, Chairman of the committee, C. Herman Pritchett, and the late Herbert Storing. Herman Pritchett excited my interest in the law. He was and still is a splendid teacher. Herbert Storing, although a few years younger than I, was professionally ahead of me and was brought into my dissertation committee after I was well along with the work. Those who have a better claim than I to having been his students can attest to his wisdom and generosity. He *lavished* criticism on the drafts I submitted and helped me greatly. It is, however, no disservice to Herman or to the memory of Herb to acknowledge that Leo Strauss was the towering intellect of the political science profession, a teacher absolutely without equal, and the guiding force of my intellectual life as of hundreds of others. To these, my teachers, I owe my profound gratitude.

As a young professor with a wife and three children to support on a $5,000 a year salary, summer teaching was essential. That, along with a 12-hour teaching load during the regular academic year made time for research scarce. The Southern Fellowships Fund helped me through one summer and the Faculty Research Fund of the College of William and Mary helped me through another. More recently, the Earhart Foundation and the Institute for Educational Affairs provided support in aid of the preparation of this manuscript. I am glad to express my gratitude to these four funds and to the Carnegie Foundation, the Harvard Law School and the National Endowment for the Humanities.

I owe thanks also to Morton J. Frisch, my good friend for nearly the whole of my academic life and to the memory of Martin Diamond who was my friend and was also my teacher in all but the institutional sense of the word.

In an age when drivers pump their own gasoline and authors drop "camera-ready copy" off at their publishers' doors, the one and the other often put their hands into things from which they were once shielded. Eagle One Graphics typeset the manuscript. I went through the result and then Philip Costopoulos and Susan Walters went over it again, and I thank them. I thought it was all done, and as the time for my going overseas for a year drew near, I left the "last minute" things to someone else. These proved to require hundreds of hours of labor and the application of keen editorial skills. My great thanks go to Scott Walter, but I see no way to thank adequately Michael P. Jackson who had the skills and who, from devoted friendship, made the time.

Introduction

A century ago an influential author said of a book which was being published more than twenty years after it had been written that it had been subjected during the interim to the "gnawing criticism of the mice."[1] Like that one, this book has lain for over twenty years protected from scholarly criticism. Even so, I have changed my mind a little about the matter it treats. In 1971, Morton Frisch and I edited a volume of essays on American political thought.[2] The last of those essays was on Felix Frankfurter. A reader remarked that it was a "powerful attack" on Frankfurter. I had not really intended it as such. Frisch and I recently brought out a second edition of that book[3] and we elected to leave all the original chapters unchanged, but if I had changed my chapter on Frankfurter, I would have done so simply by adding an opening sentence to the effect that I thought Frankfurter was the best of the twentieth century justices, but still not good enough.

I have elected not to alter this book, but to leave it as I completed it in the fall of 1962 and to offer here, in an introduction, such changes as have occurred in my thoughts, drawing on a series of articles recently or just about to be published. If I *were* to rewrite the original manuscript, I would make only two changes. First of all, I would add a sentence here and there to make sure that my high opinion of Frankfurter was not obscured by the strength of the criticism. Secondly, the criticism itself would be stronger. Frankfurter had said early in his career that the due process clauses ought to come out of the Constitution.[4] Later, on the bench, he accommodated himself to the fact of their being in the Constitution by trying to *limit* the content of due process. I now believe that his efforts to do so were built on sand. Content, any content at all, adds up to substance and invites the development of some brand of substantive due process. Substantive due process is simply self-contradictory. The notion that any taking of some liberty, whether it be freedom of contract or

ix

freedom of speech, is a violation of due process is evidently contrary to the clear corollary of the due process prohibition, namely, that liberty—any liberty and all liberty, *may* be taken if it is taken by due process. It will be useful here to offer a few autobiographical sentences to explain why my neck has stiffened on the matter of the content of due process.

I began my academic career teaching Constitutional Law. The judges seemed to be the great guides in the field. It seemed that one truly learned about the Constitution by reading more and more Supreme Court opinions. Fortuitously, I drifted into my other primary field, political philosophy, and for about ten years taught no Constitutional Law. I was free from the breathtaking addiction to the cases. When I came back to the study of the Constitution it was with a fresh point of view. This had two aspects. First, I was simply free, a free inquirer; I was no longer a thrall of the system. Second, I had not only been teaching *The Federalist* over and over, but I had been teaching Machiavelli and Hobbes and Locke repeatedly. Not to speak of the others, I developed a devoted appreciation of the monumental genius of Hobbes. From this came a flood of appreciation for the relative merit of the modern political order and, in time, a reverent awe of the comprehensive, the architectonic, genius of the Founders. What a Constitution! From this vantage I looked again at the cases and I became angry with the lawyers for pulling that Constitution apart as a puppy a shoe, with the judges for the damned incest of their intellects, with the political scientists for their trivialization of the great questions of politics, with the historians for their condescension regarding the past, and with all of them for their indulgence in what I have come to call "Gloryspeak."

From this fresh vantage I looked again at due process. Let me, by quoting at length from recent articles, indicate the view of due process to which I have come.

In a lecture to a Knox College symposium for high school teachers in June of 1985 which will shortly be published under the title "Politics, Economics and Religion in the Constitution,"[5] I made the following argument:

Hobbes reconciled everything to politics. In the Hobbesian scheme we move from perfect, individual freedom in the state of nature, where everyone has a right to everything (even to one another's bodies) but where no one has a *proper* right to anything, to a state of perfect subordination in civil society, perfect subjection to a sovereign. . . .

Without departing from the Hobbesian base, Locke sets us on the right path. *In principle,* Locke's underlying scheme does not differ much from that of Hobbes. In Locke as in Hobbes we move in principle from perfect freedom in the state of nature to near perfect subjection in civil society. The great contribution of Locke is that he provides the elements of a regime which, *in practice,* will exercise with moderation its dominion over those utterly subject to it, and he does this in such a way as to encourage constant and widespread demand for such moderation.

Perfect subjection to moderate government is the happiest solution. It allows a subordination of religion and economics to politics which is calculated to give to religion and economics the greatest freedom consistent with order. Perfect subjection to moderate government must be what Publius had in mind when he said in *Federalist* #51 that in "framing a government which is to be administered by men over men . . . you must first enable the government to control the governed; and in the next place oblige it to control itself."

The American Constitution is the completion, the perfection, of that movement toward moderation begun by Locke. It reconciles politics, economics and religion and I emphasize that it is the *original* Constitution, the unamended Constitution, the Constitution without a Bill of Rights that does this. . . .

It was Locke, of course, who legitimated the notion of near-absolute rights to property.[6] He had to contend with the traditional view, and particularly the traditional, Christian view that God had given all good things to men *in common*. That traditional view looked upon the vigorous pursuit of wealth as wrong. Locke easily admits that God gave all things to men in common but he shows that this providence of God is worth *nothing* to man until men appropriate, that is to say make *proper* to themselves, that is to say make a *property* in, things. For Locke labor, and particularly the labor of first taking, is the justification in nature for private property. By easy stages he shows that labor is worth ten times, no 100 times, no 1200 times, well, would you believe 1000 times, the miserly providence of God. God stints. It is man who is munificent. His munificence consists in his greatly increasing, by his labors, the stock of good things given by God, or by nature, thereby improving the lot of all. But a man will only labor if he has a property in the things he produces, and if that property is secure. It is not charity grounded in penury, but confident selfishness which relieves man's estate.

That confidence can only come from the security of property rights. Locke therefore teaches that the rights of property, which originate in nature, are truly secure in civil society because society *protects* one's property against the unlawful attempts of others and because it may not, itself, *take* one's property without his consent. But this is evidently silly. What sort of society would it be in which only those paid taxes who chose to do so? That problem is solved quickly, if a little darkly, by Locke. What he *means* when he says that one's property may not be taken without his consent is that property may not be taken from anyone without the consent of the *majority*,[7] but this only solves one problem to create another. What if one is in the minority? What is to prevent an overbearing majority from, say, taxing the top 5% of incomes at 95% and the remaining 95% at 5%? The more pronounced the division between rich and poor the more likely is this to happen. Can this be said to be the taking of property with one's own consent?

Locke's solution to the problems raised by near-perfect subjection to civil society is excellent but insufficient. The solution, simply stated, is that if the legislative power is vested in a *large* body, an assembly, as opposed to a single sovereign as Hobbes had preferred, and if the legislators serve for terms, rather than for life, and if the laws they pass apply to themselves in full force, and if they are applied not *by* themselves, but by a separate executive, the probability of such legislators passing laws injurious to themselves is relatively small.[8] Indeed it is small, but more is needed if the depredations of an interested and overbearing majority are to be avoided.

By completing and perfecting Locke, the United States Constitution stands as the archetype of the modern, liberal, democratic political community. It is the model of the limited, the constitutional government. It achieves limited government not by bringing limitations in from outside, for to do that would be to violate the principles of *republican* government, government grounded in the people at large. . . .

To yield, and to let virtue rule is to deny emphatically the principle of the Constitution. Perhaps that states the matter too strongly. Indeed, *freedom* and *justice* are the bottom principles of the American Constitution, but lofty as these aims are, the Constitution is unwilling to pursue them without a proper regard to means. Pursuit of the ends without regard to the means is morally and politically suicidal. . . . Single-minded insistence on freedom accepts the autonomy or supremacy of economics or religion and puts men back into that condition of mere nature which Hobbes described as a war of every man against every man where life is solitary, poor, nasty, brutish, and short. Single-minded insistence on justice might be all right, supposing there were no question about what it *is*, except that even the wisest and justest of rulers is subject to falling into a rage or of yielding to interest and, in any case, is altogether vulnerable when it comes to the problem of succession. As *Federalist* #10 puts it, to "secure the public good and private rights . . . and at the same time to preserve the spirit and the form of popular government, is . . . the great object" of the Constitution.

When *Federalist* #51 says that no government would be necessary if men were angels it speaks of perfect freedom. When it goes on to say that no control on government would be necessary if angels governed it speaks of perfect justice. But we have to face the fact that we can never hope for anything better than men governing men. It is easy to recite this fact like a catechism but we seem not to be able in great numbers to order our minds and our actions in accord with these things. They slip away from our minds.

I wish we could have a resurgence of Fourth of July oratory. But there is something else that *has* managed to survive, something which at a quick glance might look like the Fourth of July oratory whose passing I lament. That something else is what I call "Gloryspeak."

According to Gloryspeak there has been a single, straightforward progress for humanity from subjection to freedom. The difference between Gloryspeak and the Declaration of Independence is precisely that the Declaration believes such progress toward freedom is *not* merely incremental but depends altogether on a decisive break in the history of thought. It depends on the acknowledgement of the *principles* of the Declaration itself. The vital thing to remember about the Declaration and the Constitution is that they are *not* simply extensions of the wonders of English free government. America is, indeed, deeply indebted to England. Hamilton, who was perhaps the clearest-sighted of the Founders, freely and unstintingly acknowledges that debt. But America is even more indebted to two Englishmen—Hobbes and Locke—than to England. The Declaration and the Constitution are based on that debt. Together, those two documents constitute a deliberate, a profound, a fundamental and a radical break with England. It is a break grounded in principle, in doctrine.

According to Gloryspeak, the progress of liberty is the consequence of ringing declamations of a chain of hero-orators and fearless judges. Great moments in that progress are called to mind: Magna Charta, the Petition of Right, the Bill of Rights. We forget that Magna Charta is a *Parliamentary* action and is no check at all on Parliament which is, as Bagehot and Dicey and many others have shown us, *omnipotent*. We forget also, that Magna Charta is *not* a declaration of the natural rights of man but merely a declaration of the *feudal* rights of a *class* of men. We further forget that Magna Charta is a claim made against a ruler whose legitimacy is altogether denied by the principles of the Declaration and Constitution and not against a government professedly founded upon the power of the people which foundation is grounded in a higher claim to right—natural right—than the feudal claims underpinning Magna Charta. And we forget that Parliament, that omnipotent Parliament, has in the last 770 years repealed or greatly modified all but three or four sentences of Magna Charta!

Most of all, we forget that in a government professedly founded upon the rights of the people, human freedom is preserved and the public and private realms reconciled not by glorious declamations and not by government-crippling provisos, but by the proper *structure* of government leading to what Publius, in *Federalist* #51, assures us are results which would "seldom take place on any other principles than those of justice and the general good." The promise that the rightly formed government's acts will "seldom" depart from "justice and the general good" is thin soup to those nurtured on

Gloryspeak. They want absolute justice—that is, understood as perfect freedom of the individual against government—and they want absolutely the general good—that is, understood as the clear power of the government to crush "special interests" (as though any of us were without special interests). Those nurtured on Gloryspeak fail to see the tension between their extravagant demands for liberty and their extravagant demands for justice. They therefore fail to see the solution—the reconciliation.

It is not the Gloryspeakers of our history, such as Patrick Henry, who have done the most for human freedom. It is rather the steady, the clear-sighted ones, like Hamilton, to whom we are most indebted. As Hamilton reminded us in *Federalist* #1, "a dangerous ambition more often lurks behind the specious mask of zeal for the rights of the people than under the forbidding appearance of zeal for the firmness and efficiency of government." Gloryspeak has the advantage. It will always be more appealing to popular sentiment and the great weakness of popular government is that it is always subject to being led by sentiment into self-destructive acts.

Federalist #10 and #51 show well how the American Constitution completes and perfects for practical application the theoretical principles laid out by Locke. Locke had called for an assembly of fairly large size, composed of members serving terms, making laws which applied to themselves and which were applied not by themselves but by others. Building on this, the American Constitution adds these features: First, *all* government is through representatives. We do not have and we do not want what was so enticingly billed during the 60's and 70's as "participatory democracy." We don't want it because the likelihood of an interested and overbearing majority imposing its injustices on the minority is much greater if the multitude acts directly. Second, we have perfected the separation of powers and particulary the independence of the judiciary. The primary separation is between executive and legislative, but Locke still treated the judicial branch as a facet of executive power. Albert Venn Dicey explains that our independent judges are part of a separation of powers which is made *necessary* by our written Constitution which, in turn, is made necessary by our so-called federalism.[9] These are the third and the fourth contributions by the American Constitution—it is *written* and it therefore truly stands *above* the ordinary legislative process, and it establishes a novel relationship between the central and the local governments to which we have applied, somewhat misleadingly, the old label "federal."

Linked to, but distinct from, our novel, quasi-federal scheme is the Constitution's greatest contribution. We have the very first *large* republic. But, as the late Martin Diamond pointed out, it is not only *large*, but it is varied.[10] It is varied because it is a country devoted to commerce. That commerce not only leads to prosperity, as Locke was sure it would, but it also leads to that great variety of interests which makes democracy safe for the country.

In a large, commercial republic, a representative legislature of substantial size, constrained by a written Constitution, subject to its own laws, opposed by a vigorous and independent executive and monitored by a vigorous and independent judiciary, will ever so seldom form itself up into an overbearing majority dominated by a single, factious interest acting in a way prejudicial to justice and the general good.

If that still does not sound like enough, you have come to the wrong planet.

***

In a second lecture to the Knox College symposium, to be published under the title "Politics and Liberty in the Constitution,"[11] I continued my argument on the relation between public and private things in the American Constitutional order in the following way:

In *Federalist* #51, Madison suggested that the security of freedom and justice depended in the first place on the people, but he went on to say that "experience has taught mankind the necessity of auxiliary precautions." He had in mind structural things such as the separation of powers, but he surely would have allowed the idea of a bill of rights, enforced by an independent judiciary, as just such an auxiliary precaution. Indeed, it was he who shepherded the bill of rights through the proposal stage in the House of Representatives in the fall of 1789, in the First Congress.

The Bill of Rights, however, is the very focal point of Gloryspeak. The Constitution is, wrongly, said to be the product of constitutional *law*. Constitutional *law* is decided by *courts* in adversarial proceedings. In those proceedings, the Constitution is torn to shreds, by lawyers who care *nothing* for the Constitution but who snatch this or that clause from it. In fact, if you ask a lawyer about the Constitution, he never talks about *it*; he talks about the *amendments*, as though the amendments *were* the Constitution. They are *not*. They are *amendments*, and can only be understood as such by understanding the thing amended, the Constitution, in its unamended state.

Notice, for example, that the Constitution grants certain powers to the United States, but that it nowhere grants any powers to the states! That is easily explained. Each state gets *its* power from *its* people. The United States gets its power from the whole people of the United States. But notice that there *are* restraints in the national Constitution both upon the United States *and* upon the several states.

Are the states forbidden to pass laws impairing the obligations of contracts because such laws are intrinsically bad? If so, how is it that Article I, Section 9 does not forbid the *United States* to pass such laws? Are the states then simply forbidden to pass such laws because, as in the case of foreign affairs it is important not to let them interfere with the Constitutional exercise of such a power by the United States? This seems too extravagant a suggestion and certainly there is no such power explicitly vested by the Constitution in the United States.

The true answer is clear. Laws impairing the obligations of contracts are what we call "debtor legislation." It was just such legislation in some of the states that was a major cause of the calling of the convention that framed the Constitution. The Constitution forbids the states to cancel debts because, the states being small, the possibility that an unjust majority faction might unnecessarily pass such laws is very great. But the large, commercial republic of the United States as a whole is variegated enough such that its legislature would not likely pass such laws for light and transient reasons, but *in extremis*, such laws might be necessary. The salvation of the country might depend on such laws. The most foolish thing we could do would be to write a Constitution which categorically forbids the government to do what might, in an extreme case, be essential.

The Constitution does not, then, give absolute protection to property rights, the public good be damned. The protection of property rights, as of all rights, depends on what *Federalist #*10 calls the "extent and proper structure of the Union."

In the light of all this, look again at the Constitution. How many things does the Constitution *utterly* forbid government to do? The list is very, very short—only 2 or 3 things. Partly because of this there was a demand for a bill of rights—or a demand for something, for amendments. The first Congress proposed twelve amendments, ten of which were ratified. This ratification was completed in 1791. The First protects religion, speech, press, assembly, and petition. The Second and Third concern the militia and the quartering of troops. The Fourth, Fifth, Sixth, Seventh and Eighth largely protect the rights of the accused. And the Ninth and the Tenth offer some general formulations on rights.

In 1833, forty some years afterward, the case of *Barron* v. *Baltimore*[12] considered one aspect of the Fifth Amendment. Baltimore had diverted some streams of water, causing a build-up of silt next to Barron's wharf, making the water too shallow to accommodate the larger ships that had previously docked there. Barron claimed that this, in effect, took his property away—took his property for public use without just compensation—which was contrary to the Fifth Amendment which ends by saying "nor shall private property be taken for public use without just compensation."

Chief Justice Marshall dealt summarily and decisively with Barron's claim. He showed that the whole *intention* of the first ten amendments had been a protection of the individual from action by the United States, *not* a general protection against *any* government. He did this by reference to the history of the adoption of the amendments but also by a careful, internal examination of the amendments themselves.

Except for the First Amendment, which specifies *Congress* as the body which may not touch religion or abridge speech, press, assembly or petition, all of the amendments speak in the passive voice. The Fifth Amendment simply says private property may not be taken without compensation. It does not say *who* may not take it. Marshall shows that, since the whole Constitution is a constitution not of *all* governments in the United States but only of the United States itself, all language in general terms in the Constitution applied only to the government established by the Constitution, not to all governments.

Look again at Article I, Sections 9 and 10. Section 9 says "No . . . *ex post facto* law shall be passed." Section 10, however, the locus of restrictions on the *states*, says "No state shall . . . pass any . . . *ex post facto* law." If the general language of Section 9 applied to *all* governments, then the specific language of Section 10 would not have been necessary. If, by parity of reasoning, the Fifth Amendment had been intended as a restriction on the states, it would have used *specific* language like that in Article 1, Section 10 and not *general* language like that in Article 1, Section 9 which contains restrictions only on the United States.

Marshall's argument is irrefutable and, except for one cranky law professor thirty years ago, no one—certainly no one on the United States Supreme Court—has ever challenged his assertion that the first ten amendments are restrictions only upon the United States and not upon every government in the United States.

The present day claim that the first ten amendments, or some of them, are indeed restrictions on the states is not based on an attempted refutation of Marshall, but upon the supposed purpose of the due process clause of the Fourteenth Amendment.

The First Section of the Fourteenth Amendment says:

> All persons born or naturalized in the United States, and subject to the jurisdiction thereof, are citizens of the United States and of the State wherein they reside. No state shall make or enforce any law which shall abridge the privileges or immunities of citizens of the United States; nor shall any state deprive any person of life, liberty, or property, without due process of law; nor deny to any person within its jurisdiction the equal protection of the laws.

In 1884, one Hurtado was convicted in California for murder. He came to the Supreme Court of the United States with the claim that his life was being taken without due process of law because he had been convicted in a trial which had *not* been initiated by a presentment or indictment of a grand jury. The Fifth Amendment says, you will remember, that "No person shall be held to answer for a capital or otherwise infamous crime unless on a presentment or indictment of a grand jury." Hurtado claimed that when the

Fourteenth Amendment said no state shall "deprive any person of life, liberty or property without due process of law," it meant that thenceforth whatever the first eight amendments forbade the United States to do, the due process clause of the 14th Amendment forbids the states to do.[13]

That view, which is called the "incorporation doctrine," has never, even to this day, commanded a majority of the Court, but another view, which, for all practical purposes gives the same end result *has* been accepted by the Court. It is usually called "absorption." The absorption view is the view that there are certain things which are "implicit in the concept of ordered liberty," as Justice Cardozo put it in *Palko* v. *Connecticut*[14] in 1937, and these things, recognized piecemeal in a case-by-case process of inclusion and exclusion, come to be part of due process of law.

The watershed case was *Adamson* v. *California*[15] in 1947, which, by a narrow margin, upheld a view that fit more or less into the position established by the *Hurtado* case in 1884. Justice Frankfurter, in the *Adamson* case and in many other places on and off the Court, tried his best to adhere to the older view and to reject incorporation and to restrain within the narrowest limits the effects of absorption. But to support his position and to stave off what appeared to him to be the willfulness of Justices Black and Douglas and many others, he insisted that what *was* implicit in the concept of ordered liberty could best be discerned by recourse to history. I examined this matter thoroughly at the end of Frankfurter's career in 1963. I found much fault with Frankfurter's reliance on history, but I did not see as clearly then as I believe I do now, that he, even though he had the *best* position on the court, was altogether wrong. It now seems to me that nothing less resistant than the opinion in *Hurtado* in 1884 is correct. The correct view, I believe, is that *nothing, absolutely nothing* listed in the first eight amendments is *part of* due process of law by its very terms.

Frankfurter's view in no way resists the tide of absorption. So far, virtually everything in the First, Fourth, Fifth, Sixth and Eighth Amendments has been found by the Court to be *in* due process of law. What is more, if one concedes that history is the proper guide to the content of due process, it is far too easy for the absorbers and incorporators to say, well, if we want to see what history views as that which is implicit in the concept of ordered liberty, what better place is there to look than to the list of things the Founders saw fit to include in the Bill of Rights?

According to our old seducer, Gloryspeak, there was a struggle between those who were for and those who were against liberty and the forces for liberty won and the glorious Bill of Rights was adopted and, since the Constitution and the Bill of Rights are contemporaneous, they might as well be considered as simply one document.

Let us take two steps backward and reexamine these views. As a first step, let us look at the Civil War amendments themselves, the 13th, 14th and 15th Amendments. If one holds, as I do, that due process includes *nothing* of the first eight amendments—not the right to counsel, not security from unreasonable searches and seizures, not the privilege against self-incrimination, not freedom of speech or press or religion—what earthly use is it? Am I, it might be asked, suggesting that the Framers of the 14th Amendment intended simply to toy with us?

The answer is to put the due process clause into the context of the whole of the Fourteenth Amendment, in fact into the context of the whole collectivity of the 13th, 14th and 15th Amendments. While it is true that law necessarily says *more* than its framers intend, the question "more of *what*?" cannot be answered without clarity as to that intention. There can be not the slightest doubt that the overall intention of the three Civil War amendments was the alleviation of the condition and status of black Americans.

It is possible, in that context, to show that a *contentless* due process clause is not thereby a *meaningless* due process clause. First of all, note something about the rights of the accused. Unless you stand on the perfectly silly ground that the law against murder is the product of the give and take of factions to which the contributions of the faction of murderers and the faction of non-murderers are equally legitimate, you see that unlike matters of *distributive* justice, matters of *retributive* justice are not, or not so nearly, the sorts of things that depend on the large extent and commercial character of the Union for decent and moderate results. These are not party, or factional matters. One does not want a fair trial more or less because of wealth or poverty. The developments in Locke's political theory are, themselves, enough to insure a moderate development of the criminal justice apparatus, a development which adequately reconciles freedom and justice with republican forms without concern that a smaller community will have an interested and overbearing majority faction. That is, indeed, exactly why the Constitution gives commerce, war, finance, and diplomacy to the national government and *leaves* the general business of criminal justice to the states.

The history of the South, however, had shown that, eaten up as it was by the cancer of slavery, which Lincoln reminded us was just as destructive of the masters as of the slaves, individuals in the oppressed class, or individuals not supportive of that oppression, were likely to be singled out for injustice *contrary* to the law which was, otherwise, all right. It might be supposed that the equal protection clause particularly forbids discrimination by the law against a whole *class* of people—e.g., all who are black—whether that be a discrimination in the civil or the criminal law. The due process clause, on the other hand, says to the state, if you are forbidden to pass invidiously discriminatory legislation, you may be fully trusted to establish your own criminal justice system for yourselves *provided*, that whatever system you establish *for* yourselves you must be sure to *give* to each. You may not have a law which satisfies you and then get around it by taking life, liberty, or property—that is, executing, imprisoning, or fining—some black man without giving him that process which is due to him according to that law.

Here then, as in other cases, the primary security of rights is the business *not* of the Courts, but of a legislature in a soundly constructed republic.

It is now possible for us to take the second step back to the beginnings and to see with clarity the intent and the meaning of the Bill of Rights. It is surely true that there was a hesitant party profoundly suspicious of the energetic new government being proposed in the Constitution. It is *not* true, however, as the Gloryspeakers would have us believe, that the party of hesitancy held the Constitution hostage to its demand for a Bill of Rights.

One of the demands made was for a bill of rights. Hamilton answered that demand comprehensively in *Federalist* #84. He said there that there were in the Constitution several things such as one would find in a bill of rights—such for example as the prohibition against *ex post facto* laws—but, generally speaking, a bill of rights was by its nature, an understanding between an otherwise absolute king and a people otherwise wholly subject, and might really have no place in a Constitution professedly founded on the power of the people. In the rightly ordered republican regime, simple trust in majority rule was almost, by itself, sufficient security for private rights.

Hamilton further argued, perhaps disingenuously, that a bill of rights would declare exceptions to powers *not* granted and thereby give to Congress *implicitly* powers not given it *explicitly* and further, the guarantee of some rights might impliedly *deny* those rights not remembered to have been included in the bill. Finally, he argued, "the Constitution is itself, in every rational sense, and to every useful purpose, a bill of rights." What he meant is that the true and only security of private rights consistent with the public good is that security which is the legislative product of a rightly ordered republic under a sound constitution—that is, not under a bill of rights as such but under a political order soundly constituted.

What was demanded by the hesitant party in the ratifying conventions was *not* a bill of rights, simply. That notion is just Gloryspeak. What was *demanded* was *amendments*—that is, fundamental *changes* in the structure and powers of the government erected by the Constitution.

Remember, now, that when the First Congress began to confront the question of amendments, it had to confront and decide the question whether such amendments would take the form of *changes* to the body of the document, or only the form of *additions* to the text. If, instead of looking *back* on the amendments in the form and with the substance finally adopted, from our own perspective, we get *behind* the amendments and the amendment debates in the First Congress, the true meaning of those amendments is made clear.

In the First Congress, Madison moved that the House of Representatives go into a committee of the whole house to consider some amendments he would introduce. He reminded the House that amendments had been promised by the proponents of the Constitution to the hesitant ratifiers. There was great resistance to his motion, and the resistance was based on the fear that considering amendments would open the door to the complete destruction of the handiwork of the Convention. The end result was that Congress threw the hesitant party a bone by giving it in *substance* only a part of its demands, namely a bill of rights, and giving it to them in the *form* of *additions*.

The Bill of Rights is, and is rightly, *only* a limit on the United States because it was extracted by the anti-Federalists from the Federalists as a peculiar limitation *on* the strong, central, national government which the anti-Federalists feared. It was a concession the Federalists could make because it was a bunch of limitations on powers which, if they existed at all in the national government, the proponents of a strong national government didn't much care about. See the evidence of our history on this point: the First Amendment is ratified in 1791. It is not until 1919—one hundred twenty-eight years later—that you get the first freedom of speech case decided in the U.S. Supreme Court—*Schenck* v. *U.S.*[16]

The Bill of Rights is *not* a compendious list of the minimum restraints acceptable in the case of free government. The minimum restraints are listed in the Constitution itself, and they are indeed spare! Other than those few things in the original Constitution, a sound republican legislature could pretty well be trusted to protect individual rights through the normal legislative process subject to majority rule.

There is, then, no unscalable wall of "separation of church and state" except in the annals of Gloryspeak. When the First Amendment says "*Congress* shall make no law respecting an establishment of religion" it does not *at all* mean that there can be no such establishment. What it *means* is, if Maryland should choose to establish the Roman Catholic Church or Virginia should choose to establish the Anglican Church, Congress could make no law *respecting* that establishment. The strong, central, national government would not interfere in the doings of the states.

How the First Amendment has been applied to the states through the Due Process Clause of the Fourteenth is a story full of wonders.

I keep remembering an old movie with Red Skelton playing the part of a writer of pulp magazine serials. As I recall, he was dictating to three separate secretaries more or less simultaneously and, after dictating a paragraph to one in which he has his all-American boy hero welded shut in a steel cubicle and dropped to the bottom of the

Mindanao Trench by the forces of evil, he turns to his other two secretaries in turn and dictates paragraphs for his Flying Ace serial and his Cowboy serial. As he is dictating to the third secretary, the other two chat, wondering how he will ever get the all-American boy out of the steel cubicle. Finishing with the third secretary, he turns back to dictate the next paragraph to the first one. It begins "After Jack got out of the box. . . ."

This is how the Supreme Court made the First Amendment applicable to the states through the Fourteenth. Remember again that the first free speech case is *Schenck* v. *U.S.* in 1919. In 1925, the case of *Gitlow* v. *New York*[17] faced a challenge to a state statute similar to the United States statute that had been questioned in the *Schenck* case. The ruling in the *Gitlow* case was to the effect that even if the First Amendment were a restraint upon the states, New York was justified in punishing Gitlow. Two more decisions in 1927 were of a similar bent.[18] Then, in 1931, in *Near* v. *Minnesota*[19] the Court ruled that it was "no longer open to doubt that the liberty of the press and of speech" was a limitation on the states.

Leaving aside the fact that it makes a foolishment of the due process clause to rule that *any* taking of the liberty of speech is a taking without due process, and leaving aside the fact that the willful, new, liberal Court is just as wrong to produce a substantive due process of speech as was the willful, old, conservative court to cut a "liberty of contract" from whole Constitutional cloth, I am inclined to say that the Court's application of the First Amendment to the states has been about as persuasive as the saving of Jack from the deepest part of the ocean. But it is less amusing. Neither the First Amendment nor any other portion of the Bill of Rights is carried over by the due process clause or the privileges and immunities clause of the Fourteenth Amendment and made applicable against the states. What the due process clause of the Fourteenth Amendment demands of the states is just what the due process clause of the Fifth Amendment demands of the United States. A people may not adopt procedures which they are willing to have applied to themselves and then vindictively except an individual—for racial or other reasons—from those procedures and "railroad" him and execute or incarcerate or fine him. The indecorous nonsense of the Court's attempt to grapple with the definitions of obscenity and of religion show the impossibility of the ultimate substitution of judicial for legislative power in the chief business of the securing of rights.

**

Since the war in Vietnam it has become fashionable for journalists to find a "crisis in confidence" in public perception of the government. Fortunately, the public is not quite as opposed to its government as the press and the academy would have it. All the same, it is opposed to or at least suspicious of the government and its inclination to abide by the law its elected lawmakers make has lessened. That suspicion of (indeed, cynicism about) government is the fruit of a campaign of debunking which has persisted throughout the twentieth century such that as we approach the twenty-first there is every reason to fear it. It will seem surprising, then, for me to present so confidently an argument *for* government, and particularly for the legislative and executive branches as opposed to the judicial.

It would be a very strenuous work to undo the century-long attack on government and on the Constitution. What I have said here so far points in that direction but to complete the work it would be necessary to make a thorough examination of the political philosophy of Hobbes and Locke. Such would be inappropriate here. An article entitled "The Constitutional Completion of the Liberal Philosophy of Hobbes and Locke" to be published in 1987[20] moves a step or two closer to such an examination.

A few passages from that article point the way:

The sum and substance of Hobbes . . . is a movement from perfect freedom in the state of nature to very nearly perfect subjection to the sovereign in civil society. It is with regard to this movement that Rousseau tells us at the very beginning of the *Social Contract* that man is born free but is everywhere in chains. Rousseau tells us that he can explain what makes that movement legitimate. The traditional distinction had been between freedom and slavery. Since Hobbes we have tended to distinguish between freedom and authority, as though only in the absence of authority is there true freedom. How destructive an error this is! Will not every society seem like abject slavery in contrast to the engaging fantasy of perfect freedom in the state of nature? We become dissolute, even seditious, because we do not have that which is neither possible nor desirable.

While the vision of perfect freedom is destructive of good order, the lazy acceptance of near-perfect subjection is noxious to common sense and common decency. Most of us since Hobbes have tried not so much to legitimate the chains as to liberate ourselves from them. We have sought *limited* government. Our great teacher in this regard seems to be John Locke.

There is in Locke just as much as in Hobbes, a movement from perfect but worthless freedom in the state of nature to nearly perfect subjection in civil society. We try to find a check on this in Locke, and in fact, so politic and so adroit is he that we have come to regard him as having brought limited government to us, but certain problems occur.

Chapter 11 of the *Second Treatise* is entitled "Of the Extent of the Legislative Power." His use of the term "extent" suggests that there are limits to sovereignty which might be found—substantive limits. Indeed, we seem unable to resist seeing such limits as realities, and it is no doubt because of Locke that we do so. It seems to us that some things are simply "not the government's business," that there is a clear line between what we now call the "public sector" and the "private sector."

There is no such line. A close analysis of Locke's Chapter 11 disappoints one's hopes. Locke shows to the reflective and responsive reader that there can really be almost no substantive limit on the legislative power.

He shows this by stating the limits and then restating them. In the restatement, something seemingly important, and seemingly stated firmly in the original statement, slips from our grasp and we are left with only a pious inclination toward limitation.

In section 135 he disallowed absolute, arbitrary power. In section 136 he forbade ruling by extemporary decrees. In sections 138, 139 and 140 he forbade taking property without consent and in section 141 he disallowed the subdelegation of legislative power. Now, in section 142 he restates the matter as follows:

> These are the *Bounds* which the trust that is put in them by the Society, and the Law of God and Nature have *set to the*

Legislative Power of every Commonwealth, in all Forms of Government.

First, they are to govern by *promulgated establish'd* Laws, not to be varied in particular Cases, but to have one Rule for Rich and Poor, for the Favorite at Court, and the Country Man at Plough.

Secondly, These *Laws* also ought to be designed *for* no other end ultimately but *the good of the People.*

Thirdly, they must *not raise Taxes* on the Property of the People, without the *Consent of the People*, given by themselves or their Deputies. And this properly concerns only such Governments where the *Legislative* is always in being, or at least where the People have not reserv'd any part of the Legislative to Deputies, to be from time to time chosen by themselves.

Fourthly, the *Legislative* neither must *nor can transfer the Power of making Laws* to any Body else, or place it any where but where the People have.

Notice first of all that there are no other limits. This is an exhaustive list covering the limits upon the legislative power. The people sets these limits, or rather trusts in these limits in that act which we heirs of Hobbes and Locke call the "social contract."

Notice, secondly, that where the original statement had forbidden absolute arbitrary power and extemporary decrees, the restatement demands promulgated, established laws and declares that they ought to be for no other end but the public good. What appeared to be the substantive limit is now restated simply as the rule that legislative power is limited to acts which conduce to the public good.

We don't know what those limits are, then, without knowing what the public good is. Locke is, to be sure, far from silent on that matter. The public good is the end of society, the end for which men entered society. That end is, he says, the "enjoyment of their properties in peace and safety."[21] The end of society, or the public good, is the preservation of life, liberty, and property. The problem with this can be seen by examining the United States Constitution according to which life, liberty, or property may be taken if they are taken "by due process of law." This is just what Locke means, too. The crucial limit is simply this: if the legislative power is vested in a numerous body,[22] which comes from an elective system cleansed of rotten boroughs,[23] if the legislature is for a set period and if its members must again become private citizens after, if the laws enacted by the legislature are general, prospective laws and are promulgated, and if they fall equally on all people, including the ex-legislators and the legislators who made those laws,[24] and if the laws passed are passed by majority vote after debate and deliberation, then those laws will only take so much life, liberty, or property as they must take to serve the general ends of life, liberty, and property.

There cannot be any more distinct or specific limits than these and these, it must be noted, are all simply procedural limits. Thus for Locke, the question of the limits of the legislative power dissolves back into the question of legitimacy. Government is, finally, really only limited by the exigencies of the moment and by the general standard of the "public good" which is, in turn, only to be established by the judgment of the majority.

Even if one looks to the question of freedom of religion from governmental interference, one sees in Locke's *Letter on Toleration* that what can be tolerated is, after all, only what is tolerable. That *Letter* advises the majority not to regulate religious things that are *"indifferent"*—*i.e.,* which don't have any effect on civil matters. But, in the final analysis, it must be that same majority which uses its judgment to determine what is and what is not indifferent. It is no wonder that Publius later says, "In a free government the security for civil rights must be the same as that for religious rights. It consists in the one case in the multiplicity of interests, and in the other in the multiplicity of sects."[25]

Hobbes had taught a movement from perfect freedom in the state of nature to near-perfect subjection in civil society and he had preferred monarchy because it more surely perfects the coming-into-being of sovereignty, and any sovereign, no matter how harsh, is preferable to the state of nature.

In Locke we still move from perfect freedom in nature to near-perfect subjection in society. That is something which, in principle, cannot be cured. The cure must be a practical one and here Locke lays the ground-work upon which our Constitution builds. He emphatically differs from Hobbes by arguing that absolute monarchy, the sort that Hobbes preferred, is far worse than the state of nature. Locke in fact teaches us that the solution to the rigors of such monarchy is what we have come to call the right of revolution. As our Declaration of Independence puts it, whenever "any form of government becomes destructive" as opposed to preservative of the rights it was instituted to secure "it is the right of the people to alter or abolish it and to institute new government." Locke's solution to the problem of near-perfect subjection is to vest the legislative power in a "numerous" body. The problem of arbitrary seizure of property is, he says, "not much to be feared in governments where the Legislative consists wholly or in part in assemblies which are variable, whose members upon the dissolution of the assembly are subjects under the common law of the country equally with the rest."[26]

This still leaves much room for abusive government. Locke hints at the separation of powers,[27] but it is our Constitution which brings to perfection the limits sought by Locke. These limits are still only practical, but they provide as limited a government as the nature of government itself allows. To look for more is to be an idealist, than which, as Allan Bloom has somewhere reminded us, there is no more dangerous species of fool in politics. Disappointed idealism leads to despair and then to cynicism and finally to tyrannical excess.

We are reminded again of Martin Diamond's characterization of the Founding as a revolution of sober expectations, and we are reminded of the beauty, the profundity, and the correctness of the *Federalist Papers.* Locke, as we have shown, moves toward moderation, toward limited government, but he saw as we must again see that there can be no limits imposed from the outside. To begin with, the idea of limited government has its very origin in the desire of something called "the people" to limit a government which is seen as coming from somewhere outside the people. Provisionally, it would seem that a government which is, as Publius speaks of ours in *Federalist* #84, "professedly founded upon the power of the people and executed by their immediate representatives," has no need of limits. If one takes seriously the notion of the Declaration of Independence, drawn from Locke, that a people has a right in nature to give itself the law, it is seen that this right is exactly what Locke called the "Supreme Power," and it is truly limitless. It then must be, and it can only be, self-limiting, and this is what Publius means in *Federalist* #10 when he says that it is in "the extent and proper structure of the Union that we behold a republican remedy for the diseases most incident to republican government."

One of the great contributions of the American Constitution to the end of limiting government is the fact of a written constitution itself. It is as though that great, limitless power of the people, the Supreme

Power, or the Legislative Power in the most comprehensive sense, shackled itself in its most sober moments so that when it should become drunk with passion it would be unable to execute the injustices wrought by passion. There is a subtlety here which it seems Publius did and Mr. Jefferson did not understand. Publius deals with it gently but insistently in the series of *Federalist* papers from #36 to #39. The people—the legislative power in the greater sense—ought not to fiddle with the Constitution. They ought to deal with it only in their most sober moments. They ought not to "go back to first principles" lightly. If they do, the distinction between the great, self-limiting act of the legislative power in the greater sense and the lesser acts of the legislative power in the ordinary sense is lost. If that is lost the whole enterprise fails. No longer are the diseases of republican government curable with republican remedies. Limited government becomes impossible in practice just as it is self-contradictory in principle.

Locke's movement toward moderation had centered on the vesting of the legislative power in a large, variable assembly subject to its own laws as they are executed by a separate, executive power. The American perfection of this consists chiefly of five things: the written constitution; the perfection of the separation of powers; the truly independent judicial power; the extended, complicated (that is, commercial) republic; and a curious vestige of federalism grudgingly conceded by those who pressed for the Constitution.

All of these moderating influences in American government promise what Publius in *Federalist* #51 calls results which would "seldom take place on any other principles than those of justice and the general good." To ask for more is to ask for trouble.

The major complaint against the American regime stems from those who, reacting to the argument that America is modern and is therefore without religion or morality, argue in response that it is not modern. It is, they say, just as ancient as it is modern. Both of these views, it seems to me, accept the moral emptiness and moral impotence of the regime as given. In this they too readily accept the misconstruction of the Constitution by the courts. That misconstruction, in turn, rests on a silly vision of freedom, a vision which takes seriously the Hobbesian description of perfect freedom in the state of nature blinking away the Hobbesian solution, the total submission and subjection to civil society. The Founders were not such utopians as to try to have their political cake and eat it. They accepted the Hobbesian principles but they saw them through to a regime which offered the optimum security of rights. They never supposed that it would be possible to have the freedom of the state of nature without the ugliness of that state. Nor were they twentieth century moral relativists.

It is true that the American regime is not constructed of virtue and piety. It does not guarantee those things. It is also true, however, despite what the courts say, that the Constitution does not prohibit virtue or piety or their influence upon public policy. Not even the First Amendment properly understood does that. In aiming at moderation, at limited government, at republican cures for republican diseases, it protects us against zeal and against sectarian rigor. It was never intended to protect moral idiosyncracy against the common sense and the common decency of the majority.

***

Only one thing remains to be said in these introductory remarks. In this book I deal at some length with the *Murray's Lessee*[28] and *Hurtado* cases which are the historical base of any treatment of the due process clause of the Fourteenth Amendment. Here most especially, my views have strengthened over the past twenty years. In an article entitled "Due Process of Law and Due Regard for the Constitution"[29] I dealt with those two cases in the following way:

As Marshall showed in *Barron* v. *Baltimore*[30] in 1833, the Bill of Rights is intended solely as a restraint upon the United States and exists to calm the fears of those apprehensive of the power of the new, central, general government instituted under the Constitution. The absorption argument starts, as it must start, by accepting Marshall's conclusions in *Barron*. Crosskey is almost alone in insisting that Marshall is even wrong in 1833. The evidence Crosskey cites on this matter is pitiful. He says "good lawyers" in those days viewed the Bill of Rights as limits also on the states, but he cites only one lawyer who, in an off-hand remark in a note in a law journal he had started up, assumes that the Bill of Rights restrains the states. Crosskey also cites a 1796 South Carolina case involving the just compensation matter (the same matter as that in *Barron*). If one reads the four opinions in that case, which according to the older American style favored by Jefferson appear *seriatim*, rather than being compressed into an opinion of the court, one sees that even though the Fifth Amendment insistence that private property not be taken for public use without just compensation had been ratified as part of the Constitution a scant five years earlier, the four judges (and counsel for both parties, by the way) cited common law, the South Carolina Constitution, and a half dozen other things, even the Prophet, *but not one word is said about the Fifth Amendment.*[31]

Crosskey's argument here is utterly mistaken. Marshall's reasoning by the analogy of Sections 9 and 10 of Article I is manifestly correct. The intention of the Framers of the Bill of Rights was to impose thereby restraints only on the government established by the Constitution and not on the states. This is not to say that a state legislature would be prudent or just if it took private property for public use without just compensation. It is only to say that if it were imprudent and unjust and the legislature did so anyway, the correct recourse is not litigation under the Fifth Amendment.

"Ah," the absorption people say, "not by the Fifth in 1833, but, since 1868, by the Fifth through the Fourteenth because the due process clause includes at least some of the provisions of the Bill of Rights." How? By absorption. Absorption occurs through the gradual process of judicial inclusion and exclusion. How does one determine that a thing ought to be included? By a process of reasoning about "essential fairness" and what is "implicit in the concept of ordered liberty." How does one guard one's reasoning about this matter from the temptation to impose one's merely intuitive notions of fairness—mere, personal, idiosyncratic preference? By turning to history, it is said.

One of the problems of our historical condescension is that it keeps us from taking seriously the great events and the great purposes of history. History becomes a stream, a movement of merely incremental change and everything is connected to everything and everything is of equal importance and all that comes later is simply the heir of all that went before. The American experience becomes a mere extension of English history. So, there are even those who can trace the whole thing back through stages of inevitability to Aristotle and the Greek polis. This set of mind overlooks the critical distinction made by Mr. Justice Curtis in his opinion for the Court in *Murray's Lessee* v. *Hoboken Land and Improvement Co.*[32] in 1856. This case faced the question whether property taken by means of a warrant of distress from a collector of the customs whose accounts were in arrears was or was not taken by due process of law. Curtis said, "The Constitution contains no description of those processes which it was intended to allow or forbid. It does not even declare what principles are to be applied to ascertain whether [the warrant] be due process." Note well: Curtis is here construing the due process clause of the Fifth Amendment and he asserts that notwithstanding all the other provisions of the Fifth Amendment and of the rest of the Bill of Rights, the Constitution *does not define* due process of law. In other words, he makes implicitly here the distinction that Matthews was compelled to make explicitly thirty years later in *Hurtado* between the due process clause and the other clauses. The due process clause is not explained by all the other clauses. It has an "independent potency." Curtis, in *Murray's Lessee*, laid down two criteria by which to judge whether or not a process was due process.

> We must examine the Constitution itself, to see whether this process be in conflict with any of its provisions. If not found to be so, we must look to those settled usages and modes of proceedings existing in the common and statute law of England, before the emigration of our ancestors, and which are shown not to have been unsuited to their civil and political condition by having been acted on by them after the settlement of this country.

Thus, if nothing in the Constitution forbids a warrant of distress, we must see if warrants of distress were used in English proceedings. If they were, then they are all right unless the change in our civil and political condition makes them no longer all right here. But even if they were not used in English proceedings, there is simply nothing wrong with our establishing them. New process is not, as such, a denial of due process. Thus, in *Hurtado,* a California process that institutes a trial for a capital crime by way of an information as opposed to indictment by a grant jury is not a denial of due process.

No less a figure than C. Herman Pritchett, one of the of the very great scholars of constitutional law in this century and my own beloved teacher, makes a curious error about this. It is an error which stampedes the mind. Pritchett says:

> On the basis of Justice Curtis's first test in the *Murray* case, due process had clearly been violated for the Fifth Amendment makes indictment by grand jury mandatory for all capital or otherwise infamous crimes. However Justice Matthews made the *Murray* rule seem to approve the *Hurtado* result. The "real syllabus" of the Curtis holding, Matthews said, is "that a process of law, which is not otherwise forbidden, must be taken to be due process of law, if it can show the sanction of settled usage both in England and in this country; but it by no means follows that nothing else can be due process of law." Then, having recognized Curtis's first test by the clause, "which is not otherwise forbidden," he proceeded to ignore it and to work from the last thought in the sentence, which is substantially Curtis's second test—the test of historical practice.

Pritchett then goes on to say:

> For those who might find this liberal philosophy unconvincing, Matthews had a more pedantic argument. Since the Fifth Amendment contains both the guarantee of due process and of indictment by grand jury, and since it must be assumed that no part of the Constitution is superfluous, it follows that due process as used in the Fifth Amendment does not include indictment by grand jury. When the same phrase is repeated in the Fourteenth Amendment, it must be given the same meaning. Thus Matthews emerged with the remarkable conclusion, directly opposed to that of Curtis, that the due process clauses in both the Fifth and Fourteenth Amendments must be interpreted to *exclude* any rights specified elsewhere in the Constitution.[33]

But Matthew's conclusion is not "remarkable" and it is not "directly opposed to that of Curtis." To say that "due process had clearly been violated" in Hurtado's case on "the basis of Justice Curtis's first test in the *Murray* case" because "the Fifth Amendment makes indictment mandatory for all capital or otherwise infamous crimes," is to assume the point at issue. The Fifth Amendment does not make "indictment mandatory for all capital or otherwise infamous crimes." It makes indictment mandatory for all capital or

otherwise infamous crimes *tried in the courts of the United States.*
One cannot prove that due process includes indictment by asserting
that due process includes indictment. One can refute Matthews here
only if one first refutes Marshall in *Barron*, and *Barron* is irrefutable.
The scholarly honor of the incorporationists prevents their
pretending to refute Marshall, but the enthusiasm of their good
intentions, their "noble enthusiasm of liberty," makes them leap
over the difficulty. Here again, just as we cannot understand the
Constitution by looking back upon it from the Bill of Rights, so we
cannot understand the Bill of Rights by looking back upon it from the
vantage of the Fourteenth Amendment. The true intellectual course is
the other way around. As was said above, it is only open to us by way
of a constructive act of forgetting. We must strenuously act to cleanse
the mind of currently accepted notions in order to see the historical
things by their own light. To see this, let us examine the strongest case
for carrying some of the provisions of the Bill of Rights over against
the states by way of the due process clause of the Fourteenth
Amendment. Let us examine the strongest case for absorption.

Reminding ourselves, the case for absorption rests on the
concession that incorporation, as such, was not intended. It admits
with Matthews in *Hurtado* that precisely because both indictment and
due process are in the Fifth Amendment, they must be separable. One
is not simply included in the other. Admittedly, indictment is in the
Fifth Amendment solely as a restraint upon the United States and not
upon the states. If indictment is included in due process it is not
because it is in the Fifth Amendment, but simply because it is
intrinsically in due process: due process without indictment cannot be
imagined. Indictment is one of those things "implicit in the concept
of ordered liberty." But this is not evidently the case. If one reflects
on this matter, it can hardly be said that a criminal justice system that
proceeds by way of information and a preliminary hearing before a
magistrate, as opposed to presentment before or indictment by a
grand jury, must be dismissed as outright barbarous. So we are back
to history. To see what is intended as part of due process, say the
absorptionists, we have to see what the whole course of our history
has regarded as part of due process. What better place is there to
look, the argument proceeds to ask, than the Bill of Rights itself. If
the Founders saw fit to adopt these restrictions, even if we concede

that they adopted them only as restrictions upon the United States, must we not see that they, the Founders, regarded these as the right restrictions to be imposed? Thus, if the Fourteenth Amendment proscribes state imposition of death, imprisonment, or fines without due process, and due process includes what is implicit in ordered liberty, must we not concede that what the Founders included in the Bill of Rights is as good a list as we might find of what *they* regarded as implicit in that liberty?

Of course my answer to this rhetorical question is "no!" As I have argued above, the first several amendments are not a compendious list of what the Founders regarded as what is implicit in the concept of ordered liberty. Those amendments were concessions to the party of hesitancy, they were intended only as limits upon the United States, and they were phrased as categorically as they were *because* they were intended solely as limits on the United States and not on all governments within the United States and because it may well have seemed to the First Congress that those limits on the United States could be tolerated exactly because they limited things not of great consequence to the central government.

The limits on state government were, and even after the Fourteenth Amendment largely *are*, left to the peoples of the states.

R.G.S.
Washington, D.C., 1986

NOTES TO INTRODUCTION

[1]See C.J. Arthur's Preface to Marx and Engels, *The German Ideology* (New York: International Publishers, 1970), p. 1.

[2]Morton J. Frisch and Richard G. Stevens, *American Political Thought: The Philosophic Dimension of American Statesmanship* (New York: Charles Scribner's Sons, 1973).

[3](Itasca, Illinois: F.E. Peacock, 1983).

[4]Felix Frankfurter, "The Red Terror of Judicial Reform," *The New Republic*, (October 1, 1924) reprinted in Felix Frankfurter, *Law and Politics* (New York: Capicorn Books, 1962), p. 16.

[5]*Teaching Political Science,* 14 (Fall 1986), a Symposium issue ed. Lane V. Sunderland.

[6]See Locke, *Treatises,* II, ch. 5.

[7]*Ibid.,* ch. 8 and 11.

[8]*Ibid.,* especially ch. 8 and 9.

[9]A.V. Dicey, *An Introduction to the Study of the Law of the Constitution* (Indianapolis: Liberty Classics, 1982), p. 74f.

[10]As Diamond liked to put it, a large Saharan republic would simply have a few more oasis owners and many more date pickers. The tension between rich and poor would not be moderated.

[11]See note 5, *supra.*

[12]7 Pet. 243 (1833).

[13]*Hurtado* v. *California,* 110 U.S. 516 (1884).

[14]302 U.S. 319 (1937).

[15]332 U.S. 46 (1947).

[16]*Schenck* v. *U.S.,* 249 U.S. 47 (1919).

[17]*Gitlow* v. *N.Y.,* 268 U.S. 652 (1925).

[18]See *Whitney* v. *California,* 274 U.S. 357 (1927) and *Fiske* v. *Kansas,* 274 U.S. 380 (1927).

[19]283 U.S. 697 (1931).

[20]R.G. Stevens, "The Constitutional Completion of the Liberal Philosophy of Hobbes and Locke," to be published in 1987.

[21]Locke, *Treatises,* II §134, and see §§85, 88, 94, 95, 124 and 131.

[22]*Ibid.,* II §143.

[23]*Ibid.,* II §157.

[24]*Ibid.,* §§137, 138 and 143.

[25]*Federalist* #51 (pp. 339-340 in the Modern Library edition).

[26]Locke, *Treatises* II, §107.

[27]*Ibid.,* II §107.

[28]*Murray's Lessee* v. *Hoboken Land and Improvement Co.,* 18 How. 272 (1856).

[29]R.G. Stevens, "Due Process of Law and Due Regard for the Constitution," in a Symposium issue of *Teaching Political Science,* 13 (Fall, 1985), p. 25, ed. Gary McDowell.

[30]7 Pet. 243 (1833).

[31]See W.W. Crosskey, *Politics and the Constitution in the History of the United States* (Chicago: University of Chicago Press, 1953), pp. 1076, 1091 and 1056 and cf. J.K. Angell, *U.S. Law Intelligencer and Review,* 1:64, 1829.

[32]*Op. cit.* note 28, *supra.*

[33]C.H. Pritchett, *The American Constitution,* 2nd ed. (New York: McGraw-Hill, 1968), p. 593.

1963 Preface

American statesmanship, including judicial statesmanship, has faced at least three crises and is perhaps in the grip of a fourth. The first was the crisis of the founding. It need not have gone so well. That it did go so well was, I believe, due to the presence of certain excellent men. Between 1819 and 1860 the well-being of the country was again subjected to grave danger, culminating in the crisis of the Civil War, and a refoundation was required. That that crisis was resolved as well as it was was due perhaps to the excellence of a single man. During the fourth decade of the twentieth century we were once again faced with the possibility of destruction and, once again, a man of excellence preserved us, or made at least the beginnings of a preservation.

The coming of World War II, the sudden finding of ourselves in the office of chief defender of Western civilization, and the constant excitement of our contest with its chief antagonist makes it difficult to say whether the present crisis is merely a continuation of that begun thirty years ago, or a wholly new problem. But that we live every day in constant company with the possibility of destruction cannot be denied.

The excellent men who resolved the first crisis and founded the Republic bequeathed to us as a part of that foundation the United States Supreme Court. During the subsequent history of the country, and with respect to its crises, the Court has played a large part. It is, once again, playing a part. It has not always played its part well. Whether or not it does so now depends upon the quality of its judicial statesmanship. It is my belief that the quality of statesmanship is dependent upon the quality of political understanding and that proper political understanding is the affair of political philosophy. Of course, the judge is a man of *action*. But it is *considered* action and considered action is based on a prior understanding—on a *direction*.

The character of the Court's understanding, or direction, has revealed itself in the course of its division over the application of the "due process" clause to state criminal proceedings. It has appeared to me that Mr. Justice Frankfurter's view of this clause is the best view put forth by the Court, but certain aspects of his view are gravely problematic. Before treating that view, however, it seemed to me necessary to assure myself that it was in fact the best view available on the Court, for, if it were not, it would not be the one most worthy of understanding and criticism. I have accordingly gone over the ground of the alternative view, presented by Mr. Justice Black and this has permitted identification of the crucial factors in Frankfurter's view. That treatment of the alternative view has at the same time persuaded me that Frankfurter's view is in fact the superior one and is, as well, the stable and traditional view of the Court. Criticism of Frankfurter is, then, criticism of the Court as such.

The problem with Frankfurter's view may be stated thus: If Western civilization is to be preserved, it must be because it is worth preserving. If it is worth preserving it must be because it is good. If so, *can* it be preserved by reliance upon and reference to itself, or must reliance not be placed upon that by virtue of which the thing to be preserved is worthy of preservation? This problem is not new to Western civilization. Turning back into the tradition in order to find the salvation of the tradition has been an available alternative at least since Burke's response to the first great crisis in modern Western thought. To speak of Burke and Frankfurter in the same breath is to suggest that the latter is a "conservative." I think that he is, in the proper sense of the word, and if the word were not now stretched to such absurd lengths as to be used as a description of men who hold a radical, private-property, libertarian opinion wholly lacking in sophistication, it would be desirable to make something more of this fact than I have chosen to do.

Much has been written about Frankfurter, and the common descriptions of him employ the terms "restraint" and "pragmatism" to characterize his doctrines. But the treatments of these doctrines now available have not seemed adequate as criticisms. In their proper places, these doctrines have been met herein, and the intention has been to treat them as problems rather than as self-explaining conclusions.

A study of Frankfurter which claims to subject "his view" to criticism will be open to a certain charge of boldness for, necessarily, it includes the claim of having in the first instance discovered what that "view" is. That is, it must claim to have uncovered, as it were, the secret springs of all of his pronouncements. Such a claim is beset with two difficulties. The first I avoid simply by avoiding it. I have not tried to psychologize him in the sense of reducing his opinions to material causes or conditions. The second difficulty is a more real one. There is always the possibility that a living subject may yet add a word or phrase that will throw new light on the totality of his thought or that were he to hear of what is said of him he might explain to everyone's satisfaction the problems raised. But I have not sought to "interview" him. There is no reason why the living should have the advantage over the dead of supplying *post litem motam* depositions as to what they mean, and, from the standpoint of *understanding*, such interviews are more likely to divert the study into the attempt to psychologize. I have preferred to seek not what *he* means, in that sense, but rather what what he has *said* means: his *teaching* as it is contained in his writings. If I have misunderstood him it is not because of that extra word or phrase I might have gotten in an interview: I have simply misunderstood him. This preface is being written less than two months after his retirement from the bench and but a month before his eightieth birthday. He has written a mountain of words on every conceivable subject. If what he means cannot be drawn from his voluminous pronouncements there is no meaning in anything which can be discerned by prolonged industry.

A final word is in order on the volume of his work. I have not indicated in this study anything regarding the "evolution" of his thought. I have not done so because I have treated all of it as though it came out of the same pen on the same day. Of course he has changed his mind on one thing or another. He has, in fact, admitted here and there to having been wrong on occasion. None of this has seemed to me of any consequence. As far as the fundamental basis of his views is concerned I find no difference between his reference to the "Zeitgeist and the Judiciary" at thirty and his reliance on the "conscience of mankind" in his seventies. I have freely referred to and relied on all of his judicial and non-judicial writings but I have tried to rest the main burden of proof for my contentions on what he has said in the freedom of concurring and dissenting opinions in cases involving a claim made under the due process clause of the Fourteenth Amendment.

CHAPTER I

ADAMSON v. CALIFORNIA

The Court's difficulty in dealing with the due process clause of the Fourteenth Amendment and with the phrase "essential fairness" which, and no more than which, the due process clause of the Fourteenth Amendment is said to require of the states is perhaps nowhere better displayed than in the four written opinions offered in *Adamson* v. *California*.[1] We shall examine these opinions as they appear in the *Reports* in order better to understand the Court's problem, but the barest summary of the history of the case will first of all be necessary.

Admiral Dewey Adamson, a citizen of California, was charged with murder in the first degree and with burglary in the first degree; he was tried before Judge Charles W. Fricke and a jury in the Superior Court of California in and for the County of Los Angeles; and he was found guilty on both murder and burglary counts and sentenced to death. His appeal was heard by the Supreme Court of California sitting in bank[2] and his conviction was unanimously affirmed. Adamson then appealed to the Supreme Court of the United States[3] on the grounds that two particulars of the proceedings in the State courts denied him that due process of law without which the Fourteenth Amendment forbade California to take his life. The Supreme Court heard him in January of 1947 and handed down its decision affirming the California courts on June 23 of that year. Mr. Justice Reed spoke for the Court which included Chief Justice Vinson and Justices Jackson and Burton. Mr. Justice Frankfurter concurred. Mr. Justice Black, joined by Douglas, dissented as did Mr. Justice Murphy, joined by Rutledge.

The two particulars in which Adamson claimed that the California trial denied him due process of law were the admission of a certain portion of the evidence and the fact that the prosecutor had called to the attention of the jury Adamson's failure to take the stand. The matter of the evidence may be disposed of as rapidly here as it was in the opinions of Reed, Frankfurter, Black and Murphy and in that of Traynor of the California Supreme Court[4] so that full attention may be given to the other particular.

An elderly widow had been found on the floor of her apartment in Los Angeles on July 25, 1944. The indications were that she had died the previous afternoon, and it was determined that the cause of death was strangulation—and probably from a lamp wire found around her neck. She had evidently received a severe beating before she was strangled. Although she had been seen on the 24th wearing stockings and certain expensive diamond rings, she was bare-legged when discovered and the diamond rings were missing from her fingers and were not to be found. The lower half of a woman's stocking was found under her.

Six of Adamson's fingerprints were found on a delivery door—the sort of door one finds under a cabinet or sink in a small furnished apartment the likes of which abound in Los Angeles. (In some apartment hotels such a door is used for milk deliveries; in others for trash disposal. There are usually two doors, with a compartment between. The outer door may be opened without a key from the hallway and the inner door is usually latched with an ordinary spring-latch on its inside. The doors may be as small as eighteen inches square.) In this case, it was the inner door upon which Adamson's prints were found. It was off its hinges and standing in the kitchen. Tops of women's stockings were found in Adamson's apartment. No one of these tops matched the lower half found under the murdered woman's body. A witness who positively identified Adamson testified that a portion of a conversation had been overheard sometime after the murder and in that partial conversation Adamson had offered certain unseen diamond rings for sale to some unidentified person. This was the sum of evidence against him—his six prints on the door, the offer of some ring or rings for sale, and the fact that he had some stocking tops in his abode.

Since Frankfurter wrote a concurring opinion in this case, his silence on the question of the admissibility and the sufficiency of the evidence against Adamson may be taken as tacit approval of the treatment of that question in the opinion of the Court with whose decision he concurred. Black and Murphy did not need to deal with the question because they would reverse the conviction on other grounds, making the *evidence* a moot matter. Mr. Justice Reed's entire treatment of the evidence question is contained in the next-to-last paragraph of his opinion. That paragraph consists of just 120 words. That is, Mr. Justice Reed disposed of the whole question of evidence in a paragraph exactly as long as this one.

Reed's actual refutation of Adamson's claims regarding the propriety of the evidence against him was confined to the last sentence of the paragraph referred to above. It read, "we do not think the introduction of this evidence violated any federal constitutional right."[5] It is probably not overly sentimental here to suggest that, where the penalty is death, something more than Reed's one sentence would be appropriate as an answer to the charge that the evidence was improper. On the other hand, it is perhaps something more than a lawyer's trick with words to remind that there are tribunals more competent than the United States Supreme Court for the resolution of such questions.

As the case came before the Supreme Court of the United States, the matter of the evidence was confined to the question of its propriety, but in the California Courts, both its propriety and its sufficiency were questioned. Mr. Justice Traynor's answer to the sufficiency question was that "[f]rom the foregoing evidence a reasonable jury could conclude that beyond a reasonable doubt defendant committed the murder and burglary."[6]

> To be admissible, evidence must tend to prove a material issue in the light of human experience. . . . Evidence that tends to throw light on a fact in dispute may be admitted. The weight to be given such evidence will be determined by the jury.[7]

Traynor does not say that the evidence as the prosecutor set it before the jury or as it has been presented in abridged fashion here is perfect proof that must—of logical necessity—convince all sane men everywhere and in all time to come that Admiral Dewey Adamson did in fact kill and rob the elderly widow. In the American scheme of criminal justice, questions of fact are normally left to the jury and those of law to the judge. The jury must exercise practical judgment; the court exercises what Mr. Justice Frankfurter calls "judicial judgment." It is not up to the judge to substitute *his* practical judgment for that of the jury. In order for the trial judge—or, for that matter, the appellate judge—to overrule the jury on a question of fact, he must state not that some other group of twelve reasonable persons might come to a verdict other than that to which the jury has come, nor that he, the judge, comes to some other conclusion. He must state that NO group of twelve reasonable persons could have come to the verdict reached by the jury on the basis of the evidence presented to it. In other words, he must state that the jury is manifestly unreasonable.

Perhaps not *everyone* in his right mind is convinced of Adamson's guilt, but there are plenty of dozens of sane, decent, disinterested people who could be so convinced by the evidence which was presented. It is not Judge Fricke's fault, nor the fault of the California or United States Supreme Court nor of the Los Angeles jury that the penalty for first degree murder is death. That is the fault of the law of California. That of all the dozens of qualified citizens of Los Angeles, some of whom would not have been convinced and others who would have been convinced by the evidence should have ended up on Adamson's jury is due in no small part to what may be called the "law of averages."

While an outside observer may well question the wisdom of sending Adamson to his death on the basis of such evidence as was presented, the trial judge in the *Adamson* case could not be expected to forbid such an outcome as "unlawful." The law of the State of California is rather easily changed and is not of great interest to this study. The "law of averages"—i.e., the relationship of chance and practical judgment—is a more complicated matter. So much, then, for the sufficiency of the evidence against Adamson.

As far as the propriety of that evidence is concerned, Adamson claimed that the introduction of his possession of stocking-tops into the trial could have been only for the sake of prejudicing the jury against him. No stocking-top found among his belongings matched the stocking-bottom found under the corpse. It was said, since no direct connection could be drawn between one stocking-part and another, that the prosecution was obviously attempting to prejudice the jury by intimating that Adamson, a negro, had a sexually perverse interest in stocking-tops; that they constituted some sort of "fetish" for him. No such attempt is obvious on the record, although it must be admitted here that such an attempt might have been obvious in the courtroom and might at the same time have been of such a nature as to be unrecordable.[8] But, at least no overt *statement* was made by the prosecution from which such a conclusion can be drawn. All the prosecution attempted on the basis of Adamson's possession of stocking-tops was to establish that he had an "interest" in such matters which interest was sufficient as a link in the whole chain of evidence tending to show his guilt. This, said Mr. Justice Traynor, was a quite proper introduction of evidence.

But the whole question of evidence, as has been indicated, occupies but one paragraph of a case which takes up seventy-nine pages in the *U.S. Reports.* The more interesting question, the question of much greater constitutional significance, is that concerning the fact that the "prosecuting attorney commented repeatedly on the failure of the defendant to take the stand."[9] According to Adamson, this comment negated the privilege against self-crimination which was guaranteed him by the due process clause of the Fourteenth Amendment. This is a double claim and each part must be questioned in turn: does such comment negate the privilege, and is the privilege guaranteed by the Fourteenth Amendment?[10]

Once again, the latter portion of the question before us is that portion to which greater attention must be given. This is not because the question as to whether comment upon a defendant's failure to testify is of less intrinsic importance or difficulty than the question as to whether the due process clause of the Fourteenth Amendment protects the privilege against self-crimination. On the contrary, the latter may be described as "merely historical." But for the purposes of this study alone, the latter question is a more vital step in the inquiry and must, therefore, be accorded greater attention. The former question will be disposed of rather briskly of necessity.

"By statute or by decision, the majority of jurisdictions prohibit such comments," admits Justice Traynor.[11] Wigmore states that:

> . . . In England comment by the judge only is allowable, and in Canada comment by neither judge nor counsel is allowable.
> . . . Nor is it proper to go so far as to *instruct the jury* (even when no comment has been made) to disregard the inference. . . . However, by express statute in Indiana and

Washington such an instruction is required. By express statute
of Oklahoma and West Virginia (and perhaps by implication in
other statutes) no "mention" of the accused's silence is to be
made, and this may be construed to forbid even the judge's
reference to it by instructions; thus the words of the local statute
may affect the result. In two states the final absurdity has been
committed of forbidding the jury even to discuss the subject
among themselves.[12]

The question of the permissibility of comment upon the failure to
testify, like the whole matter of the judge's instructions to the jury, is
fascinating inasmuch as it is at this point that the layman receives a
"short course" in the law and is asked—if not to be a part-time
lawyer—at least to confine his lay judgment within artificial
boundaries of the law. Indeed, it is by the instructions that the
artificiality of the disjunction between the "law" of the judge and the
"facts" of the jury which is characteristic of English courts is
corrected.[13] To comment is to infer and whether and what inference
to draw from failure to testify is not everywhere agreed upon.

The layman's natural first suggestion would probably be that
the claim was a clear confession of the criminating fact. The
lawyer's natural first answer would certainly be that then the
privilege would thereby be annulled. Both of these have a truth
but only a partial truth.[14]

Can the "legal fiction" that guilt may not be inferred from the
accused's failure to testify work out in practice? Wigmore, the old
lawyers' saw that one ought to ask for a jury if he is guilty and waive
a jury if innocent, and the ordinary suspicions of any thoughtful
man, are confirmed by the fact that among veniremen to whom the
privilege against self-crimination and the bar against inference has
just been explained, a disturbing number, when asked what they
would think if a man accused of theft refused to testify in his own
behalf, answer that they would suppose he was guilty.

In order to reach the conclusion that a conclusion is exceedingly
difficult on this point, it is not necessary to chop the logical analysis
of Wigmore[15] nor the psychological analysis proffered by some of the
authorities upon whom Mr. Justice Traynor rests[16] nor to dismiss as

sentimental regard for the underdog Dean Griswold's speech on "The Fifth Amendment as a Symbol" wherein he states:

> It may well be, as has been said by high authority, that the Fifth Amendment protects against prosecution for crime (i.e., the crime of contempt for refusing to testify after immunity from prosecution has been offered in return for waiver of the privilege against self-crimination), but it cannot protect against the obvious inference which would be taken by any thinking person. I would like to suggest again that in many circumstances that inference is not wholly warranted. A person who thinks a little further about the matter may find that there are many factors in some of these situations which must be taken into account before he reaches any conclusion about the inference he should take.[17]

Although most states forbid comment on the claim of the privilege, California is one of the few states that "permit limited comment upon a defendant's failure to testify."[18] Such was not always the case in California, but the American Bar Association and the American Bar Institute conducted studies in the early thirties,[19] and in 1934, on the strength of some of the conclusions reached in these studies, the Constitution of the State of California, Art. I, sec. 13, was amended to read:

> . . . No person shall be twice put in jeopardy for the same offense; nor be compelled, in any criminal case, to be a witness against himself; nor be deprived of life, liberty, or property without due process of law; but in any criminal case, whether the defendant testifies or not, his failure to explain or to deny by his testimony any evidence or facts in the case against him may be commented upon by the court and by the counsel, and may be considered by the court or the jury. . . .[20]

In the application of this provision to Adamson, Traynor explains that comment is not made on the defendant's failure to *take the stand*, but on his failure to explain or deny evidence or facts.[21] Permission to comment extends to instances where a defendant *does* take the stand as well as to those where he does not.[22] The particular pieces of evidence which the defendant omits to lay against the prosecutor's case by his failure to "explain or deny . . . any evidence or facts . . ." are like any other piece of evidence in the case. The prosecutor does not comment upon the defendant's failure to testify, he merely calls the jury's attention to the weakness of the defense argument by showing the kinds of evidentiary statements upon which a proper defense ought to be made and then comments upon the defendant's failure to introduce evidence of that kind. It is, as it were, only coincidental that such failure is due to the defendant's failure to take the stand at all. As Chief Justice Mansfield said, "all evidence is to be weighed according to the proof which it was in the power of one side to have produced and in the power of the other to contradict."[23]

Of course, such a distinction—i.e., that between comment upon failure to provide evidence contradictory to evidence or facts in the prosecution case on the one hand and flat comment upon the failure of the defendant to take the stand—is purely academic in the nicest sense for, practically speaking, all the prosecution need do is recapitulate its evidence, item by item, and follow each item with some such comment as, "And what has the defense to say about that?—Nothing! Not one shred of evidence is offered to the contrary." In such an instance, comment by the prosecution upon the defendant's failure "to explain or deny . . . evidence or facts"—omission by omission—is tantamount to comment upon the defendant's failure to testify which, in turn, is, in many cases, the same as comment upon the fact that the defendant claimed the privilege against self-crimination guaranteed by the State Constitution. This is, in fact, just what the prosecution appears to have done on the trial in the *Adamson* case.[24] As it happens, the opinions of Reed and Frankfurter and even that of Traynor, despite the fact that the latter draws the nice legal distinction in the course of that opinion, all roughly accept the identity of the three levels of comment—comment upon failure to "explain or deny," upon failure to testify at all, upon the claim of the privilege against self-crimination—when each of these opinions is taken as a whole.

The compass of this study forbids exhaustion of the questions as to what inference may be drawn from the claim of the privilege and what comments properly may be made to facilitate such inference, or even a careful analysis of the views on this subject of Griswold,

Wigmore, or Traynor. Suffice it to say that the grant of the privilege is almost universal in English-speaking courts but that where the privilege is claimed our "first natures," so to speak, incline our suspicions of guilt to amplify. Inasmuch as perfect identification of the claim with admission of guilt is the same as conversion, *sub silentio* of a not-guilty plea into a guilty plea, however, it behooves our "better natures" to counter our "first natures" with an explanation, in an abstract or historical vein, of the reasons for the privilege. But sensible men are *bound*—whether they be lay or professional—to take into account the fact that a defendant remains silent in the face of damning evidence, and it is perhaps too much of a legal fiction to say that court and counsel may not *somehow* argue the manner of the account-taking. That the privilege might not be a baited trap, however, it makes good sense for counter-argument in the form of the historical or abstract explanations of the reasons for the privilege to come to the jury from the authoritative position of the bench in the form of instructions. In the *Adamson* case, Frankfurter points out that defense counsel's recourse, in the face of the adverse comment by the prosecution, ought to have been to prayers for such instructions.[25]

There remains to be discussed one aspect of the situation in which Adamson found himself on the trial. He had been convicted on prior occasions for burglary, larceny, and robbery. In order that evidence of *former* crimes should not influence the jury in deciding whether a defendant is guilty of a crime presently charged, the Penal Code of California provides[26] that, "In case the defendant pleads not guilty, and answers that he has suffered the previous conviction, the charge of the previous conviction must not be read to the jury, nor alluded to on the trial."[27] However, should the defendant plead not guilty and then take the stand in his own defense, his criminal record *may* be revealed to the jury in order to impeach his testimony just as in the case of any *other* witness.[28] "This forces an accused who is a repeated offender to choose between the risk of having his prior offense disclosed to the jury or having it draw harmful inferences from uncontradicted evidence that can only be denied or explained by the defendant."[29] This is an unhappy choice. The question is, is it an unfair choice? We must see how and why it is possible for it to be raised. It could not be raised in a trial in a United States Court.

The Fifth Amendment to the Constitution of the United States states: "No person. . . . shall be compelled in any criminal case to be a witness against himself. . . ." The statutory provision covering this point states the matter more strongly. A defendant may, *"at his own request, but not otherwise,* be a competent witness."[30] The law further states that "his failure to make such request shall not create any presumption against him."[31] In his concurring opinion in the *Adamson* case, Mr. Justice Frankfurter said that he was "prepared to agree that, as a part of that immunity [of the accused from the common duty to testify, written into the Federal Bill of Rights], comment on the failure of the accused to take the witness stand is forbidden in federal prosecutions. It is so, of course, by explicit act of Congress."[32] Following this statement, he cites 20 Stat. 30—the statute just quoted—and also *Bruno* v. *United States.*[33] In the *Bruno* case, Frankfurter, just ten months after joining the bench, spoke for a virtually unanimous court[34] in reversing an appellate court affirmance of a conviction to which exception had been taken because the trial judge declined to make this additional instruction to the jury:

> The failure of any defendant to take the witness stand and testify in his own behalf does not create any presumption against him; the jury is charged that it must not permit that fact to weigh in the slightest degree against any such defendant, nor should this fact enter into the discussion or deliberations of the jury in any manner.[35]

Frankfurter closed the *Bruno* opinion by dealing with the "psychological impossibility not to have a presumption arise in the minds of jurors against an accused who fails to testify" by giving the "short answer . . . that Congress legislated on a contrary assumption and not without support in experience."[36] In other words, at least for Frankfurter, comment before a United States trial jury on a defendant's failure to testify which would lead to an inference being drawn from such failure is clearly forbidden—if not by the Fifth Amendment, by the Act of March 16, 1878—and every such defendant is entitled to a charge from the bench to the jury—psychologically efficacious or not—to abjure presumption on account of such failure. Of the twenty-two justices who have sat on the Supreme Court bench alongside Frankfurter, it would be hard to find one who would deny that, in a United States court, such comment is forbidden and such a charge guaranteed.

In state trials, however, no such prohibition or guarantee is assured by the United States Constitution as it is interpreted by the Supreme Court. Adamson's conviction could have been reversed on one of two grounds. It could have been reversed on the ground that the particular dilemma in which he found himself—to remain silent and suffer the adverse comments of the prosecution upon his silence or to testify and to have his testimony impeached by the revelation of his former convictions—was essentially unfair. Or, it could have been reversed on the ground that comment inevitably negates the privilege against self-crimination. That privilege is protected in a United States court by the Fifth Amendment. But, if the court were to reverse on *that* ground, it would have to hold that the privilege is protected in a state court by the Fourteenth Amendment because the Fourteenth guarantees "due process of law" in a state proceeding and "due process of law" means all the procedural guarantees in the Fourth through the Eighth Amendments or all those guarantees and more.

The *Adamson* case was what Professor Corwin called "the high-water mark of dissent in support of the contention that the Bill of Rights, originally operative only against the Federal Government, became limitations on State action by virtue of their inclusion within the due process clause of the Fourteenth Amendment."[37] The court in the *Adamson* case was five to four against the inclusion. It appears that the tide of dissent had not ebbed twelve years later, for in *Frank* v. *Maryland*[38] and *Bartkus* v. *Illinois*[39] the mathematics were the same and the division over the meaning of the "due process" clause of the Fourteenth Amendment similar. In the *Adamson* case, Black, Douglas, Murphy, and Rutledge had been the dissenters. In the *Frank* and *Bartkus* cases, Warren, Black, Douglas, and Brennan took the side of the accused. In *Ohio ex rel. Eaton* v. *Price*,[40] the court noted "probable jurisdiction." Justice Frankfurter, with Clark, Harlan, and Whittaker concurring, wrote a separate memorandum disapproving the taking of the case on the ground that it was indistinguishable from the *Frank* case, just decided. Mr. Justice Stewart abstained, no doubt because his father sat upon the Supreme Court of Ohio from which appeal had been taken. In due course the case came up and was affirmed by an equally divided Court, with the same division and the same abstention.[41] It is time, then, for a brief historical survey of this problem.

NOTES TO CHAPTER I

[1]332 U.S. 46.

[2]165 P.2d 3. Mr. Justice Traynor delivered the opinion of the Court which included Chief Justice Gibson, and Justices Shenk, Edmonds, Carter, Schauer and Spence.

[3]Per 28 U.S.C. 344(a).

[4]165 P.2d 3.

[5]332 U.S. 46, 59.

[6]165 P.2d 3, 6.

[7]*Ibid.*, p. 7.

[8]". . . I cannot now recreate his tone of voice or the gloss that personality puts on speech." Justice Frankfurter (Separate opinion), *Von Moltke* v. *Gillies,* 332 U.S. 708, 727 at 730.

[9]165 P.3d 3, 7.

[10]Cf. *Twining* v. *New Jersey,* 211 U.S. 78, 91.

[11]165 P.2d 3, at 7.

[12]J.H. Wigmore, *A Treatise on the Anglo-American System of Evidence,* 3d ed. 10 vols. (Boston: Little Brown, 1940), Vol. VIII, sec. 2272. The "two states" to which reference is made in the last sentence of the quotation are Kansas and Texas.

[13]See the excellent fictional portrayal of this problem as it is forwarded by a technical plea of insanity in Robert Traver's *The Anatomy of a Murder.*

[14]Wigmore, *op. cit.,* Vol. VIII, sec. 2272.

[15]"The inference, as a mere matter of logic, is not only possible but inherent, and cannot be denied." *Ibid.,* p. 410.

[16]Traynor relies in part upon *State* v. *Grebe,* 17 Kan. 458, where the "instinct of self-preservation" is seen as driving the guilty to claim the privilege.

[17]*The Fifth Amendment Today* (Cambridge: Harvard University Press, 1955), p. 57. The bracketed insertion in the quotation may not be precisely the sense intended by the original, but the paragraph—at least, taken out of context—makes no sense otherwise, and it is believed that the insertion does no violence to the contextual intent of Professor Griswold. Incidentally, whatever sentimentality Griswold's little book may discover was well-deserved by the particular underdogs then receiving Griswold's support, whatever may be the long-run merits of his argument.

[18]332 U.S. 46, 55; 165 P.2d 3, 7; Wigmore, *op. cit.,* Vol. VIII, sec. 2272.

[19]American Bar Association, *Reports,* LVI (Baltimore: Lord Baltimore Press, 1931), 137-52; American Law Institute, *Proceedings,* IX (Philadelphia: Author, 1931), 202-18.

[20]Quoted in the margin, 332 U.S. 46, 48, and in the text of 165 P.2d 3 at 7.

[21]165 P.2d 3, at 8.

[22]Albeit short of contemptuous refusal to say, under cross examination, where he was, say, at nine o'clock, after freely telling, under direct examination, where he was at eight, one would suppose that the failure of a defendant who has taken the stand in his own defense to "explain or deny . . . evidence or facts" would be largely attributable to the ineptness of the prosecution in framing questions during cross-examination.

[23]*Blatch* v. *Archer,* 1 Cowp. 63 at 65, 98 Eng. Rep. (K.B.) 970; quoted in 165 P.2d 3 at 8; but miscited there as "Cowp. 66."

[24]See, for example, 165 P.2d 3, at 10.

[25]332 U.S. 46, at 61.

[26]Section 1025.

[27]332 U.S. 46, at 49.

[28]165 P.2d 3, 11.

[29]332 U.S. 46, at 49.

[30]20 Stat. 30 (March 16, 1878, ch. 37); 28 U.S.C., 632 (1946 ed.). Emphasis added. The "but not otherwise" was dropped in the recodification adopted June 25, 1948, by 62 Stat. 833; see present Code at 18 U.S.C. 3481.

[31]*Loc. cit.*

[32]332 U.S. 46, at 61.

[33]308 U.S. 287.

[34]Mr. Justice McReynolds "concur[red] in the result" without expressing an opinion.

[35]308 U.S. 287, 292. The last clause of this denied charge, which Frankfurter said was "[c]oncededly . . . correct," 308 U.S. 287 at 293, looks at bit like what Wigmore had called "the final absurdity" (*op. cit.,* p. 418). See above, pp. 5-6.

[36]308 U.S. 287, at 294.

[37]E.S. Corwin, *Constitution of the United States of America, Revised and Annotated* (Washington: U.S. Government Printing Office, 1953), p. 1115.

[38]359 U.S. 360, May 4, 1959.

[39]359 U.S. 121, March 30, 1959.

[40]360 U.S. 246, June 8, 1959.

[41]364 U.S. 263, June 6, 1960.

CHAPTER II

THE INTENTION OF
THE FRAMERS

Prior to *Admason* v. *California*, the Court, as such, had not suggested—except perhaps by occasional implication—that the Fourteenth Amendment intended the specific provisions of the first eight amendments, or any of them, as such, to be bars to state action. The Court, in fact, consistently held otherwise. Nor had more than a very little non-Court writing argued such an intention.[1] However, Mr. Justice Black's dissent in the *Adamson* case touched off a long debate in the scholarly world. The problem has been aired thoroughly, if not admirably, and a brief sketch of the exchange is in order. It begins with Black's statement, as follows:[2]

> My study of the historical events that culminated in the Fourteenth Amendment, and the expressions of those who sponsored and favored, as well as those who opposed its submission and passage, persuades me that one of the chief objects that the provisions of the Amendment's first section, separately, and as a whole, were intended to accomplish was to make the Bill of Rights, applicable to the states.[3]
> With full knowledge of the import of the *Barron* decision, the framers and backers of the Fourteenth Amendment proclaimed its purpose to be to overturn the constitutional rule that case had announced. This historical purpose has never received full consideration or exposition in any opinion of the Court interpreting the Amendment.

What immediately strikes the reader with a schoolboy's knowledge of the Civil War is the curious relegation by Black to a footnote of that "other prime purpose" (Black said "[a]nother") to "make colored people citizens." Whatever may have been the intention of the "provisions of the Amendment's first section, separately, and as a whole," there is no question but that the *Amendment*, read as a whole, shows an intention to deal with the fact of the Civil War generally and the status of the negro specifically.[4] The First Section will be set out in full below. The Second Section, perhaps worked out in answer to fears expressed during Congressional debate that the proposed Amendment might be taken as granting the suffrage to negroes, appears to leave the States free to deny such suffrage but provides for a reduction in Congressional representation in proportion to such denial. The Third Section disqualifies from future state or national office, subject to Congressional removal of the disqualification, former state and national officials who had supported the rebellion. The Fourth Section repudiates debts contracted in support of the rebellion. The Fifth Section empowers Congress to "enforce, by appropriate legislation," the Amendment.

Another curiosity of Black's dissent, which is not so apparent, is the one-sided evidence for his unsettling challenge to fixed constitutional law. That evidence is presented in the long Appendix he affixed to his opinion.[5]

Professor Fairman supplied a splendid corrective to Black's unbalanced evidence in the Adamson case in a journal article two years afterward.[6] Reference to Fairman's argument will be required, but first, something can be said about Black's assertion without going outside of the material quoted in his Appendix.

The Appendix consists of eight parts. Parts I and II[7] are devoted not to Congressional debate over the proposal of the Joint Committee on Reconstruction which finally became—in amended style and with the addition of the definition of citizenship—the Fourteenth Amendment.[8] These first two parts of Black's Appendix are devoted rather to the debate over Congressman Bingham's proposal[9] which was reported out of committee on February 26,[10] and debate upon which was postponed, following a motion by Congressman Conkling, on February 28[11] until the "second Tuesday of April next" (i.e., April 10, 1866). It might as well have been postponed until what playful boys call "the second Tuesday of next week" for an examination of the *Congressional Globe*[12] does not disclose that this proposal was ever debated again.[13] It could not reasonably be argued, even from so high a station as that occupied by Mr. Justice Black, that the substance of, and debate over, a proposal that had a life span of three days on the floor of the House could control interpretation of a Constitutional Amendment which later emanated from the same source as the earlier proposal and dealt, very generally speaking, with the same area of problems.

Granting that it would be fair to consider the general context and background of the proposal which finally became the Fourteenth Amendment and that Bingham's earlier proposal is a part thereof, the material contained in Parts I and II of Black's Appendix adds little if any weight to the proposition that the Fourteenth Amendment was meant to forbid the states to do the various things which the first eight Amendments forbid the United States to do.

The earlier Bingham proposal reads:

> The Congress shall have power to make all laws which shall be necessary and proper to secure to the citizens of each State all privileges and immunities of citizens in the several States, and to all persons in the several States equal protection in the rights of life, liberty, and property.[14]

As it reads, this proposal does not in any sense prohibit the states from doing what the United States are forbidden to do by the first eight Amendments; nor does it prohibit the states from anything. It merely empowers Congress to do something. Perhaps it empowers the Congress to forbid the states to do something. Perhaps it empowers Congress to forbid the states to do the things that the first eight Amendments forbid the United States to do. That it is not very clear just what the proposal would have empowered the Congress to do or to forbid the states to do is evidenced by the debates during its short hearing before the House.

Everyone admits that a principal object of all the Reconstruction legislation and all the Amendments passed during Reconstruction, as well as the various proposals that led to the legislation and the Amendments, was the elevation of the negro. Indeed, a good case could be made that the first and second sections of the Fourteenth Amendment, as adopted, intended merely the "equal protection of the laws."[15]

It is true that Bingham mentioned the "bill of rights" on occasion, but it is *never* fully clear what *he* meant by that phrase. At times it seemed to include for him provisions of the main body of the Constitution.[16] According to Fairman, "never, even once, does advocate or opponent say, 'the first eight Amendments.' "[17] Mr. Justice Black, however, treats "bill of rights" and "first eight amendments" as interchangeable, which could seem to be perfectly justified and does seem so until one reads through Bingham's speeches on the floor of the House,[18] and realizes that no such easy, clear equivalence can be seen in that Congressman's remarks. Just why Black should state, in reference to this late February debate, that "[s]ome took the position that the Amendment was unnecessary because the Bill of Rights was already secured against state violation,"[19] and then cite pages 1059, 1066, and 1088 as authority for that statement is a complete mystery. Argument fails at this point. The reader is invited to read these three pages of the *Globe* in search of one shred of evidence for Black's assertion.

Page 1059 consists, except for two interruptions by Congressman Chanler of New York, entirely of comments by Congressman Kelley of Pennsylvania and these comments, in turn, are all but entirely quotations from the Virginia, Massachusetts, and New York Constitutional ratifying conventions in 1788. The subject of these quotations is not the first eight Amendments or any of them but rather Art. I, sec. 4, which deals with the "Times, Places and Manner of holding Elections." Indeed, it would be difficult to see how constructive evidence could be drawn by reference to such debates. While it is true that several ratifying conventions in the states did discuss what were thought to be shortcomings of the proposed Constitution and a good deal of that discussion centered on the lack of a bill of rights, one could not draw more than illustrative evidence of the meaning of that bill of rights—e.g., its applicability—from debate over the adoption of the instrument which, if adopted, would create the body which was to draft such a bill of rights. It might be argued that the anachronism is Mr. Kelley's and not Mr. Justice Black's, for Kelley says on the preceding page [20] that the members of the Constitutional Convention "took care to arm the Government for which they were providing with power to enforce every right, privilege, and immunity accorded to the people, and to guarantee a republican form of government to each State." But, in order so to argue, one must assume: (l) that Mr. Kelley thought the "privileges and immunities" clause[21] was perfectly clear, (2) that he considered "rights," "privileges," and "immunities" as interchangeable expressions; (3) that the members of the Convention probably knew that a "bill of rights" would be appended to their work and knew the precise content of that probable "bill of rights"; (4) that he thought that the "rights" protected by the bill-of-rights-to-be-appended were "rights" "against" state action (which assumption is precisely what Black's citations purport to prove); and, finally (5) that Mr. Kelley thought that the members of the state ratifying conventions in Virginia, Massachusetts and New York thought that the members of the Constitutional Convention thought that the "times, places and manner" clause was the lever by which the national Congress was going to prevent the states from doing the things which the yet-to-be-appended first several amendments would forbid the national government to do.

The argument on page 1066 which comes closest to being what Black says it is, is Congressman Price's (Iowa) entertaining lecture to the "constitutional lawyers" in the House on the fact that the "general welfare" clause appears in Art. I, sec. 8—*not* only in the Preamble—and that the pending resolution probably would strengthen the power of the Congress so to provide by "giv[ing] the same rights, privileges and protections to the citizen of one State going into another that a citizen of that State would have who had lived there for years."[22] In other words, to use Price's own examples,[23] the sad facts of history were that, despite the "privileges and immunities" clause and the "general welfare" clause, while a Southerner could visit a Northern State and safely express his opinion on any political controversy, however agitated, then current in that Northern State, a Northerner visiting in the South dared not express an opinion on slavery which was contrary to the prevalent or the official opinion. In fact, Price points out, Northerners had been murdered in the South for just such expressions. Maybe the pending resolution could help prevent such bad things in the future. How? By enabling Congress to see to it that the Southern States did not do what Mr. Justice Black says that page 1066 shows that somebody in the 39th Congress thought the first eight Amendments—notwithstanding *Barron* v. *Baltimore*—forbade the States to do? Maybe so! But, again, one would have to assume the point the substantiation of which a perusal of page 1066 is supposed to support. A speech of Congressman Hale's (New York) which ends on page 1066 begins on page 1063. The portion on page 1066 argues only that the projected consideration by the House of the proposed Amendment is too "hasty" and is not "calm" and "dispassionate" enough for such a serious matter. It is true that Hale refers—on page 1065, not 1066—to the "bill of rights" and it is also true that the particular passage[24] taken out of context, would seem to support Black's allegation that some members of the 39th Congress thought that the first eight Amendments already applied to the States, but, if one reads all of Hale's speech—or even all that appears on pages 1065-66—the contrary is likelier, or at least as likely. Perhaps one could argue that this is a picayune complaint, that the discovery of this merely technical error in Black's argument tends rather to support his general contention that the members of the 39th Congress intended that the proposed Fourteenth Amendment forbid the states to do what Marshall, speaking for the Court in *Barron* v. *Baltimore*, said the first eight Amendments forbade only the national government to do. Mr. Hale, such an argument would run, would not otherwise have been so exercised about the radical change to the federal system he feared would be wrought by such an Amendment. In answer to this line of argument, one is compelled to state that all that evidence shows is a fear on Hale's part that the proposed Amendment would empower the national Congress to do some things that the scheme of federal relations had formerly left the states to do or undo or not to do. Nowhere is there the suggestion that the proposed Amendment would empower the United States *Courts* or any one of them to overturn a decision of one of the state Courts on the grounds that the procedures in the state court had run contrary to what the first eight Amendments prescribed for actions in the United States Courts.[25]

As far as page 1088 is concerned, remarks by Congressman Woodbridge (Vermont) and Bingham appear there. Black is obviously not referring to Bingham's remarks as tending to support the allegation that some members of the 39th Congress thought the first eight Amendments did at that time apply to the states as well as to the United States, for it is Black's argument that Bingham meant to overturn *Barron* v. *Baltimore*. What of Woodbridge? To him, the proposed amendment "merely gives the power to Congress to enact those laws which will give to a citizen of the United States the natural rights which necessarily pertain to citizenship."[26] Just what *are* the "natural rights which necessarily pertain to citizenship"? It was not until the adoption of the Fourteenth Amendment in its final form—in fact, in the amendment to the proposed Amendment offered during Senate debate on May 27 (by Senator Howard)—that the Constitution anywhere said *who* was a citizen. Nowhere does the Constitution spell out, even today, what are the rights, "natural" or otherwise, of a citizen. Did Congressman Woodbridge believe that one of the "rights" of citizenship was, say, the right to trial by jury in suits at common law, where the value in controversy exceeds twenty dollars? He does not so say. Aristotle laid as the essential feature of citizenship sharing in the administration of justice and in the holding of office.[27] Surely this was not generally held by the members of the 39th Congress as the *content* of citizenship. The Fourteenth Amendment, as finally adopted, identifies "[a]ll persons born or naturalized in the United States and subject to the jurisdiction thereof" as "citizens of the United Sates and of the State wherein they reside." But other clauses of the Constitution provide that *mere* citizenship, as the Fourteenth Amendment grants it, must be augmented by age and residence requirements for qualification for election to the presidency[28] or to the Senate[29] or to the House.[30] If the 39th Congress had agreed with Aristotle, they surely would have proposed the amendment of these clauses when they added the amendment to the proposed Amendment. Perhaps some member of the 39th Congress had failed to read Aristotle at the time that he failed to read *Barron* v. *Baltimore*.[31] And, surely again, one cannot conceive of a general definition of *citizenship* which includes the holding of office without including by implication the franchise. On the contrary, one *can* conceive of a definition of what might be called "mere" citizenship which includes the franchise (which, after all, is a kind of office) but which does not include, as such, the eligibility to elective office. Even *this* definition of citizenship was not the one entertained by the 39th Congress for it was not until the Nineteenth Amendment that female citizens were enfranchised.[32] It is not capricious to point out that even today while "all persons" are, by the Fourteenth Amendment, citizens, only "grown-up" citizens are enfranchised and the various states impose various additional requirements over and above mere "grown-up" citizenship. The Congressional debates over the proposed Amendment are ambiguous on the question as to whether the freedom granted by the Thirteenth Amendment included the franchise, or whether the power to be given Congress by the earlier proposal would or would not include the power to enfranchise the negro.[33] In fact, the Fourteenth Amendment, in final form, distinguished between citizenship and the franchise, even considering males only, by making "all persons" citizens, and leaving the states free—subject to a penalty in representation—to exclude some perons (presumably negroes as a class) from the vote. However the subject of voting may have stood, it certainly cannot be said that Woodbridge manifestly believed that citizenship implied, by necessity, protection from all levels of government against all the things noted in the first eight Amendments.

So much for pages 1059, 1066 and 1088 of the *Congressional Globe* for the First Session of the 39th Congress. A careful examination of these pages produces no support whatever for the sentence in Black's Appendix delcaring that "[s]ome took the position that the Amendment was unnecessary because the Bill of Rights was already secured against state violation."[34] Further analysis of the Appendix will be abbreviated, resting upon the foregoing discussion as an example of the doubts raised regarding Black's contention when his assertions and his authorities are subjected to a careful check. It is curious that he should have treated as simply interchangeable the expressions "bill of rights" and "first eight amendments" and that the latter phrase occurs *only* in his *indirect* quotations of Bingham. His direct quotations include only the former. It may not be overly pedantic to point out that at least one of the speeches of Bingham quoted by Black hints at the possibility that Bingham—at least at times—actually *distinguished* between the two phrases. Black quotes him as saying:

> . . . A gentleman on the other side interrupted me and wanted to know if I could cite a decision showing that the power of the Federal Government to enforce in the United States courts the

bill of rights under the articles of amendment to the Constitution
had been denied. . . .[35]

This is, of course, one of the strongest pieces of Black's evidence,
for Bingham then goes on to cite *Barron* v. *Baltimore*. But a careful
reading of this quotation from Bingham's speech suggests the
following possibility as readily as it suggests Black's contention:
Bingham had found that the "power of the Federal Government to
enforce in the United States courts the bill of rights under the articles
of amendment to the Constitution had been denied" in *Barron* v.
Baltimore. This passage only proves Black's point if one first *assumes*
that point. Just to free ourselves from that assumption, let us make
different ones, and then let us see what that passage might mean. Let
us substitute for "bill of rights" something as indistinct as a close
reading of Bingham strongly hints his thoughts may have been—say,
"the American way of life"—and let us entertain the possibility that
by the word "under" he meant "through" or "by means of." The
passage would then read "the power of the Federal Government to
enforce in the United States courts the American way of life by means
of the articles of amendment to the Constitution had been denied."[36]

This *does* show that Bingham was aware of *Barron* v. *Baltimore* as
holding that the first eight Amendments to the Constitution were bars
only to United States action and not to state action and it also shows
that he was distressed that injustices had been committed by some
states under the leeway which *Barron* v. *Baltimore* assured, and it
further shows that the proposed Amendment he was supporting
hoped somehow to correct or alleviate these injuries. But, especially if
one recalls the precise wording of the proposal under discussion *when
that speech was made by Bingham* (February 28), it does not suggest
at all that Bingham intended the states to be forbidden thenceforward
to do any and all of the things that the first eight Amendments
forbade the United States to do. Remember that the proposal then
under discussion read:

> The Congress shall have power to make all laws which shall be
> necessary and proper to secure to the citizens of each State all
> privileges and immunities of citizens in the several states and to
> all persons in the several States equal protection in the rights of
> life, liberty, and property.

Are we to conclude that what Bingham intended to do about *Barron* v. *Baltimore* was anything other than to (1) leave the federal system essentially as it was but to (2) empower Congress to give consideration to the injustices committed by some states and by individuals within any state[37] within the latitude left to state action by the Federal system as *Barron* v. *Baltimore* interpreted it and to alleviate those injustices by specific, corrective (both positive and negative) legislation? Such an Amendment would, in fact, leave the various state systems of criminal procedure intact but it would at least purport to empower Congress to change or standardize those systems. Congress might presume, under the authority of such an Amendment, even to forbid the several states to do any of the things which the first eight Amendments forbid the United States to do, although there is some difficulty in seeing just how such legislation would work out in practice.

It may be pushing the argument too far to say that Bingham *distinguished* between the "bill of rights" and the first eight (or first thirteen) Amendments, but there is certainly no warrant for arguing that he clearly intended to establish the first eight Amendments as bars to state action, or that any of his contemporaries clearly understood him to intend that. It would be better to say that it is not very clear *what* he intended.[38]

Part III of Black's Appendix is devoted to a discussion of the debates over proposed civil rights bills which took place between the postponement of the debate over the proposed Amendment discussed in the foregoing pages (which debate was, as we pointed out, never resumed) and the introduction of the proposal which, as amended, became the first section of the Fourteenth Amendment. The import of Black's discussion is that Bingham's intention to apply the first eight Amendments to the states is evidenced by his opposition on the grounds of unconstitutionality to the civil rights bills under discussion.[39]

It would be "more tedious than difficult" to refute Black. Suffice it to say that pages 1291 to 1296 of the *Globe*, read with ordinary care, disclose no such clear intent on Bingham's part, or anyone else's. The debate consists of concluding remarks after a call of the previous question on Bingham's motion to amend a motion to recommit the civil rights bill. Bingham's motion to amend would have attached instructions to the committee. His instructions were voted down and the motion to recommit was carried. It is true that he was against the bill on the stated grounds that he doubted the power of Congress—lacking an Amendment to the Constitution such as he favored—to pass such a bill. It is also true that he mentioned the "bill of rights." But what is the substance of the bill being recommitted? Essentially, it is equal protection; whatever a state does to whites it must do, say, to negroes. In all candor, there are some hints that Bingham *might* mean what Black says he means, but it is not *at all clear* that he (Bingham) does, nor that anyone else concerned so understood him. Black's subtle transposition and interchanging of terms and capitalization of key phrases as well as his careful selection of quotations is wholly misleading. An equally careful selection of quotations would as easily bear out a position contrary to that which Black holds.[40]

With Part IV of the Appendix to Black's opinion[41] there can be no dispute. It is one paragraph which links chronologically the introduction, in the Committee on Reconstruction, of the nucleus of the first section of the subsequent Fourteenth Amendment to prior occurrences. It would be gratuitous to attempt further opposition here to Black's contention. Part V of the Appendix[42] is a discussion of the debates over the proposal that, as amended, finally becomes the Fourteenth Amendment; Part VI[43] deals, *inter alia*, with Flack's book cited above;[44] Part VII[45] deals with Bingham's and others' remarks during debates in the 42nd Congress; Part VIII[46] cites Supreme Court dissents and arguments of counsel in cases interpreting the Fourteenth Amendment. Part VIII need not enter our discussion. As far as the quotations in Part VII are concerned, what Bingham said six years afterward is interesting but not controlling. Black quotes Bingham as saying, in 1871:

> Mr. Speaker, that the scope and meaning of the limitations imposed by the first section, fourteenth amendment of the Constitution may be more fully understood, permit me to say that the privileges and immunities of citizens of the United States, as contradistinguished from citizens of a State, are chiefly defined in the first eight amendments to the Constitution of the United States. (He read them verbatim.)[47]

Professor Fairman's treatment of this *post-facto* framer's intention is so compelling as to bear extended quotation.

> Maybe this statement after the event accurately expressed what lay in Bingham's mind in 1866; but it is what he said and did that counts, and never in the reported debates did he refer specifically to Amendments I to VIII.
>
> Read alone and out of context, Bingham's speech of 1871 sounds definitive. One might fancy that for the instruction of uninformed Congressmen sitting about him he was unlocking the book of history. Actually he was in the midst of a debate with Representatives Farnsworth and Garfield, Republicans, who had been there too, and who had refreshed their recollections by a study of the *Congressional Globe*. At one point Garfield retorted to Bingham, "My colleague can make but he cannot unmake history."[48] The matter before the House in 1871 was H.R. No. 320, a bill to enforce the provisions of the Fourteenth Amendment. This became the Act of April 20, 1871, commonly known as the Ku Klux Act.[49] It was aimed at Southern outrages perpetrated by the Klan. Bingham was supporting the bill as being warranted by the Fourteenth Amendment. Farnsworth was arguing that certain provisions exceeded the power of Congress.[50] (*United States* v. *Harris*[51] in 1883 held the Act unconstitutional at the very point on which Farnsworth had placed his finger.) He quoted from the record a number of comments already set out in this article. Farnsworth's argument was this: Congress had no authority to legislate generally on civil rights; its power was only to enforce the command that "No State shall . . ." Bingham's first version, he recalled had begun "Congress shall have power. . . ." That was debated to a standstill. Then Bingham had made a fresh start, and had adopted the formula "No State shall . . ." Farnsworth argued that the change had been significant, and was an evidence of the rejection in 1866 of the theory being advocated by Bingham in 1871. Here Bingham rose to give his explanation of what he had thought in 1866 and of why he had chosen the words that were finally adopted.
>
> What Bingham said in 1871 formed no part whatsoever of the facts that produced the Fourteenth Amendment. He had had a full opportunity to express his understanding in 1866, and had said a great many things. As we have seen, some of his colleagues had tried very hard at the time to commit him to a clear statement of what he thought his proposal meant. He had made history, but his afterthoughts should not be allowed to remake it.

We have dealt with Mr. Bingham in this article on the view that, however confused, he was sincere. If for a moment one were to suppose that he was astutely endeavoring to bring a wooden horse into the Constitution, certainly the result must be clear: no such fraud on the nation could be countenanced.[52]

For a discussion of the misunderstandings likely to be occasioned by Part VI of Black's Appendix, one should refer to Fairman's article.[53] And for Part V, it is necessary to follow closely the intricacies of roughly the first half of that article. The article as a whole searchingly criticizes the whole of Black's contention in the manner in which the present thesis criticized above Black's single sentence purportedly supported by citation to pages 1059, 1066 and 1088 of the *Congressional Globe* for the First Session of the 39th Congress. It amply demonstrates that Congressional debate over the proposed Amendment as well as that over related matters does not support Black—in fact, it rather supports the notion that Congressional intent centered on equal protection for negroes.[54] It argues that states with constitutions which contained provisions out of harmony with the specific procedures of the first eight amendments would not have ratified the Fourteenth Amendment without at least recognizing that the new amendment would force serious changes in those state constitutions and weighing this in their discussion of the merits of ratification,[55] and then it presents a thorough collection of debates in state legislatures over ratification and of contemporary press comments, both of which convincingly indicate that contemporary understanding by state legislators and newspapers was not at all what Black says it was.[56]

The most important correctives supplied by Fairman are that he balances Flack's and Black's reliance upon Congressman Bingham and Senator Howard by referring to the speeches of other members of the 39th Congress and he points out the significance of the fact that the ratifying legislatures of states whose constitutions and laws would have been subjected to radical change if the Fourteenth Amendment meant what Black says it means seemed not to have considered the possibility that that is what it does mean. Reference here and there in Black's Appendix and Flack's book to arguments hostile to the adoption of the Amendment which charge a centralization power and a radical transformation of the relations between states and nation are not nearly explicit enough. Many such speeches in the name of "States' Rights," then as now, are far too vague and there are a great many ways in which the powers of the national government might be expanded at the expense of the powers of the states without applying the first eight Amendments as a bar to state court proceedings.

Enough has now been said about Mr. Justice Black's Appendix and Professor Fairman's article. Perhaps some attention should now be given to Flack's book, upon which Black puts so much reliance, and to Congressman Bingham's speeches upon which in turn, Flack so strongly relies. In each case, a few general remarks and a small sample of specific criticism will suffice. Flack states that Congress:

> had the following objects and motives in view for submitting the first section of the Fourteenth Amendment to the States for ratification:
> 1. To make the Bill of Rights (the first eight Amendments) binding upon, or applicable to, the States.
> 2. To give validity to the Civil Rights Bill.
> 3. To declare who were citizens of the United States.[57]

The third "object" seems to be phrased accurately enough and, were the first two as accurate, the ranking of these objects would be quite proper. The notion that a principal intention of the framers of the Fourteenth Amendment was "to give" citizenship to the negroes overlooks the fact that that sentence with which the first section of the Amendment begins was added as an amendment in the Senate after the House had passed on the whole Amendment the first time,[58] and the equally important fact that the Civil Rights Bill enacted April 9[59] declared in its first section essentially what Howard's amendment declared.

In addition, a good many people in and out of Congress felt that the Thirteenth Amendment, ratification of which was completed on December 6, 1865, accomplished the overthrow of the *Dred Scott* decision's identification of negroes as non-citizens by the very fact of its abolition of slavery. Flack argues that it cannot be said that the *granting* of citizenship was one of the main purposes of the Amendment[60] and we are compelled to agree with him. Perhaps the best explanation of the purposes of Congress was, to use the phrase of Senator Wade who had offered an amendment which was not accepted but which in part dealt with the citizenship problem, to put the question of citizenship "beyond all doubt and all cavil."[61] Mr. Justice Swayne, on circuit in the District of Kentucky, states that the "emancipation of a native born slave by removing the disability of slavery made him a citizen."[62] Swayne here ruling on the Civil Rights Act just passed, said that even the declaration regarding citizenship in *that* act was *merely* declaratory, for free negroes were citizens anyhow, despite the dicta to the contrary in *Dred Scott* v. *Sandford.*[63]

Maybe, then, the Thirteenth Amendment involved an assumption contrary to the "dicta" in the *Dred Scott* case, the Civil Rights Act was declaratory of that assumption, and the first sentence of the first section of the Fourteenth Amendment put that declaration "beyond all doubt and all cavil."[64]

Flack's second point—"To give validity to the Civil Rights Bill"—is not so easy to support, for upon evidence analogous to that offered with respect to the import of the clause concerning citizenship, which evidence Flack himself amply cites, there is no reason to suppose that Congress as a whole regarded the Civil Rights Act, which it passed over the veto of President Johnson,[65] as unconstitutional and therefore standing in need of the proposed Fourteenth Amendment to render it valid. Flack admits that it "cannot fairly be said . . . that the men who supported the first section of the Fourteenth Amendment thereby acknowledged the unconstitutionality of the Civil Rights Bill. . . ." At least as frequent a reason, assuming the identity of the Fourteenth Amendment's first section and the first section of the Civil Rights Bill for the purpose of the argument, was the desire to put those provisions beyond the capacity of a succeeding Congress to repeal by the ordinary course of legislation and to do so before the readmission of the Southern States.[66]

If it "cannot fairly be said" that those who supported the first section of the Fourteenth Amendment believed the Civil Rights Bill to be unconstitutional without the Amendment, as Flack admits on page 95, we cannot see why he should have said on page 94 that the second—second only to applying the Bill of Rights to the States—object of the Amendment was to "give validity to the Civil

Rights Bill." In fact, in the very next paragraph on page 95, Flack contradicts himself clearly. He states:

> There is little doubt that the bill was unconstitutional, and that the Federal Supreme Court would have so declared it, had it come before that body, but the fact remains that the vast majority of those voting for it must have thought they had the power to pass it.

If the "vast majority" thought on April 9 when they passed the Civil Rights Bill over the veto of the president (April 9 is the date for House passage) that the Bill was valid, why should it be supposed that one of the main objects and motives" of those same men, when they voted for the proposed Amendment on May 10, and again—after modification by the Senate—on June 13, was to "give validity" to that Bill, unless "give validity" means "keep safe"?

There is really a deeper problem here which reflects on the whole of Flack's scholarship. If there is "little doubt that the bill was unconstitutional," but the "vast majority of those voting for it" thought otherwise, then it stands to reason that that "vast majority" did not know on April 9 how the Constitution stood on this matter. Now Flack's whole argument hopes to ascertain the truth about the intention of Congress in proposing the Fourteenth Amendment which Flack says is simply the Civil Rights Act on the Constitutional level. That argument pretends an intricate deduction from the records of Congressional debates. But if the "vast majority" did not know how the Constitution stood on the matters covered by the Civil Rights Bill, how could the same record which shows their lack of understanding show a clearly understood intention when they passed on those same matters in the form of a Constitutional Amendment? On the contrary, it would appear that Congress had no very clear "objects or motives" at all and Flack's thesis crumbles into an ash-heap of over-clever pedantry. But we do not here charge that Congress was confused. This passage of Flack's says nothing about the clarity or obscurity of Congress' intention. It does, however, say a good deal about the clarity of Flack's understanding of those intentions.

In fact, the whole of Flack's book seems defective. There is an assumed air of academic objectivity which becomes virtual neutrality—like unto the "revisionist history" and the "value-free social science" soon to become prevalent—with regard to the Civil War and Reconstruction which, superficially, has a seemly cast but which, upon examination, raises doubts as to his understanding. When the second section of the Amendment was under discussion, the Congress faced the following problem: The abolition of slavery by the Thirteenth Amendment negated the "three-fifths of all other persons" provision in Art. I, sec. 2, cl. 3, by which provision a concession had been made in 1787 to the slave states. Slaves were treated in every respect but one as property, not persons. In respect of representation, they were treated each as three-fifths of a person. With the abolition of slavery, the entire negro population was to be counted as whole persons for purposes of representation in the House. This meant a notable increase in the proportion of the House representing the former slave-owning states. It might naively be supposed that if the negroes were enfranchised they would quickly be an active political force *vis-à-vis* their former masters and that, according to republican principles, they would be *represented* and hence the very issue which had divided the Union would be mitigated soon and eventually dispelled. But no one for a moment doubted that the former masters would pursue the same objects after their return to the House that they had pursued prior to their departure therefrom for the field of battle. If the former slave States got an increase in representation based on the transformation of that class of "other persons" into "free persons" and could at the same time exclude from the franchise by state statute all those "free persons" who had formerly been "other persons" and all their posterity, to boot, they could "have their cake and eat it." What the Southern whites could not, as a minority, accomplish in the House and hence took up arms to accomplish separately, they might now, after their military defeat, accomplish as a majority of that House. The negroes would be counted as whole persons for purposes of apportionment in the House of Representatives and as no persons at all otherwise. If the three-fifths rule at the formation of the Union had been a concession, the new situation would have been, at the reformation of the Union, unconditional surrender on the part of the victors in the struggle. This snatching of defeat from the jaws of victory seemed incongruous to the 39th Congress and still seems so.

But Flack says:

> . . . Mr. Boutwell, a member of the Reconstruction Committee, declared that he did not think that two rebel soldiers

"whose hands were dripping with the blood" of Union men should have the same power in Congress as three Union Soldiers. . . . Such arguments, arguments which would now have little or no weight, had great influence at the time, it must be said with regret.[67]

Why must it be said "with regret"? Is the whole problem to be looked upon as a mere inconvenience? Does this schoolm'amish distaste for reference to the war, recovery from which was the stated purpose of Reconstruction, help or hinder genuinely scholarly understanding of the Reconstruction? Granted for argument's sake that the Reconstruction was harsh and wrong-headed, is a prudish disregard for the facts of life a necessary ingredient either of "objective" scholarship or of wise legislation?

Returning to the central question, Flack contends that the first of the "objects and motives" of the Amendment was to "make the Bill of Rights (the first eight Amendments) binding upon, or applicable to, the States."[68] We have already remarked on the undue reliance which Fairman[69] points out that Flack had placed upon the speeches of Bingham in the House and Howard in the Senate. A brief account is now in order of Flack's, and Bingham's, reasoning on this point. The strained character of Flack's reasoning can be seen in his attempt to make Congressman Stevens a witness to his contention. Flack says:

> In reference to the first section, Mr. Stevens stated that all of its provisions were asserted either in the Declaration of Independence or in the Constitution, and added: "But the Constitution limits only the action of Congress, and is not a limitation on the States. This Amendment supplies that defect, and allows Congress to correct the unjust legislation of the States, so far that the law which operates upon one man shall operate *equally* upon all." He evidently had reference to the Bill of Rights, for it is in it that most of the privileges are enumerated, and besides it was not applicable to the States. . . .[70]

We are embarrassed to point out the obvious here. The quotation of Stevens which Flack offer is *not at all* evidently a reference to the Bill of Rights. It is true that the Bill of Rights "was not applicable to the States," but Stevens had said that the Constitution—that is, the Constitution *as a whole*—was not a limitation upon the states. The Constitution as a whole was an instrument for the government of the

United States and not for the states. Generally speaking, it neither limits nor empowers the states. Article IV of the original document requires comity among the states and guarantees "a Republican Form of Government" to each. Art. I sec. 10 specifically forbids the states to do a small number of things which, if done, would—so the framers believed—defeat the great purpose of a "more perfect Union." The Tenth Amendment suggests a limitation upon the states by virtue of the delegation of certain powers to the Union. Beyond this the Constitution does not—up to the Thirteenth Amendment—pretend to give the rule either by mandate or by prohibition for the government of the states. And, as far as it being the Bill of Rights in which "most of the privileges are enumerated," this is only true if one assumes the very point which Flack's whole book purports to establish and to the establishment of which this quotation from Stevens is supposed to contribute. It is not accidental that Stevens stressed the word "equally," for this speech of his, which appears on pages 2459 and 2460 of the *Globe*, proves, if anything, that Stevens understood the essence of the first section to be equality before the law rather than a shorthand expression for the catalogue of prohibitions in the first eight Amendments.

If one reads Flack's book carefully, in fact, and does not even go to the *Congressional Globe* for additional information, he is almost compelled on the basis of the evidence Flack himself supplies to come to an opposite conclusion. The best case that can be made out for Flack's position—and, although it is not a bad case, it is by no means conclusive—is that Bingham was a principal proponent of the Amendment in the House and Howard in the Senate and that Bingham frequently mentioned "the bill of rights" and Howard once even mentioned "the first eight Amendments" and that no one in either house specifically refuted them on this point. But, except for very infrequent reference to one or another of the things contained in those first eight Amendments, by other members of the House and Senate, the overwhelming weight of the discussion centers on suffrage, equality of treatment in hotels, mixed schools, miscegenation, negro jury service and other matters related to whether or not the Congress, under the authority of sec. 5 of the Amendment, would be able to interfere with state laws which treated negroes as a class differently from whites as a class.

There was a vocal minority against the proposed Amendment in each house of Congress and the proposal had many enemies in several of the state legislatures. Surely, if the Amendment meant what Flack says it means, there would have been at least one clear-cut case of an adversary asking, say, if the Amendment were passed, whether a state court decision could be overturned by a United States court because a jury of twelve, or a grand jury indictment, or an adequate search warrant was wanting in the state proceeding and a clear-cut answer from a proponent that, yes, that would be the case. Our examination of the *Globe* for the 39th Congress turned up no such clear-cut instance and Flack does not produce such an instance from the *Globe* or from newspaper accounts or state ratifying debates.

There are not even very many instances where a torturing of the evidence would indicate that that is *probably* what was meant. Even taking Flack's best witness, Congressman Bingham, supplies only a moderate hint that that is what *Bingham* meant. Remembering that Bingham *is* Flack's best witness, consider the following: Flack quotes at length from Bingham's last speech on the proposal, immediately before the House approved it (for the first time, that is, prior to the Senate modifications) on May 10 by a vote of 128 to 37, and following these quotations from Bingham's speech he states:

> It can be inferred properly, we think, that he meant by this that no State could abridge, or could allow to be abridged or denied, any of the privileges of citizens. Besides, he had stated on a former occasion, while the resolution was still before the Committee, that the Constitution declared that no person should be deprived of life without due process of law, but that notwithstanding this life had never been protected, and is not now protected, in any State of this Union by the statute law of the United States. This clearly shows that he intended that Congress should have the power to pass laws declaring what rights should be secured to the citizens. Anyway, it matters little whether Congress was to exercise the power before the States had denied those privileges, either by acts of omission or of commission, since Congress was unquestionably empowered to define or declare, by law, what rights, and privileges should be secured to all citizens.
>
> Mr. Stevens closed the debate with a short speech, after which the previous question was ordered. The vote then was taken

immediately after Mr. Bingham had spoken, and his position must have been understood by all the members present. His statement of the need and purpose of the section must, therefore, have been acquiesced in by those who supported it, especially since Mr. Bingham was the author of it as well as a member of the Committee which ordered it to be reported, and thus could speak with authority. Furthermore, his statements do not at all contradict the position taken by Mr. Rogers and others of the minority, for nearly all said that it was but an incorporation of the Civil Rights Bill. It might be expected that the minority would ascribe certain motives to it on partisan grounds, but this does not seem to have been the case in regard to this particular section, for there was no controversy or misunderstanding as to its purpose and meaning. The minority opposed it because they objected to increasing the power of the Federal Government while the majority supported it for this very reason.

It may be said, in conclusion, that the House believed and intended that the purpose and effect of the first section of the Fourteenth Amendment would be to give Congress the power to enact affirmative legislation, especially where state laws were unequal, and that it would also make the first eight Amendments binding upon the States as well as upon the Federal Government, Congress being empowered to see that they were enforced in the States. It also seems proper to say that Congress would be authorized to pass any law which it might declare "appropriate and necessary" to secure to citizens their privileges and immunities, together with the power to declare what were those privileges and immunities.[71]

We quote now, extensively, from the speeches of Bingham upon which these conclusions of Flack rest, first from the speech of January 25, a bit of which appears early in the passage just quoted from Flack, and then from the speech on May 10, several short quotations from which appear on the immediately preceding two pages of Flack.[72] We leave out nothing that Flack puts in and, that we might not be guilty of niggardliness or suppression of evidence, we include somewhat more of those speeches than Flack does.

But I may say that the committee has under consideration another general amendment to the Constitution which looks to the grant of express power to the Congress of the United States to enforce in behalf of every citizen of every State and of every

Territory in the Union the rights which were guaranteed to him from the beginning, but which guarantee has unhappily been disregarded by more than one State of this Union, defiantly disregarded, simply because of a want of power in Congress to enforce that guarantee. I do not doubt, sir, that if the committee shall succeed in presenting in fit and proper form this proposed amendment to the Constitution, it will receive the assent, I might almost say, of every gentleman in this House. Why should it not?

I understand very well, Mr. Speaker, that there are gentlemen for whom I have the profoundest repect, not only for their great attainments, but for their generous and patriotic motives, who contend, against all past constructions and all past experiences, that the Congress of the United States has the power, implied necessarily, to enforce all the guarantees of the Constitution. In my judgment, unless some such general provision as that to which I have referred be adopted, it is in vain that you hope for future safety or future peace in the country; and I beg leave to say to gentlemen who reason in the manner I have indicated, and therefore seek to evade the discharge of this great duty incumbent upon us, that, notwithstanding the respect to which their opinions are entitled, the continued construction of every department of this Government, legislative, executive, and judicial, from that day on which Washington, for the first time, before God and his country, took the oath to "preserve, protect, and defend the Constitution of the United States," has conceded that no such power is vested in the federal Government. Gentlemen will pardon me for further reminding them of the special express powers of the Constitution, and that the general express grant is that Congress shall have power to make all laws necessary and proper for carrying into execution the foregoing powers and all other powers vested by this Constitution in the Government of the United States or in any department or officer thereof. In what I have said upon the limitation of power, I do not express my own opinion, but the opinions of others and the uniform construction.

Sir, your Constitution declares that no person shall be deprived of life without due process of law; yet, in support of what I have just said on the necessity of an additional grant of power, allow me to remind the House of the fact that this highest right which pertains to man or citizen, life, has never yet been protected, and is not now protected, in any State of this Union by the statute law of the United States. And if tomorrow, sir, your President, because of his supposed fidelity, and I might add of his real fidelity to his duty, in so far as I understand his position, crossed the line of your exclusive jurisdiction in this District into the State of Maryland, into the county of Charles, and were to be there set upon by the whole body of the community and murdered for no fault of his, but simply because of his supposed fidelity to his duty, your Government is powerless by law to avenge his death in any of your civil tribunals of justice. And this results from the accepted construction that this Government has not the power by law to enforce in the States this guarantee of life.[73]

Mr. Bingham. The want of the Republic to-day is not a Democratic party, is not a Republican party, is not any party save a party for the Union, for the Constitution, for the supremacy of the laws, for the restoration of all the States to their political rights and powers under such irrevocable guarantes as will forevermore secure the safety of the Republic, the equality of the States, and the equal rights of all the people under the sanctions of inviolable law.

. . . .

The necessity for the first section of this amendment to the Constitution, Mr. Speaker, is one of the lessons that have been taught to your committee and taught to all the people of this country by the history of the past four years of terrific conflict—that history in which God is, and in which He teaches the profoundest lessons to men and nations. There was a want hitherto, and there remains a want now, in the Constitution of our country, which the proposed amendment will supply. What is that? It is the power in the people, the whole people of the United States, by express authority of the Constitution to do that by congressional enactment which hitherto they have not had the power to do, and have never even attempted to do; that is, to protect by national law the privileges and immunities of all the citizens of the jurisdiction whenever the same shall be abridged or denied by the unconstitutional acts of any State.

Allow me, Mr. Speaker, in passing, to say that this amendment takes from no State any right that ever pertained to it. No State ever had the right, under the forms of law or otherwise, to deny to any freeman the equal protection of the laws or to abridge the privileges or immunities of any citizen of the Republic, although many of them have assumed and exercised the power, and that without remedy. The amendment does not give, as the second section shows, the power to Congress of regulating suffrage in the several States.

The second section excludes the conclusion that by the first section suffrage is subjected to congressional law; save, indeed, with this exception, that as the right in the people of each State to a republican government and to choose their Representatives in Congress is of the guarantees of the Constitution, by this amendment a remedy might be given directly for a case supposed by Madison, where treason might change a State government from a republican to a despotic government, and thereby deny suffrage to the people. Why should any American citizen object to that? But, sir, it has been suggested, not here, but elsewhere, if this section does not confer suffrage the need of it is not perceived. To all such I beg leave again to say, that many instances of State injustice and oppression have already occurred in the State legislation of this Union, of flagrant violations of the guarantied privileges of citizens of the United States, for which the national government furnished and could furnish by law no remedy whatever. Contrary to the express letter of your Constitution, cruel and unusual punishments have been inflicted under State laws within this Union upon citizens, not only for crimes committed, but for sacred duty done, for which and against which the Government of the United States had provided no remedy and could provide none.

. . . .

That great want of the citizen and stranger, protection by national law from unconstitutional State enactment, is supplied by the first section of this amendment. That is the extent that it hath, no more; and let gentlemen answer to God and their country who oppose its incorporation into the organic law of the land.[74]

Summarizing Flack's whole argument regarding Bingham's intentions, one can say that Bingham was aware of the decision in the case of *Barron* v. *Baltimore*,[75] that he somehow regarded the "no State shall" formula which is embodied in the Fourteenth Amendment as finally adopted as aimed at the same mark as the "Congress shall have power" formula in his proposal,[76] discussion of which terminated on February 28, that life was not protected in any state of the union by the statute law of the United States,[77] and that the want of the republic was the protection of the privileges and immunities of citizens of the United States from abridgment by unconstitutional acts of the states.[78]

But so far is this from showing that Bingham clearly knew what he was doing and that what he was doing was clearly overruling *Barron* v. *Baltimore* by making the first eight Amendments applicable as against the states, that it tends to prove, on the contrary, that Bingham was quite unclear about what he was doing and that, if his intention *was* to overrule *Barron* v. *Baltimore*, his H.R. No. 63 and, as well, H.R. 127 which, as modified by the Senate, became the Fourteenth Amendment, were poorly phrased and ill-calculated to accomplish that end. For, if it be granted that Bingham clearly understood that *Barron* v. *Baltimore* established the meaning of the Constitution's first eight Amendments as bars to United States action only—and this *must* be granted if one is to argue that Bingham meant to overrule *Barron* v. *Baltimore* by amending the Constitution so as to make those Amendments bars to state action as well—then *how* can Bingham possibly mean by his reference to the "unconstitutional acts of the States" such acts by the states as are by the first eight Amendments forbidden to the United States? For, if the law of the Constitution prior to the adoption of the Fourteenth Amendment was that the first eight Amendments were not in any way prohibitions of state action, then the doing of things by the states which the Constitution forbids the United States to do but *does not* forbid the states to do might be undesirable but, quite obviously, not unconstitutional.

Or, to state the problem another way, even if one takes the most generous view of Flack's explanation of Bingham's intention and grants, just for the sake of the argument, that the "privileges or immunities of citizens of the United States" which the Fourteenth Amendment forbids states to abridge include the first eight Amendments, then that clause in the Amendment was rather saved by Mr. Justice Miller in the *Slaughter House* cases[79] than destroyed by him there as has so often been said.[80] For if the "privileges or immunities of citizens of the United States" include the first eight Amendments it is something of an absurdity to forbid the States to abridge them, for it would take some doing to see how a state might abridge a United States citizen's immunity from, say, self-incrimination in a United States Court. To repeat again, the first eight Amendments were prohibitions against United States actions and not against state actions, and, also to repeat, this must be understood to be Bingham's view if Flack's argument is to have even a breath of merit.[81]

It would be far more charitable to Bingham not to suppose he was such a fool as to believe it was unconstitutional for the state to do things which the Constitution did not forbid them to do. It would save his reputation for clarity of purpose rather to strain interpretation in the opposite direction and to argue that he really *did not* mean the "first eight Amendments" when he referred to the "bill of rights" but rather meant, generally, the protection of the citizen which the whole of the Constitution threw over him by the privileges and immunities clause, the interstate comity clauses, and the guarantee of republican government in every state, contained in Article IV, and that when he referred to "privileges and immunities of citizens of the United States" he had in mind such things—vaguely—as Mr. Justice Washington mentioned in *Corfield* v. *Coryell*,[82] in 1823, such things as the owning of property and competence to testify and police protection. Then, if a state was unequal in its application of the law and sneered at a visitor's or a negro's appeal for protection of his life or property from the hostile actions of a mob, if a state itself confiscated property of visitors or negroes, or took life without even regard for its own laws or under color of one of its own laws which was unequal in application, Congress, by virtue of the authority granted in Section 5 of the Fourteenth Amendment, would be empowered to legislate protection for the life or property which the state refused to protect or itself assailed.

Or alternatively, it must be said that if Bingham really did intend to do what Flack says he intended to do, then his draftsmanship was an abysmal failure.

One last comment must be made on Flack's book. His fourth chapter is entitled "The Amendment Before the States" and runs from page 161 to page 209. His thesis being what it is, one would expect him to adduce considerable evidence from the actions of the state legislatures showing them, or some of them, to understand the proposed Amendment as intending the application of the first eight Amendments to the states. As a matter of fact he does no such thing and there are only four instances where he comes near doing this.

On page 180 he says, "An advocate of the Amendment [in the Pennsylvania legislature] said that the first section guaranteed 'state rights to every human being,' evidently having reference to the rights which were in the Bill of rights in the several States." It is not evident to us, and if it were, we should have referred to the Bills of Right, not the Bill of Rights, in the several states and, besides, this had nothing to do with the United States Bill of Rights.

On page 187 he says,

> The Committee [of the Massachusetts legislature] in its report, stated that the first section was already in the Constitution and was to be found in the second and fourth sections of Article Four, and in the First, Second, Fifth, Sixth, and Seventh Amendments. If these provisions were fairly construed, said the Committee, they would secure everything which the first section attempted to do.

Accepting without question the accuracy of Flack's characterization of the report of the Massachusetts Committee, and giving the fullest scope to the import of that report we will grant that this indicates that the Committee thought that the phrasing of the first section of the Fourteenth Amendment was equivalent to the phrasing of *some* of the first eight Amendments. We are willing to forego criticism of this point and to leave this quotation to speak for itself, stopping only to point out that in a forty-nine page chapter this is the *strongest* piece of evidence offered or, rather, the *only* piece of evidence for the main contention of the book.[83]

Immediately following this passage, Flack states, on page 188:

> This report [i.e., the Massachusetts Committee report] is entirely different from any other that we have found, for it was made by Republicans, and can't, therefore, be said to be partisan in the sense that the same statements made by Democrats were. It is also valuable from the fact that it shows that the Senate of Massachusetts, in adopting it, accepted the statements made in it that the first section was but a reiteration of the guarantees enumerated in the Amendments. The Senate ratified the Amendment March 20, 1867, the vote being 27 to 6.

This, of course, is not a separate case, but simply part of the preceding matter, quoted from page 187. We list it separately, however, simply because it is one of only four instances in the entire chapter where "first eight Amendments," "Amendments," "Bill of

Rights," or any other such phrase as might offer proof of Flack's point is used.

The last quotation we offer, from pages 63 to 65, and our last word on Flack, we leave entirely to speak for itself and therefore we quote at length. The argument from negative premises is an example of how far one must go to fetch the evidence.

> In the Senate [of Tennessee] it was proposed to submit the question of ratification or rejection of the Amendment to the people, but this resolution was defeated. Senator Frazier then offered an amendment to the resolution proposing the ratification of the Amendment. This amendment was in the following terms: "*Provided*, that the foregoing proposed Amendments to the Constitution of the United States shall not be so construed as to confer the right of suffrage upon a negro, or person of color, or to confer upon such negro or person of color the right to hold office, sit upon juries, or to intermarry with white persons, nor shall said proposed Amendments be so construed as to prohibit any State from enacting and enforcing such laws as will secure these ends, not inconsistent with the present Constitution of the United States, nor shall said proposed Amendments be so construed as to abridge the reserved rights of the States in the election and qualifications of their own officers, and the management of their domestic concerns, as provided and secured by the present Constitution of the United States." This amendment was rejected and the Amendment was then ratified by a vote of 16 to 14. There was very little, if any, debate in the Senate, but the amendment proposed by Senator Frazier shows what the minority thought would be the construction put upon the Amendment. It is, of course, evident that a State, through its Legislature or otherwise, cannot limit or extend the construction or interpretation of a proposed Amendment to the Constitution of the United States, but its effort to do so would be a clear indication of what it feared would be the construction of the proposed Amendment. The effort of the minority to do this in this particular case is of importance only as showing their views of the Amendment. It may not be altogether proper to say that the majority, by rejecting Senator Frazier's amendment, recognized that the Amendment would secure those things which his amendment proposed to include, and that they, therefore, intended to secure them. In ordinary cases, it would be perfectly proper to draw such a conclusion, but in this case the reason for the rejection of

the amendment of the minority might properly have been that the Legislature had no right to pass such a restrictive resolution, or, in other words, to make a conditional ratification of the Amendment. It is evident, however, that if Mr. Frazier's interpretation or limited construction were to be placed upon it, that the first eight Amendments would not be made binding upon the States.[84]

We suggested above[85] that, if Bingham had really intended to make the first eight Amendments applicable to the states, his draftsmanship had failed. The implication is, of course, that the words of a law have a meaning independent of the legislative intent. It does not matter what the framers intended; the words of the Amendment mean, after all, what they say. It has been argued that the plain meaning of the words of the Fourteenth Amendment is that the states are now forbidden to do any of the things which the first eight Amendments forbid the United States to do. There seems to us no way to avoid meeting this contention.

NOTES TO CHAPTER II

[1]See H.E. Flack, *The Adoption of the Fourteenth Amendment* (Baltimore: Johns Hopkins Press, 1908).

[2]332 U.S. 46, 71-72.

[3]Black inserts a footnote at this point which reads, in part, "Another prime purpose was to make colored people citizens entitled to full equal rights as citizens despite what this Court decided in the *Dred Scott* case." *Dred Scott* v. *Sandford,* 19 How. 393 (1857).

[4]See: *Slaughter House Cases,* 16 Wall. 36 at 71-72.

[5]332 U.S. 46, 92-123.

[6]Charles A. Fairman, "Does the Fourteenth Amendment Incorporate the Bill of Rights?—The Original Understanding," *Stanford Law Review,* II (December, 1949), 5-139. A companion article on "The Judicial Interpretation of the Fourteenth Amendment" was written by Professor Morrison, *idem,* pp. 140-73.

[7]332 U.S. 46, 92-94 and 94-99.

[8]That proposal, H.R. 127, was introduced by Congressman Stevens, reporting for the Joint Committee on Reconstruction on April 30, 1866. *Cong. Globe,* 39th Cong., 1st Sess., p. 2286.

[9]H.R. 63.

[10]*Cong. Globe,* p. 1033.

[11]*Ibid.,* p. 1095.

[12]Pp. 1866-77 and Index LXI.

[13]Cf. Fairman, *op. cit.,* p. 37 and note 66 thereon, and Flack, *op. cit.,* pp. 59-60.

[14]*Cong. Globe,* p. 1034. [1986 addition to 1963 note: For a correct treatment of the earlier Bingham proposal's relation to the Fourteenth Amendment, see Francis Canavan, "A New Fourteenth Amendment," *Human Life Review,* 12, (Winter, 1986).]

[15]It is interesting to note that, contrary to Congressman Bingham's statement, *Cong. Globe,* p. 1034, and quoted by Black at 332 U.S. 94 that "[e]very word of the proposed amendment is today in the Constitution . . . ," the words "equal protection" nowhere appear in that document prior to the Fourteenth Amendment.

[16]See, for example, *Cong. Globe,* pp. 1034 and 1089.

[17]*Op. cit.,* pp. 45-46. Fairman here refers to the debate in the House. In the Senate, Senator Howard did in fact refer to the first eight Amendments on one occasion. See *Cong. Globe,* pp. 2765-67 and Fairman, *op. cit.,* pp. 54-68.

[18]Black attaches much significance to the fact that Bingham cites *Barron* v. *Baltimore.* Be it noted that Marshall, in that case, refers to Art. I, sec. 9 as a "bill of rights." 7 Pet. 243, 248.

[19]332 U.S. 46 at 95.

[20]*Cong. Globe,* p. 1058, third column, near the top.

[21]Art. IV, sec. 2.

[22]*Cong. Globe,* p. 1066, second column, near the bottom.

[23]*Ibid.,* middle of the second column.

[24]*Ibid.,* first column, bottom, to second column.

[25]See Fairman, *op. cit.,* pp. 29-32.

[26]*Cong. Globe,* p. 1088.

[27]*Politics,* 1275 a23.

[28]Art. II, sec. 1, cl. 5; cf. n. 70 to ch. III, *infra.*

[29]Art. I, sec. 3, cl. 3.

[30]Art. I, sec. 2, cl. 2.

[31]Bingham cites Aristotle essentially as he is cited above. See *Cong. Globe,* p. 1291, second column, near the bottom.

[32]Cf. *Minor* v. *Happersett,* 21 Wall. 162 (1875) and *Ex parte Yarborough,* 110 U.S. 651 (1884).

[33]Is the franchise a "property" to be "equally protected"? Somewhere in the debates—just where has been lost to this record—it was suggested that the Democrats must have regarded the franchise as a property, inasmuch as they "bought and sold it." See the discussion by Fairman of the relationships among equal protection, privileges and immunities and the franchise in the Congressional debates, *op. cit.,* pp. 64-65.

[34]332 U.S. 46, 95.

[35]Quoted in *ibid.,* p. 95. The speech by Bingham will be found in the *Cong. Globe,* p. 1089, third column, bottom.

[36]A footnote seems in order here just to make doubly sure that no one mistakes this for an actual quotation of Bingham or of anyone else. It is a paraphrase of Bingham.

[37]See the *Civil Rights Cases,* 109 U.S. 3 (1883).

[38]Bingham's citation of *Barron* v. *Baltimore* was in answer to a question posed the previous day by Eldridge of Wisconsin to Bingham in the midst of a talk by Hale.

That question reads as follows: "Mr. Eldridge. I wish to know if the gentleman from Ohio [Mr. Bingham] has found or heard of a case in which the Constitution of the United States has been pronounced to be insufficient?" *Cong. Globe,* p. 1064, third column, near the bottom; bracketed name in the original. The word "insufficient" is the contrary of and in reference to the speech by Hale, immediately above that just cited, in which Hale admitted that he did not "know of a case where it has ever been decided that the United States Constitution is sufficient for the protection of the liberties of the citizens." What those liberties with which Hale was concerned are is not made plain. The context, at least, indicates a desire to see to it that negroes got to do the things that whites got to do; *not* to see to it that states were forbidden to do the things the Federal Government by the first eight Amendments was forbidden to do.

[39]Black, 332 U.S. 46, 99-103. Relevant debate at *Cong. Globe,* pp. 1291-96.

[40]One sample will have to suffice. Bingham says (*ibid.,* p. 1293, first column, top): "Sir, I have always so learned our dual system of Government by which our own American nationality and liberty have been established and maintained. I have always believed that the protection in time of peace within the States of all the rights of person and citizen was of the powers reserved to the States. And so, I still believe." (He had just quoted 1 Kent, Lecture 19, sec. 446 [p. 446 is probably intended].)

[41]332 U.S. 46, 103.

[42]*Ibid.,* pp. 104-08.

[43]*Ibid.,* pp. 108-10.

[44]See Flack, *op. cit.*

[45]332 U.S. 46, 110-20.

[46]*Ibid.,* pp. 120-23.

[47]Quoted at *ibid.,* p. 115, and in Fairman, *op. cit.,* p. 136.

[48]Fairman cites here *Cong. Globe,* 42d Cong., 1st Sess., App. 151 (1871).

[49]Fairman cites here 17 Stat. 13 (1871).

[50]Fairman cites here *Cong. Globe,* 42d Cong., 1st Sess., App. 113 (1871).

[51]Fairman cities here 106 U.S. 629 (1883).

[52]Fairman, *op. cit.,* pp. 136-37. Emphasis of the last sentence supplied by present author.

[53]*Ibid.,* pp. 78-81.

[54]*Ibid.* See especially, pp. 44-64.

[55]*Ibid.,* p. 82.

[56]*Ibid.* See, generally, the latter half of the article—say, from about p. 81 to about p. 135.

[57]*Op. cit.,* p. 94.

[58]The citizenship clause was offered by Senator Howard on May 29. *Cong. Globe,* p. 2869.

[59]14 Stat. 27.

[60]*Op. cit.,* p. 83.

[61]*Cong. Globe,* p. 2769. His proposed amendment is on the preceding page.

[62]*U.S.* v. *Rhodes,* 27 Fed. Cas. 785 at 789 (1866). We are indebted to Flack, *op. cit.,* p. 49, for finding this, the earliest case construing the Civil Rights Act of 1866. This case was in the U.S. Circuit Court for the District of Kentucky, Mr. Justice Swayne, on circuit, presiding. The home of a negro woman had been burglarized by white men; although the woman was the very one who could have given evidence

sufficient for conviction, Kentucky law excluded negroes from testifying in court. Under the terms of the new Civil Rights Act, the case was removed to Federal Court. Swayne ruled the whole Act constitutional. I believe the act has never been tested in the Supreme Court. (A misprint in Flack cites the case as *37* Fed. Cas. 785, rather than *27* Fed. Cas. 785.)

[63]27 Fed. Cas. 785 at 790.

[64]But see, William Winslow Crosskey, *Politics and the Constitution in the History of the United States,* 2 vols. (Chicago: University of Chicago Press, 1953), II, 1083-84, where it is argued that the *Dred Scott* decision was the "standing Constitutional law" up to the ratification of the Fourteenth Amendment. In order that we might pass to other things, we resolve this difficulty by suggesting that the Amendment may have accomplished more—namely the establishment of negro citizenship—than the framers intended—namely, the reassurance of negroes as to their citizenship.

[65]See, *Cong. Globe,* pp. 1857-60 and also J.D. Richardson, *Messages and Papers of the Presidents* (Washington: U.S. Government Printing Office, 1898), pp. 405-13, for the veto message. President Johnson seemed to regard the bill as much improvident as unconstitutional. At least in this veto message he appeared to be willing to let the problems of relationships between black and white work themselves out by the economic law of supply and demand. See especially, *Cong. Globe,* p. 1859.

[66]See Congressman James A. Garfield's comments on this point at *Cong. Globe,* p. 2462, and Congressman Stevens' remarks, *ibid.,* p. 2459.

[67]*Op. cit.,* p. 117. The quotation of Boutwell is from the *Cong. Globe,* p. 2508. Also see Flack, *op. cit.,* pp. 207-09.

[68]*Ibid.,* p. 94.

[69]*Op. cit.,* pp. 54-68 especially.

[70]Flack, *op. cit.,* pp. 74-75. The quotation from Stevens' speech is from *Cong. Globe,* p. 2459. The italics are Congressman Stevens'.

[71]Flack, *op. cit.,* pp. 80-82, citations omitted.

[72]*Ibid.,* pp. 79-80.

[73]*Cong. Globe,* p. 429.

[74]*Ibid.,* pp. 2542-43.

[75]*Ibid.,* p. 1089.

[76]H.R. No. 63.

[77]*Cong. Globe,* p. 429.

[78]*Ibid.,* pp. 2542-43.

[79]16 Wall 36.

[80]See, e.g., Corwin, op. cit., p. 966; C. Herman Pritchett, *The American Constitution* (New York: McGraw-Hill, 1959), p. 529; J.M. Smith, and P.L. Murphy, *Liberty and Justice* (New York: Knopf, 1958), pp. 262-63; B.F. Wright, *The Growth of American Constitutional Law* (New York: Holt, 1942), p. 99; but see Fairman, *op. cit.,* p. 139.

[81]See above pp. 20-22 and Flack, *op. cit.,* pp. 58-59; Fairman, *op. cit.,* pp. 30-37; *Cong. Globe,* pp. 1088-90, 429, and 2542-43.

[82]Fed. Cases 546, Case No. 3230.

[83]See Fairman, *op. cit.,* pp. 116-21.

[84]Flack, *op. cit.,* pp. 163-65, citations omitted.

[85]P. 54.

CHAPTER III

THE PLAIN MEANING OF
THE WORDS

William Winslow Crosskey, whose remarkable book on the Constitution appeared in 1953, concludes chapter xxxi of that book on the "True Meaning of the Fourteenth Amendment" by declaring that "what the Supreme Court has done, under this lucidly drawn provision of the document it is sworn to uphold, seems remarkable in the highest degree."[1] The chapter is long and detailed and Professor Crosskey excuses the length and complexity with a footnote to the first page thereof[2] in which he says that the "matters dealt with in this . . . chapter are very simple and very obvious. Nevertheless, they are matters which still divide sharply the Justices of our highest court. . . ."

This is a fierce accusation, for if a body of men are sharply divided over matters which are very simple and very obvious then, manifestly, at least a part of that body—if not the whole of it—is composed of fools or knaves, or at least of men unversed in the matters over which division occurs or driven to such division by blind partisanship. Crosskey, of course, does not leave it to us to draw these conclusions. He refers to Marshall's opinion in *Barron* v. *Baltimore*[3] as an "iniquitous doctrine"[4] and states that "no doubt is possible as to what the whole first section of the Fourteenth Amendment was painstakingly and skillfully drawn to mean,"[5] for, he argues, it was meant to overrule that "iniquitous doctrine."

As far as "substantive due process of law" is concerned, he states that the due process guarantee is merely—i.e., strictly—procedural and that "it is only when its words, as meaningful English words, are disregarded, that any other view is possible."[6]

> . . . The first section of the Fourteenth Amendment seems crystal clear; and since it has long been established that the framers of that Amendment *intended* it to mean all these things which, we have seen, it clearly does,[7] it is difficult to see how the Supreme Court can possibly have failed to understand the amendment, five years after its adoption, when the first cases under it arose. For the framers' intention as to the meaning of their amendment had been declared by them in Congress;[8] the Supreme Court, at the date of these first cases, must surely have been—or at the very least it could and should have been—familiar with these suggestive speeches; and it was, assuredly, not too much to ask, in addition, that the Justices have some familiarity with the earlier decisions of their own Court. So, one's wonder must be great at what we shall soon see, the Supreme Court has done.[9]

The argument of the whole book, regarding Federal-State relations, is, in brief, that the Constitution of 1787 created a truly national government, that the words of that Constitution—understood in the light of their established usage at that time—plainly call for such a national government; that the first ten Amendments to that Constitution, commonly called the Bill of Rights, were meant to be restrictions upon the government of the United States and all governments within the United States; that pressure on one side and weakness on the other gradually interpreted away that Constitution and those Amendments in the direction of States' Rights; that the Reconstruction Amendments meant to restore, at least in certain respects, the truly national character of the government; and that these, too, have in turn been construed away in favor of States' Rights. Of course, there are other propositions—relating, for example, to the respective powers of Congress and the Supreme Court within the national government—central to his argument, but, at least as far as what are called Federal-State relations are concerned, the foregoing does no violence either by omission or misstatement to his thesis.

The content of that Constitutional structure which Crosskey sees includes a general legislative power of the Congress over all those

things which might come within the scope of the grand objects
delineated in the Preamble. That there is an enumeration of powers in
Art. I, sec. 8 does not imply a restriction as to those things not
enumerated but merely emphasizes that, granting full and
unrestricted powers to the national government, the things
enumerated are to be understood as legislative powers, not executive.
It is not, that is, that the things *not listed* are forbidden to Congress
but that the things listed are forbidden to the Executive.[10] The
Supreme Court—*Federalist #78*, and Mr. Chief Justice Marshall's
mandamus decision to the contrary notwithstanding—was not at all
empowered to render invalid acts of Congress but it was empowered
to oversee, in all respects, all courts within the country.[11]

In short, Crosskey's book challenges most of the "standing
Constitutional law" of our day. Obviously, it is the business of high
scholarship to salvage history from popular nonsense and all would
agree with the reviewer who remarked that "the fact that Crosskey's
teaching is startling and contrary to the doctrines in which most of us
have been schooled does not prove him wrong."[12] But neither can we
fall into the snare, which has lately become the nonsense which is
most popular, of identifying accuracy with novelty and supposing
something to be true simply because it debunks.

> Its main significance may lie in its reflection upon the quality of
> American Scholarship as a whole, which has permitted so many
> scholars to be shaken loose from the intellectual moorings of a
> lifetime by a farrago of fancy rendered plausible only by a
> confident tone, nice printing, and an abundance of notes and
> appendices referring to obscure documents and esoteric word
> meanings.[13]

The reviews of the book are as favorable and as unfavorable as
reviews of a book by Ezra Pound might be. Some are wholly
uncritical, or reportorial,[14] others are strongly favorable[15] and others
are not very helpful because they "leave to historical specialists" the
task of assessing the adequacy of Crosskey's proof.[16] Probably the
least helpful reviews are those which reject the book on merely
traditional grounds (for it is tradition itself which Professor Crosskey
challenges)[17] and those which engage in what Hart calls "gingerly
skepticism."[18] It is foolish to criticize the findings of Crosskey and to

sandwich that criticism in between praise for "fine research" and comments that the work is "challenging."[19] If the conclusions are false the research is not "fine," it is merely ponderous and pedantic. And, as far as the work being "challenging" is concerned, so what? One of those little puzzles consisting of two interlocked, twisted, six-penny nails is "challenging" but would not be so if someone had not twisted the nails and confounded their relationship.

One reviewer was so carried away with enthusiasm for the book and for some of its dark accusations as to liken Presidents Jefferson and Madison to "germs" and Professor Crosskey to a self-less, modest and shy biologist—a kind of Doctor Salk of the legal world.[20]

Thoroughgoing criticism of Crosskey's book would have to fall into one of the following three sorts: (1) historical criticism based upon a fund of knowledge in one of the areas covered by Crosskey and consisting of an array of evidence supplementing and countering that offered by him; (2) historical criticism consisting of a re-examination and re-evaluation of the same data offered by Crosskey; or (3) internal criticism—a careful untangling of the intricate web of his argument to look for inconsistencies and logical errors. Ideally, a critique would consist of all these things, but such a critique might require as much time and effort as went into the writing of the book and in such an enterprise there is always the discouraging possibility that the expenditure might turn out to be not worth the effort. There have, after all, been some imposing books which were mere impositions.

If a large book is a bad book, countering it not only might require an effort which the book is not worth, but it might be "not a pleasant task to speak so severely of a book upon which so much effort has been spent, and into which so much ingenuity of argument is injected,"[21] as one would have to speak of a very bad book. The result might lead one to conclude "that Mr. Crosskey's performance, measured by even the least exacting of scholarly standards, is in the reviewer's opinion without merit,"[22] and one might be led to "the impression that such labor has served for the most part only to bring forth the proverbial mouse,"[23] for the argument might be "more ingenious than persuasive."[24]

There have been several adverse reviews which merit attention. A brief sample will suffice. Crosskey states that Marshall's decision in

Barron v. *Baltimore*[25] was "incorrect"[26] and "iniquitous"[27] "The Court's decision to this effect (that the first eight Amendments applied only to the national government) was announced by it, as if it were very obvious, but the fact is the decision was contrary to the considered opinion of good lawyers before that time, and it is not difficult to show that, in the scope in which the Court announced it, it was without any warrant at all."[28]

Of this problem John P. Frank says that "Mr. Crosskey suggests not a single instance between 1790 and 1833 of any unequivocal determination in his favor in any state court, and cites no other instance in which any lawyer ever came into a state court seriously relying upon the federal Bill of Rights."[29]

If Frank's statement is accurate, then one would be inclined to dismiss Crosskey's argument on this point. Conceivably there were such instances and Crosskey has simply failed to suggest them. But the burden of proof lies with Crosskey, and it is *not* conceivable that Crosskey be right and yet there be no such instances for him to adduce. For, while words do not—as in Looking Glass Land—mean whatever the speaker wants them to mean, the meaning of words in the realm of practical affairs is what it is only in relation to ordinary discourse and if there were a number of lawyers whose clients stood to profit from such a meaning as Crosskey imputes to the first eight Amendments and none attempted to serve their clients by recourse to such a meaning then therefore it did not mean that to the men who stood most to profit by such a meaning. Hence it did not mean that at all, nor does it now.

According to Ernest J. Brown:

> Almost every page calls for some question regarding completeness of statement, some remark concerning twisted dialectic or excess of venom, some note of Mr. Crosskey's saltatory method of reaching conclusions and the process of having them grow in vigor and assurance by repetition.[30]

Another reviewer said, "Sometimes (the supporting evidence) is presented without a solitary item which will withstand a fair investigation."[31]

The foregoing pages do not canvass all of the reviews of the book but they cover a goodly sample of them. Judge Clark, in his portion of a four-way symposium on Crosskey[32] accused Swisher of "an emotional investment in the constitutional status quo curious to behold,"[33] saying that Swisher suggested the "unworthiness of a university press which would stoop to publish this original new work!"[34] Professor Brown responds to this barb of Clark's by lamenting the fact that Crosskey's book has so inflamed the adversaries in the debate which followed upon it that one might only criticize the book at the peril of having his motives impugned and being charged with "emotional investment."[35] Whatever the word "emotional" means, it probably does apply to the incongruity of a reviewer who, manifesting a strongly libertarian view coupled with the advocacy of judicial supremacy, invites Professor Crosskey to burn his book.[36]

> One's first impression of Mr. Crosskey's book is a sort of shock. His pages bristle with assurance of the obvious rightness of his views. Those who, in the past century and two-thirds have taken positions contrary to that of Mr. Crosskey today are at best weaklings, oftener base wretches. His paragraphs are shot through with italic, as though in high indignation he were underlining the telling phrases of a letter to the *Times*.[37]

It is no wonder, then, that such a strong controversy has arisen over the book. In the *University of Chicago Law Review* Symposium mentioned above, Abe Krash and Professor Walton Hamilton also participated and, like Judge Clark, reacted favorably.[38] Charles Fairman, whose 134 page article (to which frequent reference was made in the preceding chapter) received exactly thirty words of attention in Crosskey's text[39] and one footnote (the very last in the book),[40] also contributed to the Symposium. Needless to say, his contribution was highly critical.[41] Crosskey paid Fairman the singular honor of replying in a 143 page article a year later[42] and Fairman, upon a point of privilege, attached thereto a thirteen page "Reply to Professor Crosskey."[43]

Occasional reference will be made to these several articles, but it is wholly unnecessary for us to include an exhaustive exposition of this vigorous and sometimes bitter exchange. The record is there for all to see.[44]

While a large portion of Crosskey's book has been subjected to criticism, the particular chapter most germane to this inquiry has not been so covered and it presents an argument which cannot be ignored. Claiming no expertise in any field of constitutional history, we shall not employ the first of the three modes of criticism suggested above,[45] but rather this discussion will have to rely on the latter two.

Part V of Crosskey's book is the last part (except for a short chapter, xxxiii, which makes up an unnumbered part entitled "In Conclusion"), and consists of chapters xxx-xxxii and is entitled "The Supreme Court and the Constitutional Limitations on State Governmental Authority." The first of these chapters, xxx, is entitled, "The Supreme Court's Destruction of the Constitutional Limitations on State Authority, Contained in the Original Constitution and Initial Amendments."[46] Fairman and others have dealt at length with this chapter.[47] For present purposes, chapter xxx may be dismissed. Prior to the adoption of the Fourteenth Amendment—indeed, prior to Crosskey's book—Marshall's decision in *Barron* v. *Baltimore* was accepted without dispute of any kind as the "standing constitutional law." The assumption on all sides of the current controversy over the meaning of the Fourteenth Amendment is that prior to the Fourteenth Amendment, Marshall's decision was the law of the land. In other words, the present study does require as a step in its progress an understanding of the meaning of the Fourteenth Amendment in the light of the accepted doctrine, prior to its adoption, of the application of the first eight Amendments. It does not require as a step in its progress examination of the question as to whether or not that accepted doctrine is correct. Passing reference may need to be made to the chronologically earlier problem but, for the most part, attention may now be turned to the later problem and the following chapter, xxxi, entitled, "The True Meaning of the Fourteenth Amendment."[48]

The argument of chapter xxxi may be summarized in this way: There are four clauses in the first section of the Fourteenth Amendment: the citizenship, privileges or immunities, due process and equal protection clauses. Everyone agrees that the citizenship clause was "intended to nullify . . . the central doctrine . . . of *Dred Scott* v. *Sandford*,"[49] and everyone is right. But everyone disagrees about the meaning of the other three clauses and nearly everyone is wrong. The true meaning of those clauses can only be discerned if one construes the words and phrases of those clauses—citizen, privilege, immunity, abridge, person, due process of law, equal—according to the standing constitutional law of the day when the Amendment was drafted. That standing law was established as far as "privileges or immunities" are concerned by the *Dred Scott* case,[50] and as far as "due process of law" is concerned by the *Murray's Lessee* case.[51] The "equal protection of the laws" clause is, of course, new to the Constitution but when the "elementary rule is satisfied, that the parts of a writing are to be so construed that all of them have some effect,"[52] the meaning of that clause becomes clear also.

Since the only point at issue here is whether or not the Fourteenth Amendment makes the first eight Amendments effective as bars to state action, we need not examine in detail the whole of Crosskey's argument on the meaning of the Fourteenth Amendment, but only so much of it as affects this issue. For the most part we may then confine ourselves to consideration of that part of the argument which relates to the "privileges or immunities" clause and the "due process" clause. The necessity for treating both clauses is that they both, according to Crosskey, impose provisions of the first eight Amendments as limitations upon the states. The "privileges or immunities" clause imposes these restrictions upon state action touching "citizens of the United States" while the "due process" clause imposes some of them upon state action touching "persons"; the distinction between the two clauses being that the former is broader. In other words, states may not abridge the privileges or immunities of citizens of the United States and those privileges and immunities include each of the things guaranteed by the first eight Amendments, and, *within* the first eight Amendments, the due process clause of the Fifth Amendment—in its turn—comprehends all the court processes named in the first eight Amendments, plus the *habeas corpus* provision of Art. I, sec. 9, plus common law practices not forbidden by the Constitution or its amendments plus a protection against court processes not forbidden by the Constitution and its amendments but which are new to the law—i.e., not to be found in the common law—and, in their nature, unreasonable. The latter clause leaves the states free to deny to aliens certain of the privileges and immunities which attach to citizens of the United States but it forbids the states to deprive even aliens of life, liberty, or property without due process of law, and as just stated, due process of law comprehends court processes guaranteed by the Constitution and its amendments and by the common law as well as a prohibition against processes neither forbidden by the Constitution nor prescribed by the common law but intrinsically unreasonable.

Throughout the thirty-first chapter one gets the impression that Crosskey is on the verge of presenting an expanded draft of the whole of the first section of the Fourteenth Amendment which will show both the meanings he finds therein and the harmony of those meanings in the whole, and, while he presents something like an expanded draft for each of the parts, he never does combine them. We therefore take the liberty of presenting such an expanded draft extruded from the whole chapter:

Professor Crosskey's Fourteenth Amendment:

> All persons born or naturalized in the United States and subject to the jurisdiction thereof are citizens of the United States and of the State wherein they reside. Every right, privilege and immunity which a citizen of the U.S. has in relation to the United States he shall also have in relation to each of the States and nothing which the United States are forbidden to do to citizens of the United States may be done to such citizens by any State; what is more, even aliens are entitled to those rights, privileges and immunities, at the hands of each State, which pertain to court processes and neither citizen nor alien may be subjected to proceedings in a State court which, while not explicitly forbidden, are both novel and intrinsically unreasonable; nor shall any State discriminate for or against any person as person by, for example, the granting of monopolies or the denial of the suffrage, although States may discriminate among classes and, for example, felons, fools, minors, women and farmers may be considered as classes but Negroes may not be so considered.[53]

Let us expand and examine the argument beginning with the *Dred Scott* case and the question of privileges and immunities. The intricacy and ingenuity of the argument is rivalled only by that of Mr. Chief Justice Taney's opinion for the Court in the *Dred Scott* case itself. Crosskey argues, and correctly so, that the purport of the *Dred*

Scott case was somewhat broader than the precise ruling in that case as that precise ruling was recounted in the *Slaughter House* cases. It will be remembered that *Dred Scott* ruled, precisely, upon two points and that that ruling held, first, that no negro could claim the privilege of suing in any court of the United States and, second, that Congress had no power to forbid slavery in any of that territory acquired beyond the boundaries of the United States as established in the treaty which concluded the Revolutionary War.

For purposes of exposition, these two matters must be separated. Crosskey argues that the full purport of the decision regarding the matter of Dred Scott's being entitled to sue in the courts of the United States was that no negro could be a member of the "people" of the United States and hence could expect no protection, no privileges or immunities, no rights at the hands of the United States. He could not even expect the "privileges and immunities of citizens in the several States." In order to do this, Taney had to perform several manipulations which were, at best, doubtful. He had first to suppose a power in each state to confer citizenship, despite the naturalization clause of the Constitution.[54] He had, then to limit the significance of the citizenship so conferred to the state where it was conferred, thereby suggesting two classes of citizens, a larger class who were citizens of the several states and a smaller class who were citizens of the several states and who were citizens of the United States as well. Taney then went on to limit the effect of the privileges and immunities clause of Art. IV, sec. 2 to this smaller class (despite the plain terms of the clause). We need not stop to inquire how, in general, distinction was to be made between the larger and the smaller class. In particular, the distinction was made in Dred Scott's case by the color of his skin. The particular distinction was based on the historically false proposition that the framers would have regarded citizenship for any negro as unthinkable.[55] Crosskey continues his discussion of the *Dred Scott* case by maintaining that it was this full purport—that no negro could claim any of the privileges and immunities of citizenship and that there were such things as citizens of a state who were not citizens of the United States—which the first sentence of the first section of the Fourteenth Amendment overrules.[56] We shall not cavil as to whether the first sentence of the Fourteenth Amendment reverses, in the first instance, the ruling of

Dred Scott or merely puts the reversal beyond cavil. Certainly, in the limited way we have reproduced Crosskey's argument, that argument does give a thorough and accurate account of the purport of the *Dred Scott* case, and we here accept, for purposes of argument, the initial-reversing character of the first sentence of the Fourteenth Amendment.

As we have indicated, Professor Crosskey's argument is intricate. Why such intricacy should be necessary for the exposition of a "lucidly drawn"[57] provision which is "clear in itself"[58] is part of the mystery. The defect in the argument is elusive and is intimately allied with the intricacy. At worst, perhaps he confused himself along with his readers and "talked himself into" an error. At best, he presents a possible solution through a complex but plausible argument. Nothing of the complexity and intricacy of that argument is reflected in the brief summary of it contained in the preceding paragraph but that exposition itself is certainly complex, not to say agile. Throughout the first section of chapter xxxi he makes frequent reference to Taney's use of the words "rights," "privileges," and "immunities." These references blossom forth in the last paragraph of his first section and the first three paragraphs of the second section[59] as conclusive evidence that the "privileges or immunities of citizens of the United States" guaranteed by the second sentence of the first section of the Fourteenth Amendment against state abridgment, included, according to the "standing constitutional law" established by the *Dred Scott* case, all the things enumerated in the first eight Amendments.

It seems advisable to reproduce in their entirety, these four paragraphs:

> In view, then, of this elaborate exemplification by the Court, as to what it meant by "rights and privileges"—or, as it sometimes said, "rights, and privileges, and immunities," or at others, "privileges and immunities"—"of citizens of the United States," no doubt seems possible that it was intended, *by the principles* of the Dred Scott case, to restrain the availability of *all* "privileges" and "immunities" under the Constitution and its various amendments, *to "citizens of the United States," only*. And bearing in mind that the Court was holding that all "men of African descent, whether slaves or not," were absolutely debarred from becoming "citizens of the United

States," this plainly means, as was stated at the beginning, that the full and true purport of the Dred Scott case was that all "men of African descent, whether slaves or not," were to be bereft thereafter of all rights and protection, *under the Constitution of the United States*, whatsoever. This, to the present-day mind, seems an unbelievable decision; but to those familiar with the political demands of the South of the time when the decision was rendered, such a tenor in the Court's holding will not be difficult to credit. For it was exactly what the South, for a long time, had been demanding.

The foregoing, then, was the general doctrine concocted in the Dred Scott case which it was one of the chief aims of the Fourteenth Amendment to undo. That undoing was accomplished, and fully and completely accomplished, by the initial provision of the amendment (which, in the [p. 1090] actual drafting, appears, somewhat strangely, to have been an afterthought) that "all persons born or naturalized in the United States, and subject to the jurisdiction thereof, are citizens of the United States and of the State wherein they reside." This, for the single purpose of making available to Negroes, *exactly as they were available to others*, all "privileges and immunities of citizens of the United States," was all that was required. Yet, for the full attainment of the ends the framers of the amendment had in view, this result was insufficient.

It was insufficient because there were two ways in which, even in the case of white men, the "privileges and immunities of citizens of the United States" had long been imperfectly secured. One of these was the result, in the main, of the Supreme Court's decision in *Barron* v. *Baltimore*, in 1833. For the Court had then held, as we know, that none of the "privileges" and "immunities" under the first eight Amendments was available and valid, as against the states. This doctrine, unsatisfactory even where the rights of white men were concerned, would, if unchanged, have left the nation's new Negro citizens wholly unprotected against various state acts that could very easily have been employed, by a state so disposed, to nullify and defeat much that the Fourteenth Amendment was framed to accomplish. So, the framers of the Amendment, apparently accepting, as part of the practical standing "law," the foregoing doctrine of the Dred Scott case, that all "privileges and immunities" under the Constitution were those "of citizens of the United States," and of no others, went on to provide, *using the language which the Court itself had used*, that thenceforth "no State sh[ould] make or enforce any law abridging *the privileges or immunities of citizens of the United States.*"

As the states antecedently, according to the Court, had been free to abridge, in any degree they thought proper, any and all those rights to which the first eight amendments related, the conclusion seems an easy and natural one, that a total extinguishment of this antecedent state power was the precise end to which this particular clause of the Fourteenth Amendment was directed.* And reflection will show that there was, as a matter of fact, nothing else, not merely nugatory, for the clause to mean. For the Supremacy Clause of Article VI had always taken care of all "privileges" and "immunities," both under the Constitution and the laws of Congress, which the Court deemed directed against the states; and the "privileges" and "immunities," covered by the first eight amendments, which, it had held, were not directed against the states, were the only other "privileges and immunities of citizens of the United States" (except [p.1091] for a few similar "privileges and immunities" in the original document) which there were *under the standing law*. The whole iniquitous doctrine of *Barron* v. *Baltimore* was, then, apparently intended to be wiped out, both as to the First Amendment, in reference to which, we have seen, the doctrine was justified, and as to all the others of the first eight amendments, in reference to which, we have also seen, it was not. So, the whole "Bill of Rights"—as it is sometimes called—was made valid, and available, by this clause of the amendment, *in favor of all "citizens,"* as against the states.

It ought, perhaps, to be noted at this point that the Ninth Amendment rather bears out the above doctrine of the Dred Scott case as to the character of the various rights created by the Constitution. It says: "The enumeration in the Constitution, of certain rights, shall not be construed to deny or disparage others retained"—not "reserved," be it noted—"by the people."* [Crosskey's note.]

This argument cannot stand if any of the following propositions, contained in it, are defective:

1. That the framers of the Fourteenth Amendment clearly knew what they were doing and did it clearly.

2. That the *Dred Scott* case clearly established that the "privileges or immunities of citizens of the United States" included the first eight Amendments.

3. That *Barron* v. *Baltimore*—or anything or anyone else—ever said that it was constitutionally permissible for States to abridge the privileges or immunities of citizens of the United States.

4. That there really is nothing other than what Crosskey says the
   phrase means, "not merely nugatory," for the phrase to mean.
For the present, we assume the first proposition, but, as to the others,
we object. Mr. Chief Justice Taney certainly does make frequent
reference to rights, privileges, immunities, and several related terms
and he varies his use, sometimes putting "rights" and "privileges" in
the same sentence; sometimes "rights" and "immunities";
sometimes "privileges and immunities." Leaving out most of those
instances where Taney refers to "rights" or "powers" of states in
relation to other states or to their citizens (and, for the sake of
readability, leaving out quotation marks), a canvass shows the
following uses of "privileges and immunities" and related phrases:

> [p. 400]: the title of himself and his family to freedom; the
> right of the plaintiff to sue in a court of the United States. [p.
> 402]: is entitled to sue there; a right to sue in a circuit court of
> the United States; not entitled to sue as a citizen in a court of the
> United States. [p. 403]: not entitled to sue as a citizen in a court
> of the United States; brought here by those who have a right to
> bring it; entitled to all the rights, and privileges, and immunities,
> guaranteed by that instrument to the citizen? One of which
> rights is the privilege of suing in a court of the United States. [p.
> 404]: entitled to all the rights and privileges which would belong
> to an emigrant; rights and privileges which that instrument
> provided for and secures to citizens of the United States. [p.
> 405]: had no rights or privileges but such as those who held the
> power and the government might choose to grant them; rights of
> citizenship which a State may confer within its own limits and
> the right of citizenship as a member of the Union. It does not by
> any means follow, because he has all the rights and privileges of
> a citizen of a State, that he must be a citizen of the United States.
> He may have all the rights and privileges of the citizen of a state,
> and yet not be entitled to the rights and privileges of a citizen in
> any other State; no rights or privileges; entitled to sue as such in
> one of its courts; privileges and immunities of a citizen in the
> other States; the rights which he would acquire; the rights and
> privileges secured to a citizen of a State under the Federal
> government; entitled to the rights of a citizen and clothed with
> all the [p. 406] rights and immunities which the constitution and
> laws of the State attached to that character. [p. 406]: personal
> rights and privileges to which the citizen of a State should be

entitled; endue him with the full right of citizenship in every other State; all the privileges of a citizen in every other State; was not entitled to sue in its courts; personal rights and privileges guaranteed to citizens; gave to each citizen rights and privileges outside of his State; rights of persons and rights of property; rights and liberties; defend their rights by force of arms; had no rights which the white man was bound to respect. [p. 409]: It is necessary to do this, in order to determine whether the general terms used in the constitution of the United States, as to the rights of man and the rights of people, was intended to include them. [p. 410]: "unalienable rights." [p. 411]: privileges secured to the citizen. [p. 412]: rights and privileges; entitled to equal rights with themselves; political rights. [p. 413]: the relative rights and position of the white and black races. [p. 414]: the equal rights and privileges and rank of citizens in every other State; rights of individuals; right of property in the master. [p. 415]; rights and privileges of citizens in the State of Connecticut; privileges and immunities of citizens in other States. [p. 416]: Civil and political rights; liberties and rights of their citizens; rights, and privilege, and rank; privileges and immunities of citizens. [p. 417]: right to enter every other State . . . to sojourn there . . . to go where they pleased. . . . Liberty of speech in public and in private upon all subjects upon which its own citizens might speak. . . . To hold public meetings . . . to keep and carry arms; privileges and immunities of citizens in the several States; entitled to demand equal rights and privileges with their own people. [p. 418]: any right of citizenship outside of its own territory; rights and immunities of citizens of one State in the other States; . . . "privileges and immunities of free citizens in the several States"; all the privileges of citizenship in any State of the Union. [p. 419]: privileges and immunities; privilege; privilege; privilege. [p. 420]: privileges of an American citizen. [p. 422]: rights which may belong to other citizens; full rights of citizenship; entitled to vote; allowed to vote; give the right to free negroes and mulattoes; privileges and immunities in other States; privileges and immunities enjoyed by its citizens; mere rights of person; political rights; no right to participate in the government; rights of person; privileges and immunities which belong to citizens of the [p. 423] State. [p. 423]: and if persons of the African race are citizens of a State and of the United States, they would be entitled to all of these privileges and immunities in every State, and the state could not restrict them; for they would hold these privileges and immunities under the paramount authority of the federal government, and its courts would be bound to maintain and enforce them, the constitution and laws of the State to the contrary notwithstanding. And if the States could limit or restrict them, or place the party in an inferior grade, this clause of the constitution would be unmeaning, and could have no operation, and would give no rights to the citizen when in another State. He would have none but what the State itself chose to allow him. This is evidently not the construction or meaning of the clause in question. It guarantees rights to the citizen, and the State cannot withhold them. And these rights are of a character and would lead to consequences which make it absolutely certain that the African race were not included under the name of citizens of a State, and were not in the contemplation of the framers of the Constitution when these privileges and immunities were provided for the protection of the citizen in other States. . . , may sue as a citizen in a court of the United States; right to convey. [p. 424]: rights of both parties, his right to sue in that character; at liberty to proceed; ability of Darnall to convey. [p. 425]: to prevent him from using its process, incapable of suing or being sued as a citizen in a court of the United States; entitled to a special privilege; rights and privileges of citizenship. [p. 426]: rights of the owner; rights and privileges. [p. 427]: not entitled as such to sue in its courts. [p. 435]: rights of person and rights of property; rights of person and of property. [p. 444]: rights of person or rights of property of a citizen, rights of person or rights of property. [p. 447]: personal rights and rights of property of individual citizens, as secured by the Constitution. [p. 449]: rights of person or rights of property; rights and privileges, rights. [p. 450]: any right; for example, no one, we presume, will contend that congress can make any law in a territory respecting the establishment of religion, or the free exercise thereof, or abridging the freedom of speech or of the press or the right of the people of the territory peaceably to assemble, and to petition the government for the redress of grievances.

Nor can congress deny to the people the right to keep and bear arms, nor the right to trial by jury, nor compel any one to be a witness against himself in a criminal proceeding.

These powers, and others, in relation to rights of person, which it is not necessary here to enumerate, are, in express and positive terms denied to the general government; and the rights of private property have been guarded with equal care. Thus the rights of property are united with the rights of person, and placed on the same ground by the fifth amendment to the constitution, which provides that no person shall be deprived of life, liberty, and property, without due process of law. And an act of congress which deprives a citizen of the United States of his liberty or property, merely because he came himself or brought his property into a particular territory of the United States, and who had committed no offense against the laws, could hardly be dignified with the name of due process of law. So, too, it will hardly be contended that congress could by law quarter a soldier in a house in a territory without the consent of the owner, in time of peace; nor in time of war, but in a manner prescribed by law. Nor could they by law forfeit the property of a citizen in a territory who was convicted of treason, for a longer period than the life of the person convicted, nor take private property for public use without just compensation.

The powers over person and property of which we speak are not only not granted to congress, but are in express terms denied, and they are forbidden to exercise them. And this prohibition is not confined to the States, but the words are general, and extend to the whole territory over which the Constitution gives it power to legislate, including those portions of it remaining under territorial government, as well as that covered by States. It is a total absence of power everywhere within the dominion of the United States, and places the citizens of a territory, so far as these rights are [p. 451] concerned, on the same footing with citizens of the States, and guards them as firmly and plainly against any inroads which the general government might attempt, under the plea of implied or incidental powers. And if congress itself cannot do this—if it is beyond the powers conferred on the federal government to exercise them. It could confer no power on any local government, established by its authority, to violate the provisions of the constitution. [p. 451]: rights and duties; rights of citizens; the rights they have reserved; the right of property of the master in a slave, provisions and guarantees; right of property; right to traffic. [p. 452]: rights.[60]

We blush at having "bathed" the reader's eyes with words but we felt we must fight bath with bath for Crosskey, in chapter xxxi, as elsewhere, has, like a bathman, poured citations and snippets of quotations over our heads until we are dizzy. It will be seen that Taney uses such words as title, right, entitled, privilege, liberty, freedom and immunity, in such a way as to make them appear, superficially, as equivalent terms. There are in excess of 129 separate instances where such terms are used. Crosskey, in fact, does treat them as being established by the "standing Constitutional law" as equivalent terms. Assuming that these terms are equivalent, and further that they are absolute (i.e., attached to the person rather than to the relationship between the person and a named or implied government—which assumption makes his contention regarding *Barron* v. *Baltimore* correct and the adoption of the privileges or immunities clause of the Fourteenth Amendment unnecessary to accomplish what Crosskey says it accomplishes) he argues that all of these rights, privileges and immunities belong to the citizens of the United States, as the *standing constitutional law*, which Taney had made available to them but not to citizens of the states who were not also citizens of the United States. And, further, he argues that *Barron* v. *Baltimore* had declared that states could abridge the privileges and immunities of citizens of the United States and therefore the privileges or immunities clause of the Fourteenth Amendment was necessary to protect citizens—white as much as black—from actions by the states which the first eight Amendments forbade the United States to employ.

Crosskey's argument has become so clever and so avaricious—and so tangled—that here it begins to bite off its own tail. First, let us observe in passing that *Barron* v. *Baltimore* never once said that states were free under the Constitution to abridge the privileges and immunities of citizens of the United States. If *that case* treated rights and privileges as equivalent terms, what it said was not that states could abridge anything at all that belonged to citizens but rather that, while the privileges of citizens of the United States might include the right not to be deprived of property *by the United States* without just compensation, those privileges did *not* include a right not to be deprived of property by a *state* without just compensation. As a matter of fact, the words "privileges" and "immunities"—or either of them—*nowhere appear* in the *Barron* case. It is an absurd word-trick to charge that Marshall anywhere stated that states were free to abridge rights guaranteed by the Constitution. So to charge requires assuming the very point at issue—namely, that the rights in question are absolute, rather than relative to the United States as Marshall ruled.

Now, so far from the privileges or immunities clause of the Fourteenth Amendment being required to undo what Crosskey says

Taney established in *Dred Scott*, if the *Dred Scott* case is to be understood fully as Crosskey exposes it, the privileges or immunities clause would be "mere surplusage." For Crosskey says that Taney had created a "smaller class" of citizens of the states who were also "citizens of the United States"—and this Taney did do—and he says that Taney limited to this smaller class the benefit of the privileges and immunities clause of Art. IV, sec. 2 and he thereby transformed those privileges and immunities to which citizens of each state were entitled, by Art. IV, sec. 2, in the several states into privileges and immunities of citizens of the United States. And that Taney also did. That is, Taney treated the first clause of Art. IV, sec. 2, as though it said that citizens of the United States were entitled to all privileges and immunities of citizens of the United States in every state; that is, that no state might abridge the privileges and immunities of citizens of the United States. In other words, the privileges and immunities clause of the Fourteenth Amendment *is* mere surplusage if the "larger purport" of the *Dred Scott* case were to be considered as the "standing constitutional law" which preceded that clause's adoption and if the framers *had* "lucidly drawn" the Amendment in the light of that "standing constitutional law" they would have been very careful not to be so foolish and so wordy as to have included the privileges or immunities clause in it. In passing, we note that, while we cannot abide Taney's *ex cathedra* expatriation of freedmen, we cannot but agree with his rendering of the privileges and immunities clause of Art. IV, sec. 2 as guaranteeing to all citizens of the United States all privileges and immunities—whatever they may be—which attach to that citizenship, in every state.

But "whatever they may be" is the question, and Crosskey commits the ultimate absurdity by maintaining that Taney's varied uses of privileges, rights, etc., established as the standing constitutional law that the privileges and immunities which attached to the person of the citizen of the United States as absolute rights included the rights listed in the first eight Amendments which *Barron* v. *Baltimore* had "iniquitously" rendered "abridgable" by the states. *Note well*, that if Taney *had* treated the first eight Amendments as privileges and immunities of citizens of the United States—as a superficial view of pages 450-51 of the Reports would suggest (see the long quotation above)[61]—*he, Taney, would thereby have overruled the Barron case.* For it will be remembered that the very thing which Taney said it was unthinkable to suppose the framers had intended to invest in negroes was the protection of the privileges and immunities of citizens of the United States against state action and that is why negroes could never be considered citizens for states would have to do what no self-respecting state would consider doing, namely, grant to them all the privileges and immunities of citizens of the United States just as the Constitution compelled them to grant those privileges and immunities to white men.

We do not believe that *Dred Scott* overruled *Barron* v. *Baltimore* by design or by carelessness. We believe that the constitutional law stood after *Dred Scott*, as it had before, rather vague as to the content of the privileges and immunities clause. The only thing we can be *sure* Taney included in it was the right to sue. That Taney may have given *no* serious thought to the bounds of that content is possible. That he did think about it and meant to leave the first eight Amendments out is not only possible but is moderately indicated by the fact that in virtually every one of those 129 or more instances in which he used the words "privileges and immunities" and words reminiscent or suggestive of them and used them in a great variety of combinations, he combined them or compared them with a disjunctive "or" or "and."

It seems more reasonable to suppose that the 39th Congress coined the Fourteenth Amendment with the same "whatever they may be" attitude toward privileges and immunities which has characterized so much court and academic usage of the term, perhaps out of an "abundance of caution," as Crosskey elsewhere admits to be within the drafting capabilities of constitutional founders.[62] It also seems reasonable to suppose that they drafted the Fourteenth Amendment with a view only to overruling the specific and narrow decision of *Dred Scott* and regarded with silent contempt the "larger purport" of that case as it affected the rights of citizens just as the "larger purport" of the case as it affected the powers of Congress to govern the territories was treated with silent contempt in the drafting of the Thirteenth Amendment which overruled only the precise point regarding slavery. If ever there was a Congress that might have laid to rest the threats to congressional power over the territories interlaced in the "larger purport" of the *Dred Scott* case it was the 39th. And so—to use Crosskey's favorite expressions—"it seems likely in the highest degree" that "the inherent probabilities" of the case are the 39th Congress, the country in general and the Supreme Court in particular have ever since the Civil War had as little to do with the "larger purport" of the *Dred Scott* case as possible.[63]

We cannot encumber this account more with further refutations of Crosskey's proposition that the privileges or immunities clause of the Fourteenth Amendment embraces, in plain terms, all of the things spoken of in the first eight Amendments, but neither can we forego the opportunity to point out that while Crosskey makes much of the use of a contemporary dictionary of his own compiling for an interpretation of constitutional clauses, he had little to say about dictionaries for the Fourteenth Amendment.[64] We know that no one in 1866 consulted a dictionary compiled by Crosskey in 1953, but we also know that some men in 1866 consulted Burrill's *Law Dictionary*[65] of 1851 and Jacob's *Law Dictionary*[66] of 1783, for Mr. Justice Swayne cites those dictionaries in the circuit court case discussed in the preceding chapter.[67] Neither of these dictionaries nor Bouvier's *Law Dictionary*[68]—editions of 1839, 1848, 1852, 1862—offers a scrap of support for his argument. In all of them "privilege" is treated as the equal of "immunity" and as a kind of right and is traced to its Latin equivalent and etymologically explained as coming from *privata lex*.[69] The term "privileges and immunities" does not appear in any of these dictionaries, nor does it appear in Thomas Tayler's *The Law Glossary* for 1861.[70] As far as the dictionary entries for "right" are concerned, the general approach of the whole lot of them is to speak, on the one hand, of right in the sense of justice or equity as those terms were generally and traditionally used and, on the other hand, of *a* right in the sense of a relative claim established by positive law. The earlier editions of Bouvier begin by offering the classical definition of natural right as a command or prohibition, but then say, "In our language it is seldom used in this sense." It can almost be said that these law dictionaries *never* offer as a definition of "right" that curious mixture of the classical notion of natural right and the traditional notion of positive legal rights which was introduced into political discussion in the seventeenth century under the name of "natural rights." Crosskey, however, implies the idea of natural rights throughout chapter xxx and here and there in chapter xxxi, and, in chapter xviii speaks explicitly of, "natural law" and a "state of nature" and by "natural law" he means the specifically modern version thereof which is equivalent to "natural rights" which arise out of that "state of nature."[71] It seems, in fact, that insofar as the lexicographers followed Hobbes, they followed him in a perfectly lawyer-like manner for Bouvier says, "Rights might with propriety also be divided into natural and civil rights; but as all the rights which man has received from nature, have been modified and acquired anew from the civil law, it is more proper, when considering their object, to divide them into political and civil rights."[72]

We entertain no doubt at all that many men in 1789 as well as in 1866 believed in some variation of the state of nature-natural rights doctrine. But how lawyers and legislators *treated* that doctrine in the business of drafting constitutions and statutes, where they "modified and acquired anew from the civil law" all those rights, is another matter. Indeed, to secure those rights, the "inherent probabilities" seem to us precisely the opposite of what Crosskey suggests, and Marshall's view that the founders secured them in the Constitution only against the government created by that Constitution—namely, the government of the United States and not the governments of the several states—is not even bent by Crosskey's thirtieth chapter. And, while the Civil War Amendments certainly affected greatly the relations between states and the United States, Crosskey's argument in the first and second sections of his thirty-first chapter that the privileges or immunities clause of the Fourteenth Amendment affected those relations by making the first eight Amendments prohibitions to state as well as to United States action is wholly unconvincing.

The *Dred Scott* case, the issue of slavery and the Civil War surely caused men to think anew about the "rights of man," but that in the heat of battle and the passions of Reconstruction they thought things all out clearly and clearly meant what Crosskey says is not at all an "inherent probability." The history of Bouvier's *Law Dictionary* is itself instructive on this problem. Prior to the Civil War, and up to and including the 1862 edition, the entry for "right" was as indicated above. But in 1867 a long addition, much reminiscent of the Lockean view of natural rights, is inserted *before* the material which had been included in that entry for the earlier editions. The entry for "right" in the latest (1914) edition, which is still used by many lawyers in preference to Black's *Law Dictionary*, is, with infinitesimal changes in wording, identical to that in the 1867 edition.

A superficial view of the entry in the 1914 edition gives the impression of a unified definition but, upon closer inspection, it can be seen that the Lockean discourse is separated from the specific definitions by the phrase, "Publicists and jurists have made the following further distinction of rights:—." And, an even closer scrutiny will show that there is just about no connection whatever between what goes before and what comes after that phrase. Perhaps the trustees who managed the dictionary after Bouvier's death were not quite as lawyer-like as he and well-meaningly dashed together a noble essay under the influence of the times. This possibility—or at least the disconnectedness of the essay and the definitions—becomes more dramatically evident if one consults not the 1914 edition but the 1867 edition wherein that Lockean essay first appears, and notices that it is squeezed in in fine print as though, as an afterthought, it had been rushed to the printers just in time.

For convenient reference we include, as Appendix I (*q.v.*) a composition of all the entries for "right" in the various editions of Bouvier from 1839 to 1914. The entries for "immunities" and for "privileges" in the current editions of Bouvier and Black are reasonably like the entries for those words in all of the dictionaries, of whatever date, mentioned in the foregoing paragraphs except that, we mention again, there is no entry for the phrase "privileges and immunities" in any of the pre-Civil War dictionaries.[73]

And so not only Professor Crosskey's imaginary dictionary but the real dictionaries lawyers and legislators consulted, in the 1860's and before fail to support Crosskey's contention as to the meaning of the privileges and immunities clause of the Fourteenth Amendment.

The third section of Crosskey's chapter xxxi[74] is devoted to an exposition of his understanding of the equal protection clause of the Fourteenth Amendment, but it will not be necessary to discuss that section since Crosskey's views, whether right or wrong, have no more than a peripheral bearing on the problem of this study.

The fourth and fifth sections,[75] however, are concerned with the due process clause and attention must be given to those sections for they argue, first, that the due process clause covers with the protection of the first eight Amendments—or most of them—against state actions aliens who had been left out of such protection by the privileges or immunities clause because that clause, being broader, confined its protection to citizens and, second, that the doctrine of so-called substantive due process of law is an entirely impermissible construction of the due process clause.

This latter point does not touch upon crucial matters, at least at this stage of the argument, and so, provisionally, it may be dealt with rather quickly. Crosskey says that the due process guarantee does not "invest the Supreme Court with such a discretionary reviewing power" as it has claimed, since the Fourteenth Amendment's adoption, over the "wisdom or reasonableness, of all the acts that the Congress of the United States might pass."[76] Coining the apt phrase "due substance of law" he treats as heresy the trend begun in New York in *Wynehamer* v. *The People*.[77] He admits that the *Dred Scott* opinions on the majority side "had, to a certain extent, fallen in with this New York heresy" but, although he had in the case of the privileges or immunities clause made much of the broader purport of the *Dred Scott* case, he here dismissed *this aspect* of that broader purport *by describing the Dred Scott* case as "thoroughly discredited."[78] This seems like having one's cake and eating it.

> So, remembering that the first beginnings of the "substantive" view were a discredited heresy, rather than an accepted tenet, when the Fourteenth Amendment was drawn, it does seem that, if "due substance" was meant, the framers of the amendment would have said so plainly. And this they did not do.[79]

This seems to work both ways, too, and if "first eight Amendments" was meant, the framers might have saved us all a lot of bother by saying so plainly. And this they did not do.

He sums up his treatment of "due substance" by arguing that the inclusion of the "equal protection" clause in the Fourteenth Amendment proves that the due process clause could not involve substance, for—and one must take the equal protection clause to mean what Crosskey says it means and it means that to Crosskey partly because that's all it could mean because the other clauses mean what Crosskey says they mean—the equal protection clause already covers "interpersonal inequality" and that means unjust laws (which are, be it noted, only forbidden to the States and not to the United States). But Crosskey had treated legislation as to farmers, for example, as legitimate class discrimination, and not as "interpersonal inequality,"[80] and it is impossible not to ask what would be the case of an act of Congress or a state legislature expropriating all agricultural lands. Would this not be legitimate class legislation which somehow deprived farmers, whom, despite Marx's jibe about the "idiocy of rural life"[81] the Constitution treats as "persons," of their property without doing so through "due" court "process"?

> . . . The Equal Protection Clause proves the draftsmen of the amendment were aware that their Due Process Clause, in accord with its plain, literal terms, was a guaranty of appropriate "process" only.[82]

The framers may or may not have been aware of this—supposing such a question to be legitimate in our inquiry. But, although the clause well may be a guarantee of appropriate "process" *only*, it at least *is* a guarantee of that. While we accept the generally prevalent view today that the Supreme Court exercised for many years an undue discretion over social legislation in the name of the due process clause but really based on limited views of the economic processes of society, we cannot accept Crosskey's dismissal of what he calls "Due Substance" without further inquiry.

The "distinction between public and private matters is itself a public matter expressed in law by the makers of the law."[83] The founders of the Constitution, if not those of all the Amendments thereto, were surely aware of this, and, when they drew that distinction in the act of founding, they were, without doubt, wise enough to draw it broadly so as to leave it to future publics to define and redefine. And certainly the Constitution does not warrant an unbending protection of "dynamic" property coupled with a niggardly construction of the clauses granting governmental powers, but it *does* say that persons shall not be deprived of property without due process of law either by the United States or by the states.

The Constitution provided that no person shall be deprived of life, liberty, or property without due process of law. This is a guarantee of appropriate process only. But it is not possible to read it as though it read—as Crosskey implies over and over again in the fifth section of chapter xxxi—"Whenever life, liberty or property is taken by court process that process shall be the due and appropriate process."[84] It is just as much within the realm of the possible for a tyrant to take life, liberty, or property without *any* court process as it is to take them with or by inappropriate process. And, if a tyrant does that, it might very well be in substance a deprivation of life, liberty or property without due process of law. However far afield the Court may have gone on this leg, however much it may deserve the censure of the country and of the political departments of the government and of sincere scholars of the law and successors on the bench, the doctrine of substantive due process of law cannot be laughed or stricken off as a bad joke, a bad dream, or a bad plot.

Accepting, then, that aspect of Crosskey's argument which maintains that the due process clauses of the Fifth and Fourteenth Amendments were not drafted consciously with a view to legislation as such but were rather drafted in order to guarantee due, or appropriate, court process in all cases of deprivation of life, liberty or property, it remains only to inquire whether that guarantee is, or includes a guarantee of all the specific modes of process, in terms, catalogued in the first eight Amendments. It is not necessary or desirable to exhaust this topic at once. The history of the interpretations of the due process clause of the Fourteenth Amendment is too familiar to bear repeating. Such parts of that history as are necessary will be called forth as the argument progresses. What must be done here is deal with the assertion that the clause plainly, and therefore without reference to the framers' intentions, embraces the procedural commands and prohibitions of the first eight Amendments.

A part of Crosskey's argument regarding the due process clause is dependent upon acceptance of his argument touching the privileges or immunities clause and that has already been seen to be defective. However, other portions of his argument might claim to stand alone and these portions must be discussed. These independent portions argue, as did the argument for the privileges or immunities clause, in the name of the standing constitutional law of the time of the adoption of the Amendment. That standing law is found in the only

Supreme Court case to construe the "due process" clause of the Fifth Amendment as an incident to decision, namely, *Murray's Lessee* v. *Hoboken Land and Improvement Co.*[85] Crosskey offers a three-part interpretation of the "due process" clause and maintains that the *Murray's Lessee* case established the first two of those parts—which was as far as that case needed to enter the question—and that the third part of his interpretation is "inferable on [the] same basis" as that upon which the *Murray* case rested.[86]

It is easy to agree with Professor Crosskey when he states that "due process of law" means "appropriate" or "required"[87] and that whatever is unreasonable or unfair is inappropriate and forbidden,[88] and if one gives to everyone what is due to him as in justice one must, it is appropriate to praise Crosskey for doing here what few enough researchers do in their legal studies—he goes beyond the law as such to the purpose served by the law in order to attach this, the third part of his interpretation, to the "due process" clause. For, if one supposes that "due process of law" means nothing other than "the law of the land" as has often been supposed,[89] and "law of the land" is construed wholly uncritically so as to allow unrestrained statutory amendment, one ends up with absolute legislative supremacy and legal as well as moral relativism. No one, for example, could sensibly say that the process of law rendered by Nazi Germany was in all cases due process of law simply because it was the process ordained as the law of the land.[90]

The "due process" clause cannot mean "law of the land" in the sense of the Common Law exactly as it stood upon the adoption of the Fifth Amendment for that would preclude adjustments in process of any kind by subsequent action of Congress,[91] nor could it mean, as Coke seemed to say, merely "indictment and presentment of good and lawful men, and trial and conviction in consequence,"[92] for that would make the "due process" clause of the Fifth Amendment a redundancy[93] and so it must be "that the phrase 'due process of law' therein simply means 'the appropriate process of law' *in a general way* and contemplates various sub-categories of 'propriety' thereunder."[94]

The "various sub-categories" which are contemplated by the "due process" clause of the Fifth Amendment are the provisions of the Constitution, the elements of the Common Law not altered by the

Constitution, and such processes as are neither forbidden by the Constitution nor prescribed by the Common Law—that is, novel processes—and which are not in their nature unreasonable or unfair.

Up to this point, and, on the surface, it is possible to agree with Professor Crosskey. But there are three particulars in which we cannot agree: (l) his understanding of "appropriate", (2) his application of the provisions of the Constitution; and (3) the manner and extent to which he calls upon Mr. Justice Curtis' opinion in the *Murray* case for support.

As to the term "appropriate": Crosskey seems to overlook the fact that some things may be appropriate to one polity or to one civil relationship and yet inappropriate to others. Some things may be inappropriate to any and all civil societies—i.e., tyrannical—but other processes may suit one situation and not another. What is due a man from his wife is not what is due him from his sister. What is fitting for a man to say to his neighbor it may not be suitable for him to say to a stranger. What it behooves the United States to do in its dealings with one of its citizens may be an unnecessary encumbrance upon a state in its dealings with the same man who is also one of its citizens.[95]

Concerning the application of the provisions of the Constitution, Crosskey says:

> The most obvious of the sub-categories of "appropriate" legal process which the Due Process Clause comprehends is that comprising all those elements of "process" that are specifically covered, and enjoined upon the Government, by the various particular process guarantees in the Fourth, Sixth, Seventh, and Eighth Amendments, and in the other clauses of the Fifth.[96]

Since, he argues, "due process of law" in the Fourteenth Amendment must, "under an elementary rule"[97] mean exactly what "due process of law" in the Fifth Amendment means and the latter includes as one of the "most obvious of [its] sub-categories" the process guarantees of the Fourth through the Eighth Amendments, then, of necessity, the "due process" clause which the Fourteenth Amendment imposes upon the states imposes the specific processes of the Fourth through the Eighth Amendments. Superficially this argument is irrefutable, but it presupposes the misuse of "appropriateness" noted just above. We agree that the clause in the later Amendment means *exactly* what the clause in the earlier Amendment means and we agree that the clause in the earlier Amendment means the specific processes of the Fourth through the Eighth Amendments. We do *not* agree that the clause in the later Amendment "means" the specific processes of the Fourth through the Eighth Amendments. For, both clauses require that life, liberty and property be not taken without the appropriate, the fitting, the suitable, the due process of law, and the standing Constitutional law at the time of the adoption of the Fourteenth Amendment clearly and unequivocally held that, for example, it was fitting that a man be brought to trial by the United States for a capital crime only in consequence of an indictment or presentment of a grand jury, but it did not hold that such an indictment or presentment was due him before trial for a capital crime by a state.

In other words, neither state nor nation may take life, liberty or property except lawfully; not everything one or the other might choose to enact is truly lawful for some things are so unreasonable as to be unthinkable and undue; there are certain implications and certain specific limitations imposed by the higher law of the Constitution upon what may be considered lawful in the case of either state or nation or both; but the first eight Amendments stand as specific limitations only upon what the nation may make lawful.[97]

As far as the *Murray* case is concerned, Crosskey states that Curtis established there as the standing law of the land two-thirds (which was all the case called for) of what he, Crosskey, contends for.[98] This is simply not true. Mr. Justice Curtis, of course, could not foresee the adoption of the Fourteenth Amendment twelve years after the *Murray* case, but he can only be said to rule what Crosskey contends for *if* one assumes Crosskey's attitude regarding "appropriateness" and the "provisions" of the Constitution. Reading the *Murray* case with these assumptions in mind, and in check, one finds not a single sentence in support of the proposition that the "due process" clause of the Fourteenth Amendment, by its "plain words" imposes upon the states all the prohibitions and commands which the first eight Amendments, or any of them as such, impose upon the United States.

Mr. Crosskey argues that the words of the Fourteenth Amendment are clear. Perhaps they are, but they clearly do not or, at least, do not clearly impart what he says they impart. He says they are so clear that historical inquiry into the intention of the framers such as that carried on by Fairman[99] is "illegitimate,"[100] and yet he employs the benefits of such inquiry alleging the opposite of Fairman's conclusions—and hence in support of Crosskey—by allowing them in through the side door of implication. He says the Fourteenth Amendment "was intended" to nullify the *Dred Scott* case[101] and that "no doubt is possible as to what the whole first section of the Fourteenth Amendment was painstakingly and skillfully drawn to mean,"[102] and that "one of the chief aims of the Fourteenth Amendment" was to undo *Dred Scott*.[103] And, he says, "for the full attainment of the ends the framers of the amendment had in view" the first sentence of the Amendment was insufficient,[104] and that "the framers of the Amendment, apparently accepting, as part of . . . the . . . standing 'law' . . . *Dred Scott*. . . went on to provide . . . the privileges or immunities" clause,[105] and that the "extinguishment" of certain "antecedent state power was the precise end to which . . . the Fourteenth Amendment was directed."[106] He further states that the "iniquitous doctrine" of *Barron* v. *Baltimore* was "apparently intended to be wiped out,"[107] and that "there can . . . be no . . . doubt as to what 'privileges' and 'immunities' were meant," and that "the framers . . . apparently desired to cure" other difficulties with the equal protection clause for such "a cure, they undoubtedly believed, was desirable even for the protection of white men."[108] The "Equal Protection Clause was meant, primarily" to do so and so.[109] There was an "over-all scheme of the whole first section,"[110] and it "falls into good order as a careful, skillful, and consistent example of the drafting art."[111] "There remains the question of the intended meaning of the Due Process Clause,"[112] and "it is perfectly understandable that the framers . . . might wish to set up precise Constitutional categories of 'propriety.'"[113]

Crosskey claims that inquiry into the intentions of the framers is in this instance illegitimate because, as he quotes Holmes opposite the title page of each volume:

> We ask, not what this man meant, but what those words would mean in the mouth of a normal speaker of English, using them in the circumstances in which they were used.

But perhaps what a word means to a normal speaker of English in given circumstances cannot really be discerned—especially nearly a century after that use in those circumstances—without recourse to such evidence as "the intention of the framers" might supply. Mr. Justice Holmes also said:

> A word is not a crystal, transparent and unchanged, it is the skin of a living thought and may vary greatly in color and content according to the circumstances and the time in which it is used.[114]

Surely the frequency with which Crosskey has such recourse in chapter xxxi suggests its utility even though Crosskey brands others' recourse to such as "illegitimate."

NOTES TO CHAPTER III

[1]*Op. cit.,* II, 1118.
[2]*Ibid.,* p. 1083.
[3]7 Pet. 243.
[4]Crosskey, *op. cit.,* II, 1091.
[5]*Ibid.,* p. 1084.
[6]*Ibid.,* p. 1115.
[7]Crosskey cites at this point Flack's book which was discussed at length in the preceding chapter.
[8]Crosskey here cites as follows: "These are conveniently collected in an appendix to the opinion of Black, J., in *Adamson* v. *California,* 332 U.S. 46, 92 (1947)." Chapter xxxi of Crosskey's book is thirty-six pages long and there are forty-five footnotes to the chapter. His apparent lack of concern for the "intentions" of the framers is indicated by the fact that these references to Flack and Black are the only ones that have anything to do therewith. See below, pp. 75-77.
[9]Crosskey, *op. cit.,* II, 1116-17, Crosskey's italics.
[10]*Ibid.,* chapter xv.
[11]Cf. A.E. Sutherland, Book Review, *Cornell Law Quarterly,* XXXIX (1953), 164.
[12]R.L. Stern, Book Review, *Northwestern University Law Review,* XLIX (1954), 107.
[13]Henry M. Hart, Jr., Book Review, *Harvard Law Review,* LXVII (June, 1954), 1486. Professor Crosskey's book is very large. It runs to two volumes, with 1,175 pages of text, 73 pages of appendices and 127 pages of notes. The sheer statistics of

the thing are as awe-inspiring as an advertisement for a Cecil B. DeMille spectacular. The book took thirteen years to write; there are 2,209 notes; the text, exclusive of notes and appendices, runs nearly two-thirds of a million words, or, a little longer than the Old Testament.

[14]See, e.g., James A. Durham, Book Review, *California Law Review,* XLI (1953), 209; Oliver P. Field, Book Review, *New York University Law Review,* XXVIII (1953), 1197.

[15]Arthur L. Corbin, Book Review, *Yale Law Journal,* LXII (1953), 1137.

[16]Hessel E. Yntema, Book Review, *American Journal of Comparative Law,* II (1953), 584.

[17]See C.P. Patterson, Book Review, *Texas Law Review,* XXXII (1953), 251.

[18]67 H.L.R. 1486 referring to the review by George D. Braden, *Yale Law Journal,* LXII (1953), 1145, *inter alia.*

[19]Dean F.D.G. Ribble, Book Review, *Virginia Law Review,* XXXIX (October, 1953), 870.

[20]Sylvester Petro, Book Review, *Michigan Law Review,* LIII (1954), 349. Petro's review is intended as a reply to that by J. Goebel, Jr., Book Review, *Columbia Law Review,* LIV (1954), 450.

[21]*Ibid.,* p. 483.

[22]*Ibid.,* p. 451.

[23]R.K. Gooch, Book Review, *American Bar Association Journal,* XL (1954), 313.

[24]Nathaniel L. Nathanson, Book Review, *Northwestern University Law Review,* XLIX (1954), 1118.

[25]7 Pet. 243.

[26]Crosskey, *op. cit.,* II, 1076.

[27]*Ibid.,* p. 1091.

[28]*Ibid.,* p. 1056.

[29]Book Review, *Northwestern University Law Review,* XLIX (1954), 135. An example of some of the difficulties with Crosskey's evidence is that one of the "good lawyers" who believed that the first eight—or at least several of them—Amendments were restrictions upon State activity was Joseph K. Angell (Crosskey mentions Angell on p. 1076; the citation for that mention appears as n. 51 on p. 1376). Angell had begun a periodical on the law in 1829 called *U.S. Law Intelligencer and Review,* which he edited. He inserted what in today's newspaper parlance would be called a "feature" which he called "Restrictions upon State Power in Relation to Private Property" and which was roughly equivalent to the "comments" in a present day law review, in serial form. This item ran two or three pages per issue for the first four issues. (The Library of Congress has Vols. I, II, and III of Angell's Journal and we believe that that is as far as the journal progressed. Crosskey's citation is to I, 64, which is the third of the four items under this head.) Angell does indeed show at the place Crosskey cites that he believed the Amendments to apply to the States. However, while we will not question that Angell was, in general, a "good lawyer," he was, in particular, a poor citer, for in support of his opinion about the applicability of the Amendments to the States, he cites the 1796 case of *Lindsay* v. *The Commissioners,* 2 Bay 38 (now also found at 1 S.C. [II Bay] 16). This was an eminent domain case involving the question of just compensation. Three of the four judges came out in favor of the eminent domain power of the Commissioners appointed by the city council of Charleston but one of them along with the fourth judge called for compensation. Since the court was equally divided on the

compensation question, Lindsay's application failed. Lindsay had cited *Magna Charta* and Art. IX, sec. 2 of the Constitution of South Carolina. Judge Waites, who wrote the opinion calling for compensation cited Blackstone, the prophet (Mohammed), and several civilians, but *not one word* from either bench or bar was said about the United States Constitution or its Amendments although the action of the Commissioners would have been *clearly* contrary to the "just compensation" clause of the Fifth Amendment if the Fifth Amendment *had* been thought to apply to South Carolina.

For further discussion of Crosskey's evidence re *Barron* v. *Baltimore's* wrongness, see the Frank book review cited at the beginning of this note and the Fairman critique, "The Supreme Court and the Constitutional Limitations on State Governmental Authority," *University of Chicago Law Review,* XXI (1953), 43-44.

[30]Book Review, *Harvard Law Review,* LXVII (1954), 1455.

[31]Irving Brant, Book Review, *Columbia Law Review,* LIV (1954), 446.

[32]*University of Chicago Law Review,* Vol. XXI, No. 1 (Autumn, 1953), entire issue.

[33]*Ibid.,* p. 27. Referring to C. Swisher, "Evolution of a Document," *Saturday Review,* April 4, 1953, pp. 33, 34.

[34]*Ibid.,* p. 28.

[35]Brown, *op. cit.,* p. 1456.

[36]R.C. Pittman, Book Review, *American Bar Association Journal,* XL (1954), 390.

[37]Sutherland, *op. cit.,* p. 169.

[38]*Op. cit.,* pp. 1 and 79, respectively.

[39]*Op. cit.,* II, 1171, "And the latest contribution from the legal learned world is an elaborate attempt to justify the Supreme Court's continued flouting of the plain and simple provisions of the Fourteenth Amendment."

[40]*Ibid.,* p. 1381, "Entirely apart from the questions of the adequacy, and of the handling, of the evidence which Mr. Fairman presents, it is to be remembered that a recurrence to evidence of the sort he presents, is illegitimate in the case of a provision, like the first section of the Fourteenth Amendment, which is clear in itself, or clear when read in the light of the prior law. It is doubly illegitimate when it is remembered that most of what the first section requires, was also required by Amendments II-VIII. . . . Mr. Fairman forgets that the ultimate question is not what the legislatures meant, any more than it is what Congress or the more immediate framers of the amendment meant: it is what the amendment means. Cf., Holmes, *The Theory of Legal Interpretation,* 12 H.L.R. 417 (1899)."

[41]*Op. cit.,* pp. 40-78.

[42]"Charles Fairman, 'Legislative History,' and the Constitutional Limitations on State Authority," *University of Chicago Law Review,* XXII (Autumn, 1954), 1.

[43]*Idem,* p. 144.

[44]It is urged that the whole exchange ought to be taken as a single inquiry and taken chronologically. See (1) the appendix to the dissenting opinion by Mr. Justice Black in *Adamson* v. *California,* 332 U.S. at 92-123; (2) Fairman, "Does the Fourteenth Amendment Incorporate the Bill of Rights?—The Original Understanding," *op. cit.,* pp. 5-139; (3) Crosskey, *op. cit.,* II, 1049-58; (4) Fairman, "The Supreme Court and the Constitutional Limitations on State Governmental Authority," *op. cit.,* pp. 40-78; (5) Crosskey, "Charles Fairman, 'Legislative History,' and the Constitutional Limitations on State Authority," *op. cit.,* pp.

1-143; and (6) Fairman, "A Reply to Professor Crosskey," *op. cit.*, pp. 144-56. The book by Flack (1908) can, we think, safely be ignored.

[45]P. 50.

[46]*Op. cit.*, II, 1049-82.

[47]*Op. cit.*, p. 40, and see Frank, *op. cit.*, pp. 132, 135.

[48]*Op. cit.*, II, 1083-1118.

[49]*Ibid.*, p. 1083.

[50]19 How. 393.

[51]*Murray's Lessee* v. *Hoboken Land and Improvement Co.*, 18 How. 272 (1855).

[52]Crosskey, *op. cit.*, II, 1102.

[53]Again, a footnote is in order to emphasize that we are here paraphrasing and summarizing—not quoting—Crosskey.

[54]Art. I, sec. 8, cl. 4.

[55]For evidence to the contrary, see the dissent by Mr. Justice Curtis, especially at 19 How. 393 at 572-76.

[56]See Crosskey, *op. cit.*, II, chapter xxxi, sec. 1, 1083-89, especially p. 1087, and pp. 1089-90, and *Dred Scott* v. *Sandford*, 19 How. 393, 405.

[57]Crosskey, *op. cit.*, II, 1118.

[58]*Ibid.*, p. 1381, n. 11.

[59]*Ibid.*, pp. 1089-91.

[60]19 How. 393, *passim*, as noted in the text. The periods preceding each page citation, every semicolon except those occurring within the long quotations from p. 423 and pp. 450-51, and every colon in the preceding series of quotations are inserted for the purpose of separating the individual quotations. All other punctuation is Taney's. The quotation marks around the item from p. 410 indicate that item as being quoted from the Declaration of Independence; those for the item from p. 418 indicate the Articles of Confederation.

[61]Pp. 62-63.

[62]Crosskey, *op. cit.*, I, 499.

[63]See especially Mr. Justice Matthews for the Court in *Murphy* v. *Ramsey*, 114 U.S. 15 at 44-45 (1885) and Mr. Chief Justice Waite for the Court in *National Bank* v. *County of Yankton*, 101 U.S. 129 at 133 (1879). Crosskey admits, as everyone does, that the *Dred Scott* case was "thoroughly discredited" at the time of the adoption of the Fourteenth Amendment (p. 1115). But he does not draw the conclusions we draw.

[64]See Crosskey, *op. cit.*, II, 1117-18.

[65]A.M. Burrill, *A Law Dictionary and Glossary* (New York: John S. Voorhies, 1859).

[66]G. Jacob, *A New Law Dictionary* (London: 1772 and 1797).

[67]*U.S.* v. *Rhodes*, 27 Fed. Cas. 785 at 786 and 788 (1866) See *supra*, pp. 45-46.

[68]J. Bouvier, *A Law Dictionary*, 2 vols. (Philadelphia: 1914).

[69]See Burrill and Bouvier for the years indicated and Jacob for 1772 and 1797.

[70](7th ed.; New York: Lewis and Blood, 1861). Crosskey's use of the term "privilege" as an equivalent for "qualifications" when he speaks of the "privilege" of serving as President (p. 1085) constitutes a purely private language. Cf. *supra*, p. 21.

[71]See Crosskey, *op. cit.*, I, 564-68, and see also thereon Goebel, *op. cit.*, p. 458, and Lord Mansfield in *Millar* v. *Taylor*, 98 Eng. Reports (K.B.) 201, 253 (1769) (cited in Goebel). Lord Mansfield's dismissal of the idea of a judicial decision being

based on theories of "gathering acorns and seizing a vacant piece of ground" very likely has reference to Locke's *Second Treatise,* chapter v.

[72]The entry, as quoted, in Bouvier, *op. cit.,* II, 2961, in the current edition is the same as that appearing from 1839 on.

[73]For suggestive passages on this phrase see: Corwin, *op. cit.,* pp. 967-71, and cases cited therein; and see the entries for that phrase in the current *Words and Phrases.*

[74]*Op. cit.,* II, 1096-1102.

[75]*Ibid.,* pp. 1102-16.

[76]*Ibid.,* pp. 1110-14.

[77]13 N.Y. 378 (1856).

[78]Crosskey, *op. cit.,* II, 1115.

[79]*Ibid.,* p. 1116.

[80]*Ibid.,* p. 1099.

[81]*Communist Manifesto,* Part I, about the middle.

[82]Crosskey, *op. cit.,* II, 1116.

[83]See J. Cropsey, "The Relation Between Political Science and Economics," *American Political Science Review,* LIV (1960), 3, 6.

[84]Once again, that we be not misunderstood, this is not a quotation from Crosskey, nor from anyone else.

[85]18 How. 272 (1856).

[86]Crosskey, *op. cit.,* II, 1109.

[87]*Ibid.,* p. 1104.

[88]*Ibid.,* p. 1107.

[89]See, e.g., 16A C.J.S. 5682 and cases cited there; and 2 Co. Inst. 50-51 cited in Crosskey, *op. cit.,* II, 1337, and in A. Hamilton, *Works,* ed. H.C. Lodge (New York: Federal Edition, Putnam, 1904), pp. 231-32; and Sir William Blackstone, *Commentaries on the Laws of England,* ed. J. Chitty, 4 vols. (London, 1826), I, 133-34.

[90]Our sentence construction was intended to avoid the suggestion that Coke, Blackstone or Hamilton were legal positivists or moral relativists, a point not here at issue.

[91]Crosskey, *op. cit.,* II, 1105.

[92]2 Co. Inst. 50-51 and Hamilton, *op. cit.,* pp. 231-32.

[93]Crosskey, *op. cit.*

[94]*Ibid.,* Crosskey's emphasis.

[95]Attention is called to the relation between justice and what is "suitable" or "fitting." The connection between specific justice and the terms "vestments," "vested" and "investments" and between "property" and "propriety" should not be overlooked, either. For a case of what may be called "undue process of law"—inappropriate, that is, in ANY society and certainly in that in which it took place—see *The Trial of Sir Thomas More for High Treason,* in *State Trials,* I, No. 30 (London: 1535), 385, and especially 393-94. It is to the credit of Henry, who, as a student of justice knew that giving benefits to friends was a rough approximation thereto, commuted More's sentence to beheading.

[96]Crosskey, *op. cit.,* II, 1106.

[97]D.O. McGovney, then of the University of Iowa Law School, argues something of the same thing with regard to the "privileges and immunities" clause of the Fourteenth Amendment. See "Privileges or Immunities Clause, Fourteenth

Amendment," *Iowa Law Bulletin,* IV (November, 1918), 219 at 231-32; reprinted in *Selected Essays on Constitutional Law* (Chicago: Foundation Press, 1938), pp. 402 at 413-14. Crosskey dismisses McGovney's argument as "really fantastic." Crosskey, *op. cit.,* II, 1091-93, especially at p. 1093.

[98]*Ibid.,* pp. 1108-10 and see 18 How. 272 at 276-77, 280.

[99]"Does the Fourteenth Amendment Incorporate the Bill of Rights?—The Original Understanding," *op. cit.,* p. 5.

[100]Crosskey, *op. cit.,* II, 1381.

[101]*Ibid.,* p. 1083.

[102]*Ibid.,* p. 1084.

[103]*Ibid.,* p. 1089.

[104]*Ibid.,* p. 1090.

[105]*Ibid.*

[106]*Ibid.*

[107]*Ibid.,* p. 1091.

[108]*Ibid.,* p. 1097.

[109]*Ibid.,* p. 1098.

[110]*Ibid.,* p. 1099.

[111]*Ibid.,* p. 1102.

[112]*Ibid.*

[113]*Ibid.,* p. 1105. Almost any page of chapter xxxi shows similar reference to the "intentions of the framers."

[114]*Towne* v. *Eisner,* 245 U.S. 418, 425.

CHAPTER IV

NATURAL LAW

The words of the Fourteenth Amendment do not, as Professor Crosskey argues, plainly impose the same limits upon the states as those imposed upon the United States by the first eight Amendments. nor does the legislative history of the Fourteenth Amendment plainly show, as Mr. Justice Black argues, an intention to impose such limits. But, plainly, the Amendment does impose limits upon the states. The problem that has troubled the Court—and still troubles it, for even *Mapp* v. *Ohio*[1] does not reverse the essential holding of the *Adamson* case—is: What are those limits?

Happily, it will not be necessary to recapitulate the Court's treatment of the Amendment, nor even of any clause in it, to further the present argument. It will be enough to summarize very briefly what the Court has said thematically about the due process clause. Of course it is essential to refer to the pre-history of the Amendment to find the Court's stand on the due process clause of the Fifth Amendment, for everyone concerned readily admits that the words "due process of law" in the Fourteenth Amendment mean precisely what is meant by those identical words in the Fifth. To say the contrary would be to deny that there is any such thing as law at all for it would be to say that there is no assurance which can be given in words which cannot be circumvented by interpretation, and if law were stripped of every other attribute, it could not be stripped of assurance and still remain law. That is, the very idea of law includes the principle of stable expectations.

Mr. Justice Curtis, about whom so little has been written but whose devotion to justice may perhaps be gathered from the fact that he retired from the Court and from public life after the worst excesses of the slave power prospered over his dissent in the *Dred Scott* case,[2] only to return to public life successfully to defend President Johnson against the excesses of the Radical Republican Congress, wrote the opinion for a unanimous Court in *Murray's Lessee* v. *Hoboken Land and Improvement Co.*[3] in which he offered the exposition of the words "due process of law" upon which all later discussion is based. Although that exposition is quoted in every text it must be quoted again here:

> That the [distress] warrant [taking property to recompense the government for a default in the accounts of a customs collector] now in question is legal process is not denied. It was issued in conformity with an act of Congress. But is it "due process of law"? The constitution contains no description of those processes which it was intended to allow or forbid. It does not even declare what principles are to be applied to ascertain whether it be due process. It is manifest that it was not left to the legislative power to enact any process which might be devised. The article is a restraint on the legislative as well as on the executive and judicial powers of the government, and cannot be so construed as to leave congress free to make any process "due process of law," by its mere will. To what principles, then, are we to resort to ascertain whether this process, enacted by congress is due process? To this the answer must be twofold. We must examine the constitution itself, to see whether this process be in conflict with any of its provisions. If not found to be so, we must look to those settled usages and modes of proceeding existing in the common and statute law of England, before the emigration of our ancestors, and which are shown not to have been unsuited to their civil and political condition by having been acted on by them after the settlement of this country.[4]

Twenty-eight years later, and sixteen years after the Fourteenth Amendment forbade states to "deprive any person of life, liberty or property without due process of law," Mr. Justice Matthews for the Court—over the lone dissent of the first Mr. Justice Harlan—affirmed a conviction for murder got in a trial initiated by a prosecutor's information in California, despite the fact that, had the accused been tried in a United States court, the Fifth Amendment would have forbidden trial except pursuant to an indictment or presentment of a grand jury.[5]

Matthews explained that "due process" meant in the Fourteenth just what it meant in the Fifth Amendment and therefore could not be understood as "intended to include, *ex vi termini*, the institution and procedure of a grand jury in any case" for it would be absurd to suppose that the framers of the Fifth Amendment would demand *both* a grand jury *and* due process if the latter included, *ex vi termini,* the former and so the term "due process of law" must mean something other than the specific terms of the Fifth Amendment, or, by extension, of any other amendment as such.[6] Quoting a portion of the passage from the *Murray* case which we quoted above,[7] Matthews also explained that if a process has the sanction of settled usage in both England and America and is not otherwise forbidden[8] it is certainly "due process" but "it by no means follows that nothing else can be due process of law."[9]

It has been argued that, according to "Justice Curtis's first test in the *Murray* case, due process had clearly been violated [in the *Hurtado* case], for the fifth Amendment makes indictment by grand jury mandatory for all capital or otherwise infamous crimes." But, Matthews, "having recognized Curtis's first test by the clause, 'which is not otherwise forbidden,' . . . proceeded to ignore it and to work from the last thought in the sentence, which is substantially Curtis's second test—the test of historical practice."[10] But we do not believe Matthews' treatment to be out of harmony with that of Curtis. A few sentences before, Curtis had said that we "must examine the constitution itself, to see whether this process be in conflict with any of its provisions," he had said that the "constitution contains no description of those processes which it was intended to allow or forbid. It does not even declare what principles are to be applied to ascertain whether it be due process." There is an apparent contradiction between these two sentences, but perhaps they can be explained so as to restore harmony between them and between the passage as a whole and Matthew's explanation of it.

Perhaps Matthews understood Curtis in the following way: If one wants to know what is "due process" he looks first to the Constitution. The Constitution contains no list of processes which the due process clause allows or forbids, but that Constitution does forbid the government to do certain things and, surely, if the government behaves toward an accused in defiance of an explicit prohibition of the Constitution, the accused cannot be said to have been treated with due process of law. But the Constitutional limitations by no means exhaust the possibilities. If some process is nowhere mentioned in the Constitution and has always been a part of the Anglo-American tradition then the accused got what he had a right to expect—that is, he got due process of law. But it would not be due process for the government to go against an accused in defiance of a specific statutory or constitutional provision simply because the process employed, while now prohibited, was once a part of the Anglo-American tradition. But if a process is not explicitly forbidden by statute or constitution and is wholly unheard of by the Anglo-American tradition or is sometimes and somewhere accepted by the tradition and sometimes and somewhere not, then it is due process of law as long as it is established in an orderly (i.e., lawful) way and is not in and of itself impermissible. Finally, while an accused would have his liberty taken without due process of law if he were imprisoned by the United States for a capital crime after a trial which did not follow an indictment or presentment of a grand jury, his liberty would not necessarily have been taken without due process of law had he been imprisoned by a State after such a trial. For, in the former instance, it is not that the phrase "due process of law" subsumes the phrase "presentment or indictment of a grand jury." It is simply that the due process clause includes the promise of treatment according to the regular course of the law and, by the regular course of the law an accused has the right to expect a presentment or indictment of a grand jury if he is tried for a capital crime *by the United States*, for the Fifth Amendment forbids the United States to try any person otherwise.

To put it all another way, the due process clause promises that one will not have his life, liberty, or property taken by an irregular proceeding. If anything is taken from him it will be by a process which he has a right to expect. That expectation may rest upon various bases; the nature of that right may be complex. For example, if an administrative officer promises on his own motion always to behave in a particular way, it would be contrary to due process for him to take something from someone in a manner which belies his promise.[11] Nor may an administrator break a statutory promise,[12] nor a statute break a constitutional promise.[13] We suggest that it would contravene the principle of due process for the Constitution to permit that which was, in itself, impermissible. That is, to make the argument by the shortest route, such a permissiveness would stand in contradiction to the promise of due process and that contradiction would frustrate the principle of expectation itself. No one would know what to expect and, as we have suggested, if law had no other principle it would have to have the principle of expectation.

The longer way through the argument is to phrase this last proposition as follows: There are some things which one has a right to expect from civil society itself. Indeed, one could say that the very ranking of societies—some better and some worse—consists precisely in measuring the fulfillment and disappointment of these expectations. Such a proposition raises the question of natural law. To that question we must now turn.

In his dissenting opinion in the *Adamson* case, Mr. Justice Black says that the Court's

> decision reasserts a constitutional theory spelled out in *Twining* v. *New Jersey*, 211 U.S. 78, that this Court is endowed by the Constitution with boundless power under "natural law" periodically to expand and contract constitutional standards to conform to the Court's conception of what at a particular time constitutes "civilized decency" and "fundamental liberty and justice."[14]

While the latter two of the three phrases enclosed in quotation marks in this passage do appear from time to time in the Reports, it should be noted here that the phrase "natural law" nowhere appears in either of the two opinions—Moody for the Court; Harlan dissenting for himself—in the *Twining* case as is implied by Black. It is true that various passages in Moody's opinion in *Twining* do suggest some such underlying doctrine but Moody's opinion as a whole rests explicitly not on "natural law" but on English history. It is possible that neither Moody nor Black adequately distinguishes between the two. But perhaps somehow the problem does come down to the problem of natural law.

No doubt responding to Black's imputation, Frankfurter writes in his concurring opinion, "In the history of thought 'natural law' has a much longer and better founded meaning and justification than such subjective selection of the first eight Amendments for incorporation into the Fourteenth."[15] The issue, then, comes to this: the Court has consistently denied that the Fourteenth Amendment had meant to impose upon the states the full catalog of prohibitions which the first eight Amendments laid against the United States.[16] But, of course the Amendment does impose limits, and the Court was pressed to say what they were. In the *Hurtado* and *Twining* cases Matthews and Moody identified the phrase "due process of law" with the phrase "law of the land" in Magna Charta. But, to paraphrase the original treatment of due process by Curtis in the *Murray's Lessee* case, it is not to be supposed that the land could make *anything* law "by its mere will." While the Court "has always declined to give a comprehensive definition" of the due process clause, preferring "that its full meaning should be gradually ascertained by the process of inclusion and exclusion in the course of the decisions of cases as they arise,"[17] it has agreed that any taking which is not in consequence of a hearing before a court which has jurisdiction and acts in keeping with general laws is a taking without due process.[18] Continued pressure has brought from the Court only the negative explanation that due process is lacking where are lacking things without which "a fair and enlightened system of justice would be impossible."[19] A whole host of familiar and favored procedures "might be lost and justice still be done,"[20] for due process is simply that without which one could not conceive of "a scheme of ordered liberty."[21]

These are all very fine phrases but Mr. Justice Black's view is that what is "implicit in the concept of ordered liberty" depends on who is doing the conceiving. He uses the phrase "natural law" in a deprecatory—not to say accusatory—sense on ten separate occasions in a twenty-four page opinion.[22] The clear implication is that nothing is just by nature or, at least, if any such natural justice there be, long study by judges will not find it. The whole cast of Black's deprecation of natural law is that of legal positivism which we believe ill-represents his essential position. For, if Black were a thoroughgoing legal positivist, there would be no place for the moral indignation he displays throughout his opinion. It might make sense, on the surface at least, to say as Black says in one place:

> . . . to pass upon the constitutionality of statutes by looking to
> the particular standards enumerated in the Bill of Rights and

> other parts of the Constitution is one thing; to invalidate statutes
> because of application of "natural law" deemed to be above and
> undefined by the Constitution is another.[23]

That is, accepting *arguendo* Black's recounting and interpretation
of the legislative history of the Fourteenth Amendment, one could
make a stand for judicial restraint.[24] Such a stand might, perhaps, be
based on the rejection of the possibility of natural law at all, or upon
the impossibility of men grasping it, or upon the contention that
judges are simply not authorized in America to employ standards
other than those established by the positive law of the Constitution.
The first of these possible bases would be legal positivism proper, the
second might be said to add up to it in the long run, but the third is at
least a few steps removed. One might sensibly argue, for example,
that the natural law is more nearly approximated by legislative choice
or by historical accretion than by the decision of judges. While such
an argument might break down in due course, it is, initially at least,
not absurd.

But Mr. Justice Black does not so argue. The whole temper of his
opinion is that of a complete, not to say sarcastic, dismissal of natural
law. And, in the context of that dismissal, it seems strange for him to
say:

> I think [the *Twining*] decision and the "natural law" theory of
> the Constitution upon which it relies degrade the constitutional
> safeguards of the Bill of Rights and simultaneously appropriate
> for this Court a broad power which we are not authorized by the
> Constitution to exercise.[25]

Change for the worse is reason for one's deploring degradation,
but if there is no natural or intrinsic standard of what is better and
what worse, what right and what wrong, what lawful and what
arbitrary, then mere change could not call forth the moral
indignation which pervades Black's opinion. If there is nothing which
is naturally worthy of being guarded, then one could not speak in a
laudatory manner of "constitutional safeguards," nor complain of
their "degradation." He could only speak of constitutional
"clauses" or "provisions," and remark on their change or passing.
And, why be upset by the Court's appropriating for itself broad

power not authorized by the Constitution? If nothing is naturally lawful then it is not unlawful for the Court to run counter to the Constitution. That is, if nothing is by its nature right and just, then being constitutional is no more right and just than being, say, "creative." Unless a judge were simply lazy, which no one would accuse Mr. Justice Black of being, he would have no call to criticize his brethren for appropriating power as long as they got away with it. That is, a mere transfer of power from the dead words of the Constitution to the lively fiat of the judiciary ought not to disturb anyone unless it disturbs the public and one should only be disturbed *then* if he believes, as Hobbes did, that civil peace is *naturally* preferable to civil war. If *nothing* is naturally preferable, then what others call "civil war" the sophisticated would simply regard as an interesting social science datum—a laboratory experiment in democratic action—if, indeed, one thing is by its nature more interesting than another.

It must be supposed, at least provisionally, that the inconsistency between the apparent legal positivism and the manifest moral indignation in Black's opinion is resolvable by some underlying principle of unity but that resolution is outside the scope of the present study. We turn now to Frankfurter's defense of his allegedly "natural law" position.

The charge by Black that the power "appropriated"[26] by the Court is "boundless"[27] is the charge that there are no natural boundaries to judgment, that one must stay within the specific bounds of the detailed provisions of the Constitution or one is left wholly at large to impose upon the litigant by judicial fiat entirely private predilections; there is no other choice. But Frankfurter contends that the positive law of the Constitution and personal whim are not the only available choices. There are, throughout his opinion in the *Adamson* case, intimations of a third possibility. He speaks of the Fourteenth Amendment as being "concerned . . . with matters fundamental to the pursuit of justice"[28] and he does not put the word justice in quotation marks. He believes that there is such a thing as "ultimate decency in a civilized society"[29] which implies a distinction between civilized and uncivilized societies—between civilization and barbarism. That is, some societies are more decent than others, for what is decent and what indecent is not established by the fiat of a society. If the Bill of Rights contains "safeguards" it is not that the Founding

Fathers, by force of will, rendered the things guarded worthy of guarding.

Frankfurter speaks of "just-minded" and "right-minded" men.[30] In 1942, dissenting from the Court's strict enforcement of the contractual obligations of the Government on the grounds, pressed by the Government, that the contractor had taken advantage of the desperate public need for ships to equip the Navy in World War I, Frankfurter asserted, "The law is not so primitive that it sanctions every injustice except brute force and downright fraud."[31] There is such a thing, then, as fraud which is fraud because it is downright and not because it is defined by statute as fraud. There is such a thing as justice, simply, for its contrary is not such because the law made it so. The very measurement of law's departure from the primitive state is its refusal to sanction what it *recognizes*—not makes—as certain kinds of injustice. In 1952 he stated that "[c]riminal justice is concerned with the pathology of the body politic."[32] That political bodies require the science of pathology means they are sometimes diseased. To speak of a disease means to admit a state of ease, or health—properly speaking. There is, then, by nature, a healthy state for the body politic. A society might make itself healthy, but it cannot *make* health. Health is. Whatever one may say about the particular tasks the Supreme Court is designed to perform in the light of the existence of state and lower United States courts, or whatever one may say about the limitations upon all courts implied by the existence of other public agencies, "courts of law are, after all, in the service of justice."[33]

Black's contention that if there were no catalog of standards in the positive law to which judges might turn, then judges would be left at large to press their whims amounts to a negation of judgment as such. If that contention were true, then "judicial" tasks could be performed by clerks, or, perhaps even by machines. But Frankfurter rejects "mechanical jurisprudence."[34] We cannot have "IBM machines doing the work instead of judges,"[35] for "judges are not automata."[36] Ultimately, "judgment cannot be escaped—the judgment of this Court."[37] Even if one were to consider only statutory construction, Frankfurter has said:

> The judicial function is confined to applying what Congress
> has enacted after ascertaining what it is that Congress has

enacted. But such ascertainment, that is, construing legislation, is nothing like a mechanical endeavor. It could not be accomplished by the subtlest of modern "brain" machines. Because of the infirmities of language and the limited scope of science in legislative drafting, inevitably there enters into the construction of statutes the play of judicial judgment within the limits of relevant legislative materials.[38]

If it be argued that this very passage refutes the foregoing argument for it shows that the necessity for judgment rests not on the fact that there is such a thing as justice but rather on the fact that language is infirm, we must answer that so to argue begs the question. One need only move from the problem of statutory construction to that of constitutional construction and reflect on what "infirmities of language" means to see this. The latter must mean in the case of statutory construction that the language of the law cannot be fed into a data-processing machine. In the case of constitutional construction, "the limits of relevant . . . materials" are as broad as "union," "justice," "tranquility," "defense," "welfare" and "liberty." Indeed, one would have to forget the *Dred Scott* case[39] not to know that even the word "ourselves" in the Preamble allows enough "play" to satisfy the most industrious judge. To put it another way, what is the cause of the concern over the due process clause if not some difficulty—let us here call it "infirmity"—in the words "law" and "process" and, especially, in the word "due"?

Frankfurter may not be the "most industrious judge" but the volume of his output—a volume sufficient to irritate some[40]—shows that he no more than Black can be accused of laziness. That volume has been explained away by Mr. Justice Douglas as a result of Frankfurter's having two law clerks instead of the standard allotment of one.[41] And, if it is true that Frankfurter "willingly . . . assumes the intellectual heritage devised by other men"[42] it may be that that "heritage" includes a "style" and so, according to his own measure, his clerks have been able to imitate that style quite easily.[43] But even if the implication of Douglas' explanation—the implication that the law clerks, not Frankfurter, write the Frankfurter opinions—were true, they are so many and so lengthy that even to read and sign for them would require considerable industry.[44] And the fact that he has on occasion simply refused to share responsibility for a decision because he had doubts and was preoccupied with other matters[45] together with the fact that his hesitancy to finish—or to regard as finished—his opinions holds many decisions up until the last Monday of the term[46] indicates more than nominal responsibility for those opinions. Perhaps his consciousness of the problem of the relationship between judge and law clerk would stand by itself to cover this matter. In a 1947 lecture to the New York City bar he spoke of Mr. Justice Brandeis' "law clerk, whom he always treated as a co-worker."[47] Although his good opinion of Brandeis is not doubted by anyone, this statement while not explicitly an accusation is from its context obviously not praise. We are inclined to rest content with the public impression that the vigor which Frankfurter displays in the Courtroom is carried over into conference room, chambers, and study, and simply to assume that he is in fact responsible for his own opinions.

That vigor, that vivacity which always entertains the tourists, sometimes exasperates the Chief Justice, and must often terrify counsel, calls our attention specially to his great concern for limiting the Court's work load as strictly as it can be limited. In the June, 1928, issue of the *Cornell Law Quarterly* Frankfurter argued at length for the end of diversity jurisdiction.[48] If that jurisdiction was ever really necessary it no longer is, according to Frankfurter, because of what he called, in 1954, "the increasing permeation of national feeling and the mobility of modern life."[49] In company with the stand on diversity jurisdiction is his strict application of the principles of the Judiciary Act of 1925 which provides the Court with ample power to refuse to hear cases, thereby—in principle—reducing its work load.[50] His desire to see the Court's workload lessened through Congressional restriction of diversity jurisdiction and through the Court's use of its discretionary power over review is said to be aimed at improved treatment of those cases for which there could be no other answer than Supreme Court decision. Such reduction in quantity would lead to an increase in quality, to "wise decisions and luminous opinions."[51]

> The judgments of this Court are collective judgments. Such judgments are especially dependent on ample time for private study and reflection in preparation for discussion in Conference.

> Without adequate study, there cannot be adequate reflection; without adequate reflection, there cannot be adequate discussion; without adequate discussion, there cannot be that full and fruitful interchange of minds that is indispensable to wise decisions and persuasive opinions by the Court. . . .[52]

By requiring that opinions be "luminous" or "persuasive," Frankfurter reminds us of the importance of the precise choice of words in those opinions and so calls special attention to *his* particular choice of words. Study of and reflection upon them reminds us that the word "judgment" from the pen of a Justice—like the word "organize"[53] from the Congressional pen or the words "due process" from the pen of the Founders—suffers certain "infirmities." In the first place, the word "judgment" may mean either an activity or an event. That is, judgment may be what the judge engages in, or it may be what he issues. Explanations of the word in the one sense will therefore not be sufficient if the word is being used in the other sense. Further and different sub-divisions of meaning—further ambiguities or infirmities—suggest themselves when we see that the word requires modification by an adjective when it comes from Frankfurter's pen. He repeatedly speaks of "judicial judgment."[54]

In the current (i.e., 1914) edition of Bouvier's *Law Dictionary* there is a twelve-and-one-half page entry (in excess of 12,000 words) for the word "judgment." That entry is entirely confined to the sense of the word which has to do with an *event* and only as an event produced by a *judge*. That is, it does not concern itself even by explicit abstention with other than judicial judgment (say, parental judgment or fiscal judgment) nor—again, not even by explicit abstention—with that judicial judgment as anything other than an event (say, with that activity which caused Frankfurter on one occasion to speak of the "pains of judicial judgment,"[55] and on another to speak of the "agony" of the judge's duty).[56] Very early in Bouvier's definition we are reminded that the

> language of judgments . . . is not that "it is decreed," or "resolved," by the court; but "it is considered" (*consideratum est per curiam*) that the plaintiff recover . . . or that the defendant do go without day. This implies that the judgment is not so much the decision of the court, as the sentence of the law pronounced and decreed by the court, after due deliberation and inquiry.[57]

The entry in Bouvier for *consideratum est per curiam*[58] cites Sir Frederick Pollock on Contracts[59] but, as often happens with law dictionaries, reference to the place cited is unproductive. *Words and Phrases*, under that heading, quotes two cases.[60] One of these is the 1841 Arkansas case of *Baker* v. *State*[61] which, in turn, cites three sources for its opinion,[62] but reference to those three sources is *wholly* unproductive.[63] The other case from which *Words and Phrases* takes a quotation is a 1936 case in the United States Circuit Court of Appeals for the Fifth Circuit, *Wilson* v. *Aderhold*.[64] *Words and Phrases* quotes *Wilson* v. *Aderhold* as follows:

> Form of judgments, *"consideratum est per curiam,"* implied that judgment was not so much decision of the court as the sentence of law pronounced after due deliberation and inquiry.

But Circuit Judge Holmes had said in the *Wilson* case:

> The old form of judgments, *"consideratum est per curiam,"* implied that the judgment was not so much the decision of the court as the sentence of the law pronounced after due deliberation and inquiry.

That is, what is merely suggested by the past tense in the passage as it appears in *Words and Phrases* is made explicit in the *Wilson* case by the fact that the passage begins with the words, "The old form of judgments. . . ." For, while Blackstone, who offers the same explanation of the phrase,[65] cites no ancient authorities, it is evident that not only the *form* but the explanation is old. It is a worthy old explanation but it cannot be divorced from its old context.

To say that judges merely pronounce what the law decrees, that they are impersonal vehicles of lawfulness itself, is no more than to say that they are, or mean to be, impartial. If this is all that Mr. Justice Frankfurter means by modifying the word "judgment" with the adjective "judicial," there can be no quarrel with him. But it must be remembered that the old context within which the phrase *"consideratum est per curiam"* appeared was the view that the law somehow *is*, and the judge's duty is to *find* it. That is, the *law* which expressed itself through the impersonal vehicle of the judge was not simply a congeries of *leges*; it was the *ius*. There has been in modern jurisprudence a steady tendency to dismiss that view as naive, or unrealistic. That tendency is best illustrated by Mr. Justice Holmes:

> The common law is not a brooding omnipresence in the sky but the articulate voice of some sovereign or quasi-sovereign that can be identified; although some decisions with which I have disagreed seem to me to have forgotten the fact.[66]

The rejection of that "brooding omnipresence" in Holmes' dissent in the *Jensen* case became the stand of the majority in the *Tompkins* case.[67] (In passing, it must be noted that Brandeis' opinion in *Tompkins* rejected "transcendental" law not only because of the unconstitutionality of the attempt to enforce such, but because of the "injustice.")[68] Frankfurter quotes Holmes with approval in the *Lincoln Mills* case:

> There are severe limits on "judicial inventiveness" even for the most imaginative judges. The law is not a "brooding omnipresence in the sky," . . . and it cannot be drawn from there like nitrogen from the air.[69]

But to substitute for the ancient meaning of the word "law" the view that law is a congeries of *leges* and no more, for *leges* are the things *legislated,* and yet *retain* the judicial self-abnegation of the "old form of judgments" is simply to take a more sophisticated flight into the very "mechanical jurisprudence" which Frankfurter claims to reject, for to "find" or "be the impersonal vehicle of" the sum of what has been enacted by a "sovereign" whose "sovereignty" exists by virtue of its successful assertion is to be no more than "the subtlest of modern brain machines."

One prominent commentator who has been an alert and industrious student of Frankfurter for some time believes that he has found the essential difference between Black and Frankfurter.[70] That difference is said by Mendelson to be "starkly revealed"[71] in the *Youngstown* case,[72] and it is said to be a difference of "approach."[73] But, in criticism of Mendelson it has elsewhere been suggested that merely to be more complicated is not to be different in any essential respect.[74] There may be an underlying agreement between the two which must be grasped for an understanding of either of them.[75] The view that the measure of a judge can be had by understanding his "approach" is a view which can readily be drawn from Frankfurter's own writings. It has been accepted uncritically—not to say in a transport of enthusiasm—in some quarters.[76] And, in some ways, it is a correct view. But it must not be left at that.

Frankfurter's "approach" of "judicial restraint" is so well known as not to require establishment here by elaborate and tedious citation. A few passages, as the argument progresses, will do. In one of the Jehovah's Witnesses cases he reminds us that judges are to eschew "private notions of policy."[77] For, private notions of policy lead judges to a usurpation which "properly deserves the stigma of judicial legislation."[78] For:

> it can never be emphasized too much that one's own opinion as to the wisdom of a law must be wholly excluded when one is doing one's judicial duty.[79]

The imputation by Black in the *Adamson* case that judges must either follow the letter of the positive law or sail on an endless sea of what Frankfurter admits ought to be called "subjective" judgments has led Frankfurter to emphasize repeatedly that using judgment does not mean and must not mean "private notions of policy" or the judge's "own opinion as to the wisdom of a law." As we have suggested, if this simply means impartiality, everyone must agree. But what impartiality is—what are its attributes—is itself a question. At times it appears that impartiality or disinterestedness is a part of or identical with "restraint" and restraint is in action what "humility" is in mood:

> What becomes decisive to a justice's functioning on the Court in the large area within which his individuality moves is his general attitude toward law, the habits of mind that he has formed or is capable of unforming, his capacity for detachment, his temperament or training for putting his passion behind his judgment instead of in front of it. The attitudes and qualities which I am groping to characterize are ingredients of what compendiously might be called dominating humility.[80]

The "large area within which his individuality moves" is an attribute of judging which must concern us in due course. For now it will do to note the identification of detachment and humility. But putting passion behind judgment has been a theme of writers on human affairs for a very long time, and Plato, for example, who dealt at length with the subject was certainly not of the opinion that such an ordering of the soul led to or amounted to "dominating humility." Certainly a parent tries to be impartial as between his children but he does not humble himself before them. The man of science hopes always to be detached but his very boldness in proposing to discover answers to what he regards as the highest questions is the antithesis of humility. The results of his research are published as emanating not from his "humble" but from his "considered" opinion.

On occasion Frankfurter has disjoined these qualities by speaking of humility *and* disinterestedness as attributes of the judge.[81] But there are certainly instances where it would appear that they are identical in his view, or, at least, that in the case of *judges* they are identical, or, perhaps that disinterested judgment only occurs if a judge is restrained in the performance of his duty and the only thing which *can* restrain judges is humility. In justice to Professor Mendelson, it must here be admitted that one cannot tell whether it is he, Mendelson the critic, or his subject, Frankfurter, who is the originator of the doctrinaire elevation of humility to the rank of a science.[82] Whether Frankfurter has indeed founded a veritable sect of "humilitarians"[83] or rather it is Mendelson who has given undue emphasis to certain sayings of the former is rendered at least doubtful by two factors. First of all, there is the frequent confusing in Frankfurter's writing between detachment and humility of which we have been speaking. Secondly, even a cursory reading of *Felix Frankfurter Reminisces*[84] causes one to apply to Frankfurter what he has elsewhere said of others: "One wonder whether English judges are confined psychologically as they purport to be legally."[85] Indeed, the fact that journalists are normally very poor interpreters of judges and their work does not deny significance to the fact that one has dared to call him "rude."[86]

In one place, Frankfurter goes so far as to admit, even if only by implication, that one can go too far with the business of humility. In a 1955 memorial article he spoke of Mr. Justice Roberts' "judicial self-depreciation,"[87] and in fact, as we shall try to show in the proper place, Frankfurter's bottom view of what judges do to law and what law does to men stands in uneasy suspension with the doctrine of humility.

But the term itself has a variety of shades of meaning and, despite its having become a "household word" by virtue of recent presidential campaigns, it is not everywhere received as a term of praise. While the word is congenial to both the Christian and the democratic traditions it is not simply obvious that to be lowly is the highest thing. And so, whatever the "psychological" basis of judicial behavior, it will perhaps be better for the time to speak of the behavior itself and the standards which measure it rather than measuring what lies behind it. To return then to this aspect of judicial "approach," Frankfurter tells us:

> The outlook of a lawyer fit to be a Justice regarding the role of a judge cuts across all his preferences for this or that social arrangement.[88]

That is, those only are qualified to sit on the Supreme Court who put the question of the "role of the judge" ahead of the question as to whether "this or that social arrangement" is preferable. But is the horse really before the cart here? Can it really be more important for a judge to ponder the preferred behavior of judges whether they be in the Soviet Union or the United States than to ponder whether it is preferable to be a judge *in* the Soviet Union *or* in the United States? Obviously the term "social arrangements" cannot be so broad as to include the difference between the Soviet and American regimes, for:

> The conception which a judge has of his own function . . . depends first on the judge's philosophy, conscious or implicit, regarding the nature of society; that is, on his theory of the clash of interests. This, in turn will influence his conception of the place of the judge in the American constitutional system.[89]

"Social arrangements," then, must mean those lesser social arrangements within the larger social arrangement called "the American constitutional system." Frankfurter must be talking about what would be called the "role of a judge in the American system," or, more particularly, the "role of a United States Supreme Court judge in the American system."

But this won't do. For even if one could say that Frankfurter is concerned with the role of a particular kind of judge in a particular society, he refers for the resolution of that concern to the "nature of society" as such. That he should identify the "nature of society" with the "clash of interests" raises a great many problems[90] and Frankfurter has indicated an awareness of some of them by denying that a court (of equity) is "just an umpire between two litigants,"[91] but even admitting these problems, it must also be admitted that the movement from the question of the "role of the judge" to that of the "nature of society" is an improvement.

Frankfurter, then, frequently admits that there is such a thing as justice. While he tells us that the term "'natural law' . . . was not much more than literary garniture" in Marshall's day, "even as in our own,"[92] he admitted in the *Adamson* case that there was more to it than that. But in *Textile Workers* v. *Lincoln Mills*[93] he quoted approvingly Holmes' proposition that the law is not a "brooding omnipresence in the sky,"[94] which certainly complicates the issue. Because of such complications, Professor Crosskey has indicated that Frankfurter is simply inconsistent[95] and Professor Rodell accuses him of preciosity, pedantry, and dereliction of duty as well as inconsistency.[96] Despite the defect in the manner of Rodell's so saying, the accusations themselves cannot be dismissed out of hand. In a way they are a summary of all the criticisms now being made of Frankfurter, for his detractors in recent years never accuse him of being an enemy; rather, always of being a clumsy or timid ally.

To Frankfurter's admission that there is some such thing as justice must be added his admission that courts and judges are involved in finding or applying it. That judicial involvement is not mechanical, but is characterized by judgment. Because that judgment is difficult, the most important court must constantly limit or have limited the quantity of its work that the quality of it might be as high as is humanly possible. The court's work is not only to be limited quantitatively, however. It must avoid or be freed of responsibility for tasks which are not meet for courts. That is, its judgments must not only be high quality judgments; they must be high quality *judicial* judgments. Because judgment is not simply an event, but an activity as well—an activity fraught with the dangers of human weakness, and judges are human beings[97]—and because the line between what is and what is not meet for judicial judgment is not clear enough for externally imposed prohibitions, the judge must be humble in his approach to his work or, at least, restrained in the performance of it.

It would then follow, according to Frankfurter, that the questions which *must* be answered by the Supreme Court will more likely be well answered.

What are those questions and where, if not to the black letters of the Constitution or into one's own viscera, does one look for the answers?

NOTES TO CHAPTER IV

[1]367 U.S. 643, June 19, 1961.
[2]19 How. 393 (1857).
[3]18 How. 272 (1856).
[4]18 How. 272 (1856) at 276-77.
[5]*Hurtado* v. *California,* 110 U.S. 516 (1884).
[6]*Ibid.,* pp. 534-35.
[7]Matthews quotes from 'To what principle, then, are we to resort . . .'' to ''. . . having been acted on by them after the settlement of this country.'' *Ibid.,* p. 528.
[8]We offer as an example of a ''settled usage'' now forbidden, but not clearly in the name of due process, the exclusion of negroes from juries trying a negro.
[9]110 U.S. 516, 528.
[10]Pritchett, *op. cit.,* p. 529.
[11]*Vitarelli* v. *Seaton,* 359 U.S. 535 (1959). And see Frankfurter concurring there: ''An executive agency must be rigorously held to the standards by which it professes to be judged'' (p. 546). Mr. Justice Harlan, for the Court, does not ''reach the Constitutional issue'' but he speaks of Secretary Seaton's action as ''illegal'' (p. 545) although no law forbade Seaton to act as he had acted. According to Frankfurter, ''He that takes the procedural sword shall perish with that sword'' (p. 547). What we here suggest is that what Vitarelli asked for was not due him from the Constitution; it was due him from Seaton. Seaton owed it to Vitarelli because he promised it to him. Behind Seaton's promise was the Constitution's promise that promises are to be kept.
[12]That is, expectations established by statute may not be disappointed by administration. See *Peters* v. *Hobby,* 349 U.S. 331 (1955). As in the Vitarelli case, the constitutional question was not reached here.
[13]*Reid* v. *Covert,* 354 U.S. 1 (1957).
[14]332 U.S. 46, 49.
[15]*Ibid.,* p. 65.
[16]For the lone dissenting voice, see Harlan in *Twining* v. *New Jersey,* 211 U.S. 78, 114 at 118-27. Harlan agrees that the Fourteenth Amendment protects ''fundamental liberties.'' He argues that the adoption of the first eight Amendments—even though they might have held only against the more feared

central government—shows conclusively what the American tradition *regarded* as fundamental liberties and hence what the framers of the Fourteenth must have understood to be such.

[17]*Twining* v. *New Jersey,* 211 U.S. 78 at 100.

[18]*Ibid.,* p. 111.

[19]*Palko* v. *Connecticut,* 302 U.S. 319, 325.

[20]*Ibid.*

[21]*Ibid.*

[22]332 U.S. 46 at 69, 70, 75, 77, 79, 80 (twice), 90 (twice) and 91. He also uses the terms "natural right and justice" (p. 77) and "natural justice" (p. 78) as equivalents.

[23]*Ibid.,* p. 91. Citations omitted.

[24]It is curious to note that public discussion has accepted the distinction between a restrained Frankfurter and a judicially active Black. See W. Mendelson, *Justices Black and Frankfurter: Conflict in the Court* (Chicago: University of Chicago Press, 1961), chapter v. But it has been asked, "Who is more 'active'—the judge who would make a ruling on the applicability of the first eight amendments once and for all because he says he believes that the Fourteenth Amendment meant to apply them to the States, or the judge who brings down upon the Court a continuing torrent of individual cases which cannot be decided without reviewing intricate sets of facts and comparing them with the whole *corpus* of the common law?" R.G. Stevens, Book Review, *William and Mary Law Review,* III (1961), 212-13. And see Walter Berns, *Freedom, Virtue and the First Amendment* (Baton Rouge: Louisiana State University Press, 1957), p. 177.

[25]332 U.S. 46 at 70.

[26]*Ibid.,* p. 70.

[27]*Ibid.,* p. 69.

[28]*Ibid.,* p. 62.

[29]*Ibid.,* p. 61.

[30]*Ibid.,* p. 60.

[31]*United States* v. *Bethlehem Steel Corp.,* 315 U.S. 289, 326. It appears that the government stood here to Bethlehem in the relation of a Little Nell to the mortgagee.

[32]*Sacher* v. *United States,* 343 U.S. 1, 37.

[33]Frankfurter dissenting in *Elkins* v. *United States,* 364 U.S. 207, 233 at 235 (1960).

[34]Frankfurter concurring in *United States* v. *Spelar,* 338 U.S. 217, 222 at 224.

[35]Felix Frankfurter, "The Judicial Process and the Supreme Court," a paper for the American Philosophical Society in 1954, reprinted in P. Elman, ed., *Of Law and Men: Papers and Addresses of Felix Frankfurter, 1939-1956* (New York: Harcourt-Brace, 1956), p. 31. (Hereinafter cited as *L and M.*)

[36]*Universal Camera Corp.* v. *Labor Board,* 340 U.S. 474, 489. Frankfurter for the Court. Cf. his opinion for the Court in *Addison* v. *Holly Hill Co.,* 322 U.S. 607 at 618.

[37]Frankfurter concurring in result in *Sweezy* v. *New Hampshire,* 354 U.S. 234 at 267. And see Frankfurter concurring in *Pennekamp* v. *Florida,* 328 U.S. 331 at 367.

[38]Frankfurter for the Court in *Carpenters Union* v. *N.L.R.B.,* 357 U.S. 93, 100.

[39]19 How. 393.

[40]See Miss Thomas' defense of his prolificness. *Felix Frankfurter: Scholar on the Bench* (Baltimore: Johns Hopkins University Press, 1960), chapter xv.

[41]The explanation by Douglas was to a group of students from the College of William and Mary on April 23, 1962.

[42]Thomas, *op. cit.*, p. viii. But compare *ibid.*, p. x. "Justice Frankfurter's concepts are uniquely his."

[43]In F. Frankfurter, *Felix Frankfurter Reminisces,* ed. H.B. Phillips (New York: Reynal, 1960), pp. 142-44, there is an account of a document wholly prepared by someone else but issued by President Wilson which Frankfurter says the *New York Times* described as having the "inimitable Wilson touch." Frankfurter says that this was possible because Wilson's style was itself "synthetic."

[44]Frankfurter's amused account of Wilson's "inimitable touch" admits the same responsibility in Wilson's case which we here attribute to Frankfurter. *Ibid.,* p. 144.

[45]*United States* v. *Public Utilities Commission of California,* 345 U.S. 295 at 321.

[46]According to Clerk (now Judge) James R. Browning in a conversation at the Court in the spring of 1961.

[47]Printed in *Columbia Law Review,* XLVII (1947), 527. Reprinted in *L and M,* p. 44, "The Reading of Statutes," p. 51.

[48]"Distribution of Judicial Power Between United States and State Courts," *Cornell Law Quarterly,* XIII (1928), 499.

[49]Frankfurter concurring in *Lumbermen's Mutual Casualty Co.* v. *Elbert,* 348 U.S. 48 at 56. That Hamilton and Madison expected and hoped for such an "increasing permeation of national feeling" and a consequent movement of power and stature from the states to the United States is convincingly argued by Martin Diamond. See G.C.S. Benson, M. Diamond, *et al., Essays in Federalism* (Claremont: Institute for Studies in Federalism, 1961), pp. 42-51 and the passages in the *Federalist* cited therein. We do not mean here to imply any view by Hamilton or Madison on the diversity clause. That must remain, from the viewpoint of this study, an open question.

[50]See *United States* v. *Shannon,* 342 U.S. 288 where Frankfurter would dismiss the writ of certiorari as improvidently granted and *Ferguson* v. *Moore-McCormack Lines,* 352 U.S. 521, Frankfurter dissenting. Cf. *Brown* v. *Allen,* 344 U.S. 442 at 491, and see Mendelson, *op. cit.,* chapter iv.

[51]Frankfurter dissenting, *Ex parte Republic of Peru,* 318 U.S. 578 at 603.

[52]*Ferguson* v. *Moore-McCormack Lines, supra* at 547.

[53]See *Yates* v. *United States,* 354 U.S. 298.

[54]See his opinion for the Court in *Carpenters Union* v. *Labor Board,* 357 U.S. 93 at 100; concurring in *Adamson* v. *California,* 332 U.S. 46 at 68; dissenting in *Irvine* v. *California,* 347 U.S. 128 at 147; disqualifying himself in *Public Utilities Commission* v. *Pollak,* 343 U.S. 451 at 467. Compare his opinion (judgment for the Court for reasons supported by a minority) in *New York* v. *United States,* 326 U.S. 572 at 581.

[55]*Irvine* v. *California,* 347 U.S. 128 at 147.

[56]*L and M, p. 43.*

[57]*Bouvier, op. cit.,* I, 1718.

[58]*Ibid.,* I, 619.

[59]Pollock *Contracts,* p. 177, as cited *ibid.*

[60]*Words & Phrases* (St. Paul: West Publishing Co., 1951), 8A, p. 325.

[61]3 Ark. 491.

[62]"1 Chitty's Crim. Law 701; 8 B. & C. 196, and authorities there quoted; 1 Chitty's Black., 312-13."

[63]The whole of the short opinion in *Baker* v. *State* is concerned precisely with the question that concerns us here, but none of the three places cited has anything to do with the subject. If this is not due to typographical or editorial error, we leave it to others to determine why Judge Dickinson of the Arkansas Supreme Court should have embellished his opinion with three absolutely meaningless citations.

[64]84 F.2d 806 cited by *Words and Phrases, as 806 at p. 808.*

[65]*Op. cit.*, III, 396.

[66]Dissenting in *Southern Pacific Co.* v. *Jensen,* 244 U.S. 205 at 222. We need not pursue the fact that Holmes' effort to tidy up the definition of "law" involves reliance upon the word "sovereign," a word at least as "infirm" as, and the use of which is dependent upon a doctrine as problematic as, the view of law Holmes means to refute for such an examination would, ultimately, bring us back to the question here being pursued.

[67]Mr. Justice Brandeis for the Court in *Erie R. Co.* v. *Tompkins,* 304 U.S. 64. See especially Brandeis at 77-80 and the cases quoted and cited at 79.

[68]*Ibid.,* p. 77.

[69]Dissenting in *Textile Workers* v. *Lincoln Mills,* 353 U.S. 448 at 465. Cf. his opinion for the Court in *Guaranty Trust Co.* v. *York,* 326 U.S. 99 at 101-02 and see Philip B. Kurland, "Mr. Justice Frankfurter, the Supreme Court and the Erie Doctrine in Diversity Cases," *Yale Law Journal,* LXVII (December, 1957), 187.

[70]Mendelson, *op. cit.* See, e.g., p. 41.

[71]*Ibid.,* p. 10

[72]343 U.S. 579.

[73]Mendelson, *op. cit.,* p. 10; and see pp. 13-14.

[74]Stevens (1961), *op. cit.,* pp. 208-09.

[75]See Berns, *op. cit.,* pp. 166, 178-79.

[76]See Thomas, *op. cit.,* especially p. 347; see also chapters v and xiii and pp. 265-66.

[77]*West Virginia State Board of Education* v. *Barnette,* 319 U.S. 624, Frankfurter dissenting at p. 647.

[78]Frankfurter for the Court in *Kirschbaum Co.* v. *Walling,* 316 U.S. 517, 522 and again in *Addison* v. *Holly Hill Co.,* 322 U.S. 607, 618.

[79]Frankfurter for the Court in *Osborn* v. *Ozlin,* 310 U.S. 53, 66.

[80]Frankfurter, "Mr. Justice Jackson" (1955), reprinted in *L and M,* p. 193.

[81]Frankfurter, "Chief Justices I Have Known," *ibid.,* p. 138.

[82]Mendelson, *op. cit.,* p. 124, and see Stevens (1961), *op. cit.,* p. 210.

[83]The word is Mendelson's *op. cit.,* p. 124.

[84]*Op. cit.* The final chapter, entitled "Function of a Judge" disappoints the expectation of a thematic treatment of the subject, but one cannot complain of this for the contents support the title not of the chapter but of the book.

[85]Frankfurter, "The Reading of Statutes," *L and M,* p. 64.

[86]Arthur Edson, "Frankfurter—Man and Judge," Baltimore *Sun,* July 22, 1962, Section A, p. 3.

[87]*L and M,* p. 205, and see his only partly ironic reference, in his concurring opinion in *Woods* v. *Stone,* 333 U.S. 472 at 478 to Mr. Justice Jackson's "immoderate restraint."

[88]*L and M,* p. 41.

[89]Felix Frankfurter, *Mr. Justice Holmes and the Supreme Court* (Cambridge: Harvard University Press, 1961), p. 56.

⁹⁰Berns, *op. cit.*, pp. 134-48, discusses this problem at length.

⁹¹*Chrysler Corp.* v. *United States,* 316 U.S. 556, Frankfurter dissenting, at p. 325. And in his dissenting opinion in *Johnson* v. *United States,* 333 U.S. 46, at 54 (1948) he states, "Federal judges are not referees at prizefights but functionaries of justice."

⁹²Frankfurter, "John Marshall and the Judicial Function" (1955), reprinted in *L and M,* p. 13.

⁹³353 U.S. 448, 465.

⁹⁴Holmes had denied that the *common* law was such an omni-presence, *Southern Pacific Co.* v. *Jensen,* 244 U.S. 205, 222, but we do not doubt that Frankfurter's rendering of the phrase adequately represents the intention of Holmes.

⁹⁵Crosskey *op. cit.,* II, 1393. Whatever criticism may be offered to Crosskey's book, and we have offered some above, it must be admitted that all of it—even the Index, to which this note is a citation—is interesting.

⁹⁶F. Rodell, Book Review of, *Of Law and Men,* in *Saturday Review of Literature,* September 1, 1956, p. 15. We cannot quote from Rodell to show how he makes these accusations for, indeed, we simply cannot quote from Rodell. His review is a burlesque of its subject over which the editors of the magazine have stated that this is proof that he has long been a student of Frankfurter's prose. If the burlesque were coherent—and done with a lighter stroke—it might be entertaining although it still might not be instructive. As it is, it is simply unintelligible, and, as a burlesque, we cannot see how it could please anyone other than a pre-determined detractor of Frankfurter or an intemperate consumer of burlesque, good or bad. The review does employ a great many words and phrases favored, overtaxed and/or coined by Frankfurter, but they are put together after the manner of the book being compiled in Gulliver's Lagado (Jonathan Swift, *Gulliver's Travels,* Third Part, chapter v). While some of Frankfurter's articles and opinions raise questions as to ultimate intelligibility he has, in half a century of academic and judicial writing, hardly rendered a single sentence which, as sentence, is not perfectly and immediately intelligible to anyone whose reading was not learned in a speed-clinic. (For a much *better* burlesque in the *Saturday Review* see that on speed-reading by Clifford Owsley in the "Phoenix Nest" of the edition of June 8, 1962, p. 8, "Confessions of the World's Fastest Reader.")

⁹⁷See Frankfurter dissenting in *Craig* v. *Harnev,* 331 U.S. 367 at 392 (1947).

CHAPTER V

HISTORY

Everyone would admit that all the other courts in the United States could not be abolished and all their work given to the United States Supreme Court. Even if the desirability of local institutions and the convenience of litigants did not matter, division of labor would. Some line or some scheme must divide the labor, and nearly everyone who is informed would admit that the present line or scheme still leaves the Court a work load it is hard put to dispose of excellently.[1] To do its work well, of course it must engage in "adequate reflection" and of course it must render "luminous opinions." Mr. Justice Frankfurter's argument that it ought only to consider those cases for which there is no alternative to Supreme Court consideration is, we believe, unanswerable. If a way could be found so that the Court decided only one case per term we ought not to begrudge the Justices their salaries even if they drank and caroused for eight months out of every year, provided the one case decided was of the importance of, say, *Youngstown* or *Dennis*, and provided the opinions were not only "luminous" but unanimous and downright compelling as well.

Lord Bryce taught us that judicial review is rendered necessary by a written constitution and a federal division of governmental activity.[2] Understanding this is a fair beginning on understanding Frankfurter's view of the essential minimum of Court duties.[3] Mr. Justice Roberts explained in 1936 that judicial review consisted in laying the Constitution beside the statute to see if "the latter squares with the former."[4] Professor Berns has described this as "ingenuous,"[5] and well it may have been in that case. But Roberts' statement was virtually a replica of that made by Bryce in his *American Commonwealth*[6] and a close reading of Bryce shows that he was fully aware that his statement was only a partial truth. The statement was made as a defense of the principle of judicial review, a brief discussion of which is not outside the present purpose.

Bryce's argument for judicial review is identical with his argument for the existence of the Court. The Court exists *in order to* engage in judicial review *because* of a written constitution and a federal division of governmental activity. The argument is very similar to that offered by Hamilton in *Federalist* #78 and by Marshall in *Marbury* v. *Madison,* in 1803.[7] Recent attempts at refutation of Bryce by arguments in the name of democracy or in the light of comparison with European countries with written constitutions and federal divisions are as unsuccessful as early attempts at refutation of Marshall. With respect to the comparison of other countries, a short route may be taken through a very long problem by pointing out that the fate of the Weimar Republic and of the several French Republics thoroughly discourages looking to them to see what is "essential," given a written constitution. No one would be so silly as to say, for example, that a stronger French judiciary would have saved the Third Republic from Hitler's troops, but neither should one be so bold as to look to such volatile and unhappy civil polities as the French from 1789 to 1940 or the German from 1919 to 1933 for evidence as to what is "essential." That the French in 1946 preferred to start afresh says something about the Third Republic. One cannot look to the present German Federal or Fifth French republics for authoritative evidence for no one knows what will happen in those countries when the two old men die as die they must.

The precise element which is common to the views of Hamilton, Marshall, and Bryce is the position that the fact of a written constitution containing express limitations on the legislature requires that something give effect to those limitations. The Constitution, like statutes, is a law—that is, it is a thing legislated. Laws are what judges apply; if two conflict, the later takes precedence, but where the two conflicting laws are of differing authority, the more authoritative—even if earlier—takes precedence. The answer is often made that this doctrine elevates the judiciary to a position of supremacy over the legislature. Overlooking the various means by which the legislature can counter judicial action, one may concede that this charge of judicial supremacy is in some ways and in some cases a true charge. But it only follows that judicial review is unwarranted if one *assumes* a simply democratic regime. The Constitution no more contains an express command for simple democracy than it does an express command for judicial review. We are back at the beginning.

The clearest response to the Hamilton-Marshall-Bryce position is that offered by Mr. Justice Gibson of the Pennsylvania Supreme Court in the case of *Eakin* v. *Raub*[8] in 1825. Explicitly disputing Marshall, Gibson argues that invalidation of an act of the legislature is an act of sovereignty and he maintains by the authority of Blackstone that "sovereignty" and "legislative power" are "convertible terms."[9] So they may be by tradition or by necessity. But where *is* the "legislative power" in the United States? To identify legislative power with Congress is to misconstrue the American Constitution by a facile transmission of Locke through Blackstone to that Constitution. When Locke speaks of legislative power[10] he clearly means the power of the whole people to give itself the law. Surely, for Locke, this power is represented by the legislature. But, whatever may have been the intention of some of those at the Philadelphia Convention, the jealous if short-sighted stand of Paterson and Sherman and the habits of a large proportion of the other delegates insured the continuance in nearly full vigor of the several state legislatures. Congress is not "*the* legislature," it is *a* legislature.

In however high esteem Locke might have been held in America in 1787 the Founders no more *enacted* Locke than they, esteeming the British Constitution as they did, enacted *it*. The "executive power" is by Article II given to a President, the "judicial power of the United States" is by Article III given to "one Supreme Court and such inferior courts as Congress" may establish; only "all legislative powers herein granted" are by Article I given to Congress. Clearly Congress is not sovereign. It does not have the legislative power. The legislative power is in America held in abeyance. It has acted on eighteen occasions—to adopt the Constitution itself, to adopt ten of the first group of twelve proposed amendments, and on thirteen subsequent occasions to adopt and three subsequent occasions to reject other proposed amendments. This amounts to oftener than once in every ten years. Whether or not this is "often enough" depends upon a long argument but if one notices that the tempo has greatly increased in recent years—there was, after all, a period of over sixty years between the fourth and fifth exercise of the legislative power (between, that is, the Twelfth and the Thirteenth Amendments)—and remembers that "it is a *Constitution*" we are amending, the argument appears shorter.

One could say that the great merit of the American Constitution is its failure to enact in pure form the more exciting of the newer theories about government. Locke's *Second Treatise* was less than a hundred years old, Montesquieu's *Spirit of the Laws* less than forty when the Convention was in session. There is in the Constitution a certain common sense, a certain preservation of other and older views in company with the theories of Locke and Montesquieu. Approving comment upon this preservation may, but does not necessarily, disclose a simple preference for tradition over theory after the apparent manner of Burke. Such an approval is no more compelling proof of such a preference than would preference for the Oregon woods over, say, the slums of Peiping prove preference of nature over art nor preference of London over the Sahara prove the contrary. One could simply prefer particular aspects of a particular tradition to particular aspects of a particular theory, in the name of something else.

The identification of sovereignty and legislative power which Gibson attributes to Blackstone and which one can find in Locke means simply that the highest human thing is the faculty of a whole people which enables it to give itself the law—to say what is right and not to be gainsaid. It is this faculty which Rousseau was compelled to call the "General Will." To say that this is the highest thing is ultimately reducible to saying that what the multitude demands is right. The insistence of the demand of the multitude carries with it the implied threat of force. Deference to that threat may in practice be compelled by prudential considerations. Deference in theory amounts to simple approval of the proposition that might makes right. The connection between the legislative sovereignty of the people and force is indicated by that rather purer adherent of the modern theories, Thomas Jefferson, in his perhaps wistful suggestion that there ought to be a revolution from time to time. The connection is also indicated by Madison in his argument against occasional appeals to conventions of the people for altering or preserving the constitution.[11]

Bryce's argument that judicial review is a necessary consequence of a written or of a federal constitution takes the form of an unsmiling assertion that American judges have no extraordinary power but do exactly what English judges do. They interpret the laws.[12] The only interesting difference is the written constitution in America. In England, "Parliament is omnipotent,"[13] but in America, it is not that the *Court* is omnipotent for "American judges do not, as Europeans are apt to say, 'control the legislature,' but simply interpret the law."[14] Just *how* interesting is this difference is indicated by the fact that Bryce tells us that "the position of Congress may for this purpose be compared to that of an English municipal corporation or railway company."[15] It would be too much to say that Bryce simply regarded the Constitution and laws of the United States as equivalent to the charter and by-laws of a railway company, for Bryce was not a fool. If any notion that Bryce was blind to the vast power of American judges has survived the recent paperback abridgment of his work, and its consequent cheap availability, it deserves to be dispelled now by two rather long quotations, one of which is, the other of which is not, reproduced in the abridgment.

> Now the American judges have no will in the matter any more than has an English court when it interprets an Act of Parliament. The will that prevails is the will of the people, expressed in the Constitution which they have enacted. All that the judges have to do is to discover from the enactments before them what the will of the people is, and apply that will to the facts of a given case. The more general or ambiguous the language which the people have used, so much the more difficult is the task of interpretation, so much greater the need for ability and integrity in the judges. But the task is always the same in its nature. The judges have no concern with the motives or the results of an enactment, otherwise than as these may throw light on the sense in which the enacting authority intended it. It would be a breach of duty for them to express, I might almost say a breach of duty to entertain, an opinion on its policy except so far as its policy explains its meaning. They may think a statute excellent in purpose and working, but if they cannot find in the Constitution a power for Congress to pass it, they must brush it aside as invalid. They may deem another statute pernicious, but if it is within the powers of Congress, they must enforce it. To construe the law, that is, to elucidate the will of the people as supreme lawgiver, is the beginning and end of their duty.[16]

To press this point is not to minimize the importance of the functions exercised by the judiciary of the United States, but to indicate their true nature. The importance of those functions can hardly be exaggerated. It arises from two facts. One is that as the Constitution cannot easily be changed, a bad decision on its meaning, i.e. a decision which the general opinion of the profession condemns, may go uncorrected. In England, if a court has construed a statute in a way unintended or unexpected, Parliament sets things right next session by amending the statute, and so prevents future decisions to the same effect. But American history shows only one instance in which an unwelcome decision on the meaning of the Constitution has been thus dealt with, viz. the decision, that a State could be sued by a private citizen[17] which led to the eleventh amendment, whereby it was declared that the Constitution should not cover a case which the court had held it did cover.

The other fact which makes the function of an American judge so momentous is the brevity, the laudable brevity, of the Constitution. The words of that instrument are general, laying down a few large principles. The cases which will arise as to the construction of these general words cannot be foreseen till they arise. When they do arise the generality of the words leaves open to the interpreting judges a far wider field than is afforded by ordinary statutes which, since they treat of one particular subject, contain enactments comparatively minute and precise. Hence, although the duty of a court is only to interpret, the considerations affecting interpretation are more numerous than in the case of ordinary statutes, more delicate, larger in their reach and scope. They sometimes need the exercise not merely of legal acumen and judicial fairness, but of a comprehension of the nature and methods of government which one does not demand from the European judge who walks in the narrow path traced for him by ordinary statutes. It is therefore hardly an exaggeration to say that the American Constitution as it now stands, with the mass of fringing decisions which explain it, is a far more complete and finished instrument than it was when it came fire-new from the hands of the Convention. It is not merely their work but the work of the judges, and most of all of one man, the Great Chief-Justice Marshall.[18]

Although it has long been the habit of the Americans to talk of their Constitution with almost superstitios reverence, there have often been times when leading statesmen, perhaps even political parties, would have materially altered it if they could have done so. There have, moreover, been some alterations suggested in it, which the impartial good sense of the wise would have approved, but which have never been submitted to the States, because it was known they could not be carried by the requisite majority. If, therefore, comparatively little use has been made of the provisions for amendment, this has been due, not solely to the excellence of the original instrument, but also to the difficulties which surround the process of change. Alterations, though perhaps not large alterations, have been needed, to cure admitted faults or to supply dangerous omissions, but the process has been so difficult that it has never been successfully applied, except either to matters of minor consequence involving no party interests (Amendments xi. and xii.), or in the course of a revolutionary movement which had dislocated the Union itself (Amendments xiii. xiv. xv.).[19]

According to Bryce, then, Congressional statutes *must* be tested by the Constitution, judges are charged with doing the testing and ultimately the judges of the Supreme Court have the say. That testing and that say involve the *activity* of judgment, the art of interpretation. The Constitution which is to be interpreted is brief and general and leaves the judges enormous latitude. The subject matter over which this interpretation holds sway is not narrowly legal but broadly—indeed, well nigh exhaustively—political. What is more, those judges have virtually the last say on earth on these great political matters for the legislative power, in the full sense in which Locke meant the term, that is, the amending process, is exasperatingly difficult to convene and control. Notwithstanding Frankfurterian doctrines of judicial self-restraint, we believe Bryce's view to be an accurate view of the American Constitution and the "role of the judiciary" thereunder.

Frankfurter would agree with Bryce at least in that his delineation of what work *must* be done by the Court would be based on the fact of a written federal constitution. But not a few problems arise. Frankfurter has told us:

In the past this Court has from time to time set its views of policy against that embodied in legislation by finding laws in conflict with what was called the "spirit of the Constitution." Such undefined destructive power was not conferred on this Court by the Constitution. Before a duly enacted law can be judicially nullified, it must be forbidden by some explicit restriction upon political authority in the Constitution. Equally inadmissable is the claim to strike down legislation because to us as individuals it seems opposed to the "plan and purpose" of the Constitution. That is too tempting a basis for finding in one's personal views the purposes of the Founders.[20]

On and off through most of the first few decades of this century the Court had invalidated acts of Congress as well as of state legislatures with great frequency. This had often been done in the name of due process. The weight of opinion presently condemns these invalidations and we are in agreement with the present condemnation. President Franklin D. Roosevelt, in 1937 proposed a thoroughgoing reformation of the makeup of the national judiciary. Tremendous opposition met Roosevelt's plan, not all of it from those Roosevelt called the "economic royalists." Many who had been his strongest supporters in other matters thought the plan devious and perhaps unconstitutional. More "direct" counter-proposals were offered in Congress. Frankfurter is described as being among the supporters of Roosevelt who disapproved of the proposal. The following paragraph from *The 168 Days* sums up the opposition from that quarter:

> Other men with Frankfurter's sympathies were even more upset than he by the indirections of the plan, but the plan's indirections were not the only thing about it that upset the liberals. The precedent it set, the prescriptive right to tamper with the judiciary it gave the executive and legislative branches, frightened many liberals who feared its use in the future by conservative or semi-Fascist administrations. The fact that it failed to provide a permanent remedy for the Court's right of review annoyed many others who held the left-wing opinion that the Court's right is no right but a wrongly assumed power.[21]

But convincing argument is currently being offered that the beauty of Roosevelt's plan was precisely its failure "to provide a permanent remedy for the Court's right of review."[22] Roosevelt, who was perhaps our strongest president, like Lincoln, who was our greatest, in his most critical dispute with the Court did not propose a fundamental revision of the constitutional place of that Court. By means eminently within the letter of the Constitution he proposed to accomplish what we believe would have been soundly within the spirit of the Constitution—namely a quiet change in the course of its decisions by a mere speeding of the rate of change of the personnel. That speeding would in no material way have tampered with the tenure of sitting judges. Rather than destroy the Court's power over the Constitution by what pious liberals would have regarded as an "above-board" constitutional amendment that would have satisfied not only the country's needs but the liberals' impatient feelings as well, Roosevelt proposed simply to alter the relative weight of the combined executive and legislative branches in contests with the Court. There is more than statistical significance to the fact that he meant to change not 9 to 0 failures into 10 to 9 successes but 5 to 4 failures into 6 to 5 successes. The liberals who, failing to appreciate this significance, denounced his "indirection," entertained the same wooden distinction between law and politics which burdened the Court majority.

When Roosevelt finally did, without benefit of his judiciary bill, change the course of decision by changing the character of the Court personnel he was not long in appointing Frankfurter. Given the then very recent history of the Court's obstinate stand against social legislation, there was a refreshing air to Frankfurter's refusal in 1943 to substitute *his* notions of policy for those of the West Virginia Board of Education. But some of those who had been most impatient with the Court for its refusal to let the New Deal legislate were now disappointed with Frankfurter for his stand here in the *Barnette* case and two years before in the *Gobitis* case, which *would* allow West Virginia and Minersville to legislate. Not wishing to enter the much extended debate over whether or not the First Amendment stands in a "preferred position," we can here take the shorter course by pointing out that supporters of Frankfurter's stand argue that his critics in this matter had previously hidden their substantive views behind procedural arguments and the supporters further show that Frankfurter's stand was a consequence of his lawyer-like consistency.[23]

Consistency is a virtue. A simply inconsistent judge would be of little use to society. To say that someone is lawyer-like is usually a kind of praise. But the inquiry cannot stop there. Judges are, after all, *more* than lawyers; and consistency is an attribute of, not a substitute for, law. Or, to put it another way, there may be a higher consistency than lawyer-like consistency. And, however appealing Frankfurter's restraint may have been in 1943, to say that the "plan and purpose" or "spirit of the Constitution" must not guide judges is to say too much on the subject too quickly. What does it mean to say, as he says elsewhere, that "the letter killeth,"[24] unless it means that the spirit giveth life? It won't do to answer that he was there speaking of statutory construction as he was when he told us that "blind literalness" is the "cardinal sin"[25] for Frankfurter is not such a fool as to suppose that a whole bookshelf of the technicalities of the United States Statutes at Large are to be construed liberally while the comprehensive political pronouncements of the Constitution are to be pieced out of their brief context and read like the instructions on an electric can-opener. Even if the Court were, as one man, to make a conscientious effort so to construe the Constitution, the effort would immediately betray its own impossibility. For the parts of the Constitution are often meaningless outside the context of the whole and the meaning of the whole has therefore to be ascertained. What the Constitution *itself* says *explicitly* about the meaning of the whole it says in the fifty-two words of the Preamble and what *that* means only reveals itself to long study.

In fact, despite his disavowals of constitutional spirit, Frankfurter has told us that:

> due regard for the presuppositions of our embracing federal
> system, including the principle of diffusion of power not as a
> matter of doctrinaire localism but as a promoter of democracy,
> has required us not to find withdrawal from the States of power
> to regulate where the activity regulated was a merely peripheral
> concern of the [Congressional] Act.[26]

In *Knapp* v. *Schweitzer* Frankfurter told us for the Court that the due process clause "does not blur the great division of power" between nation and states.[27] We agree, but not because the Constitution anywhere says anything explicit about the "great division of power." Neither does it say a word about the "separation of powers" upon which Frankfurter, despite his circumlocution, flatly depended for his concurring opinion in *Youngstown Sheet and Tube Co.* v. *Sawyer.*[28] The problem of *Knapp* v. *Schweitzer* and *Adamson* v. *California*—what the due process clause of the

Fourteenth Amendment imposes on the states—could not have occurred if Marshall had not ruled as he did in *Barron* v. *Baltimore* in 1833 and the entire basis of Marshall's ruling there is *not* on what the Constitution *says* but on what it need not have said. It is based on what everyone is supposed to have understood that the movers of the first ten Amendments were worried about. Marshall's problem in *Barron*, his resolution of which is the necessary condition of Frankfurter's need to teach over and over again what "due process" means, is analogous to the problem of statutory construction regarding which Frankfurter tells us:

> The starting point for determining legislative purpose is plainly an appreciation of the "mischief" that Congress was seeking to alleviate.[29]

That problem is the problem of the "plan and purpose" of the thing being construed. What else *is* a concern for "our embracing federal system" as a "promoter of democracy" except a concern for the "spirit of the Constitution"? The words "democracy" and "federal" *never once appear* in the Constitution. Maybe they are "between the lines." Maybe they are not there because they *need* not be there because everyone is supposed to know what they are and that the Constitution is constructed *for* them. Then again, it may be that the Constitution avoids the word "federal" as carefully as it avoids the word "slavery." Certainly one cannot come away from the records of the Philadelphia Convention with the unmixed view that the "mischief" the legislators there were seeking to alleviate was excessive centralization or a defect of democracy. Frankfurter, then, is also an applier of constitutional spirit. The whole apparatus of "judicial self-restraint" is nothing more than deference to "our federalism" and "our democracy" and "our separation of powers," none of which appears in words in the Constitution.

Professor Berns has pointed out that Frankfurter comes about as close as any present-day judge to opposing judicial review altogether.[30] This near-complete opposition can be appreciated if one looks behind his view that the Court ought only to perform those functions which "our federal system" compels it to perform and sees that he at one time held explicitly (and, in a way, may have continued to hold) the view that an enormous portion of those functions, as Frankfurter found "our federal system," ought to be taken away. For a very long time now a very large part of the Court's work has been generated by the due process clauses, and there was a time, fifteen years before Frankfurter's appointment to the Court, when he thought the clauses ought to be stricken from the Constitution. But there has been a movement from his outspoken condemnation of the clauses to an apparent acceptance of them.

In 1924 Frankfurter maintained that the "due process clauses ought to go,"[31] but in 1951 he regarded due process as "perhaps the most majestic conception in our whole constitutional system."[32] This needs to be explained. The fast answer—too fast—would be to say that he reversed himself during the course of those twenty-seven years. An equally fast and much more facile answer would be to say that his stand on due process had "evolved." The former answer is that which a critic of Frankfurter would offer; the latter that of a supporter. Both are at about the same level and neither explains very much. The imputation of thoughtless inconsistency is so easy to make and to support by contrasting the 1924 and 1951 utterances as to be suspect in dealing with a man of Frankfurter's obvious excellences. The defense of "evolution," on the other hand, too glibly employs a term of "convenient vagueness." A number of alternatives present themselves. In the first place, the contexts are different. In 1924 Frankfurter was referring to the Court's invalidation of economic legislation and in 1951 he was referring to administrative regulation of speech and assembly. In the second place, it was not the "same man" who spoke in 1951 as the one who had spoken in 1924. That is, what a law professor might say in criticism of the Constitution in the columns of a provocative magazine is not necessarily what a justice of the Supreme Court, charged with the care of the Constitution, might say in an opinion, for the gown *does* change the man.[33] In dealing with someone as literate and as witty as Frankfurter, one cannot refuse to entertain, at least momentarily, one other possibility. His doctrine of judicial restraint is based in large part on his firm belief in democracy.[34] Such a believer in democracy who is also adept at ironic utterance[35] might use the adjective "majestic" and not intend it as a term of praise, for the essential attribute of majesty is precisely the personal authority which Frankfurter often tells us judges ought not to wield.

The context of the 1951 description of due process as majestic discourages the conclusion that the description was deliberately ironic. But while he might not have intended to use the word ironically, it is perhaps ironic that he used it. That is, seeing the usage as an irony might best disclose the full meaning of his stand on due process. It is, of course, a long way from the suggestion to its establishment and it is first necessary to see the surface aspects of the change between the 1924 and 1951 remarks.

In a 1934 article for the *Encyclopedia of the Social Sciences*[36] Frankfurter states that "the duties of the Supreme Court have on the whole been kept within the capacities of nine judges who are not supermen."[37] As we have agreed, the only way to insure excellence in the Court's work is to confine its work to that which it and only it can do. Congress has kept its duties within its capacity by decreasing its business.[38] But the superhuman attributes judges lack are qualitative as well as quantitative. In his 1924 suggestion that due process ought to come out of the Constitution Frankfurter said:

> An informed study of the work of the Supreme Court of the United States will probably lead to the conclusion that no nine men are wise enough and good enough to be entrusted with the power which the unlimited provisions of the due process clauses confer.[39]

Twelve years earlier, constitutional amendment had not seemed the best alternative because "back of the constitutional amendment is the construing power of the courts."[40] But amendment seemed unnecessary then because the "stream of the *Zeitgeist*" had been "allowed to flood the sympathies and the intelligence of our judges."[41] But his reflection on subsequent conduct of the Court led him in 1924 to conclude that that earlier hearkening to the *Zeitgeist* had come about because Theodore Roosevelt had put the "fear of God" into the judges.[42] Such fear is, however, "too capricious, too intermittent,"[43] and the God-fearing judges had gone off on their own course again after 1912. Apparently a man of liberal good will could not put his trust either in the judges or in God himself and so the answer to the construing power of judges was to be sought in giving them less to construe. The due process clauses had to be excised from the text. So obvious must it have been to all men in 1924 that the trouble lay in due process and the companion equal protection clause that "not a single constitution framed for English-speaking countries since the Fourteenth Amendment ha[d] embodied its provisions."[44]

Contrary to later statements that judges can find due process without recourse to their "personal" views, the 1924 article emphatically declares that Democratic presidential candidate

> Davis must know that these broad "guarantees" in favor of the individual are expressed in words so undefined, either by their intrinsic meaning, or by history, or by tradition, that they leave the individual Justice free, if indeed they do not actually compel him, to fill in the vacuum with his own controlling notions of economic, social, and industrial facts with reference to which they are invoked.[45]

Coolidge, in his innocence, might be forgiven. But Davis must know better. He must know better because he is a lawyer. Frankfurter and Davis, the lawyers, must know that the seat of the country's difficulty in passing "economic, social, and industrial" legislation is the entrenchment of crabbed economic, social, and industrial notions in the judiciary. It is then with a view to the "substantive," or dynamic-property, stand of the Court on due process that the 1924 demand for excision is made. Whatever may have been the merits of the Matthews opinion in *Hurtado* and the Moody opinion in *Twining*, in 1884 and 1908 respectively, Frankfurter was concerned in 1924 with the latitude due process gave judges to bar legislation necessary for the general welfare and not with the effect of the clause on state criminal proceedings.

The general shift from the vigorous demand in 1924 for amendment of the Constitution to shear the horns of due process from the Court's bull head to the support of due process in 1951 *is* adequately explained by the fact that the citizen's duty in 1924, as Frankfurter saw it, was to promote the curbing of the Court and the judge's duty in 1951, as everyone must see it, was to support and defend the Constitution—all of it—as it was. But that does not explain enough. The 1951 statement was made within the freedom a justice has in a concurring opinion. If Frankfurter had still believed, in his heart of hearts, that "the due process clauses ought to go" he could easily have done his judicial duty in applying due process, because the clauses had *not* gone, without going so far as to teach bench and bar that the clause was a leading contender for the position of "most majestic"—i.e., grandest, noblest, most beautiful and worthy—concept in the Constitution. Something must have changed his mind in some way or other.

It is not within the realm of possibility that Frankfurter was in 1924 unaware of the use to which Mr. Justice Holmes had put the due process clause the year before in overruling an Arkansas federal court's refusal of *habeas corpus* to five negroes sentenced to death by a state court which had gone through the motions but had obviously not given a fair trial.[46] But apparently that was not enough. Perhaps the incorporation of the First Amendment into the Fourteenth by the series of cases from *Gitlow* v. *New York*[47] in 1925 to *Near* v. *Minnesota*[48] in 1931 softened Frankfurter's antipathy to the due process clause. But we believe that Mr. Justice Sutherland's opinion in *Powell* v. *Alabama*[49] in 1932 and Mr. Justice Cardozo's opinion in *Palko* v. *Connecticut*[50] in 1937, both expounding on due process (the one ruling for the accused, the other for the state) may have had most to do with his turn in favor of the clause. Immediately after the *Powell* decision, Frankfurter wrote favorably on it for the *New York Times*,[51] and as far as the *Palko* case is concerned, writing on Mr. Justice Cardozo in 1955 for the *Dictionary of American Biography*, he chose six of Cardozo's 140 opinions in order to illustrate the latter's "judicial prowess" and *Palko* was one of them.[52]

If the assumption of judicial duties necessitated Frankfurter's reconciliation to the due process clause, his heavy reliance in the *Adamson* case upon not only the general reasoning but also the particular phrasing of the *Palko* case persuades us that it was Cardozo's opinion there which eased that reconciliation. That is, what the assumption of judicial duties did to him in letter, Cardozo's opinion did for him in spirit. If in 1924 he believed that the due process clauses allowed or perhaps compelled judicial flights into personal whims, *Palko* showed him how the clauses might be applied impersonally. Fully to appreciate the character of that reconciliation and to judge of its worth it is necessary to see how Frankfurter distinguishes between what is "personal" and what "impersonal."[53]

The beginning of that task is a survey of his reliance upon the element which Professors Jacobs and Thomas rightly identify as history, but first, a brief recapitulation will be useful here.

Adamson contended that California's forcing him to choose between the revelation of his former crimes and allowing comment by the prosecutor on his failure to testify deprived him of life without due process by negating the privilege against self-incrimination. The Court rejected his contention on the grounds that the standing doctrine with respect to the due process clause of the Fourteenth Amendment denied that states were compelled to continue the privilege. Mr. Justice Black countered that the standing doctrine was in error. He maintained that an examination of the legislative history of the Fourteenth Amendment showed that the intention of its framers was to incorporate the first eight Amendments. But Fairman and others answer, and we agree, that the legislative history is *at best* equivocal and, properly read, by no means supports Black. Crosskey then suggests that legislative intent does not matter and, *whatever* the framers intended, what was *adopted*, by its plain terms, incorporates the first eight Amendments. But our examination of Crosskey persuades us that his reasoning is circular and self-destroying and that, Adamson, Black, and Crosskey to the contrary, the Court's standing doctrine that due process means, and was intended by its 1866 users to mean, "essential fairness" rather than a fixed list of processes is correct.

Mr. Justice Black, however, admonishes us that such an interpretation perpetuates in American constitutional law the discredited natural law doctrine by means of which the Court had wrongly interfered with social and economic progress prior to 1937. Such a doctrine, Black argues, leaves judges free to impose their personal whims upon country and legislature. But Frankfurter counters that "natural law" has a better and older meaning than "merely personal" or "subjective" standards. One is not confined, he says, to a choice between rigid written formulae and boundless whim. There *is* such a thing as essential fairness and judges are compelled to find it—to engage in the activity of judgment, however agonizing. How does a judge go about finding it; where does he look?

Answers to this question have been attempted by two comprehensive works on Frankfurter published in the past two years by young political scientists. With sympathetic appreciation of the complexity of the task, we are yet bound to express our dissatisfaction with them. The first, *Felix Frankfurter: Scholar on the Bench,* by Shirley Thomas,[54] was adversely reviewed by Maurice Merrill who explains that the book was probably doomed to failure at the outset, for, "Dr. Thomas . . . has had no training in law. Apparently, she has not ever studied at a university sheltering a law school. Her listing of 'intellectual debts' includes no lawyer or teacher of law in a law school. This is hardly the basis for an understanding of judicial activity. Constitutional law, after all is *law.*"[55] This does not seem to us a valid complaint. We are far from disparaging disciplined and expert training but it is a bit ungracious for lawyers, who regard themselves, and are in America publicly regarded, as experts-in-everything-under-the-sun, to dismiss everyone else as laymen. Law, after all, gives the rule for human affairs. As such, it is subject to critical examination by disciplined students of human affairs. Perhaps what Professor Merrill really means is that law and political science are not discrete but contending disciplines and that the former is the true and the latter the false contender. If that is what he meant, he should have said so. That is an interesting question. Its resolution might begin by pitting Merrill's supposed contention against that of Aristotle that *politics* is the queen of the sciences.[56] But, whatever the underlying *reason* for the defects in Miss Thomas' book, we are not far from agreeing with Merrill's account of them.

> For the most part, [the book] consists of a . . . running comment upon . . . Frankfurter's judicial decisions. . . . While there are references also to judicial method and to philosophy, they are superficial. There is no acute analysis, no adequate explanation of what makes the judge "tick."[57]

"What makes the judge 'tick'" may escape lawyers and laymen alike, but acute analysis of the printed record of Frankfurter's views is possible and is demanded. Such analysis is very difficult in the case of a judge, for his views are scattered and compromised and are drawn forth not by the force of logic as the result of an unemcumbered pursuit of the truth but by the self-seeking demands of advocates who "have a propensity for claiming everything."[58] The judge's practical responsibilities as a statesman further shroud his meaning. It goes without saying that the views of statesmen with more immediate responsibility for the conduct of affairs—that is, the views of legislative leaders, princes, and presidents—must, on the same grounds, be many times as unyielding as those of judges. This is because a much larger proportion of what the judge decides results in a written opinion supported by argument and because the argument is addressed at least in the first place to the reason of the legal profession and not to the passions of constituents. A Supreme Court justice of long tenure is pressed to opine about or at least to vote upon a sufficient array of questions such that determining his views does not suffer by comparison with determining those of president or legislator. While subtle shades of his character may elude the "cold record," while forceful aspects of personality may be hidden in conference, he faces a great array of questions and what he decides he decides and what he says he supports with argument; even his disinclination to decide—the negative vote on petitions for *certiorari*—are often enough revealed in recent years to aid the understanding of the student. The student of the Court, be he blessed with the sciences of archaeology and psychiatry may *never* find out what makes the judge "tick," but he *can* find out what the judge *teaches*—what he does to law and to law abidingness.

The judge's views are not only scattered and compromised and shrouded by political responsibility, they are necessarily delivered in a repetitious fashion for decision and opinion are confined by the forms of litigation and, case by case, different aspects and different levels of the same problem arise as separate problems and so, case after case, the judge must decide upon and opine about repeated instances of what, at bottom, are all one question. All this being true, analysis of those views involves a great quantity of dreary clerical work. But it must not lose itself in routine nor in the simple pleasures of the cataloguer. The analysis begins after the clerical work is done. It consists in identifying the several superficial classes of the views, ordering and relating them, resolving ambiguities, noting apparent contradictions, reducing the latter to what might be called "the least common denominator"—that is, determining what one or few broad views encompass and rectify the several lesser ones—and then analyzing those. *Analyzing* them means not resting at the level of the judge's explicit statement of them. It means exposing the meaning and consequence of them. It is not possible to describe adequately without explicating and explication means criticism—evaluation. To evaluate, to say what is truer and better and what the reverse, is to judge the judges. If to presume to judge the judges appears to be arrogance it must be confessed to be so. But the judgment of scholarship, like the judgment of judges, is a part of public—that is, political—life, and all political life has, of necessity, an element of arrogance in it.

If Miss Thomas had been willing to call a spade a spade, if she had recognized her own arrogance in presuming to appraise the life's work of a man engaged in one of the highest human pursuits, she might have been more sensitive to and critical of Frankfurter's "humility." The statesman knows that he is not an angel but that he will have to do until one comes along. To know this is to know himself for a potential devil. Statesmanship has in one place been described as the realization that one has the wherewithal to be a tyrant coupled with the preference for not being a tyrant.[59] He who lacks the gifts of a tyrant will never be a statesman, but at best a public administrator. He who, having these gifts, lacks self-awareness will be a slave to the gifts and will enslave his people. He will be, to use a phrase introduced into American politics about seventy years ago and restored as an epithet against Franklin D. Roosevelt, "intoxicated with the exuberance of his own verbosity." His crime, though criminal folly, will be none the less a crime.

But self-awareness is not self-effacement. The ruler who ignores the needs of the ruled or the judge who flies from judgment out of preoccupation with his lack of fitness is guilty of a kind of selfishness. To rule means not to not rule but, as Lincoln put it, to rule rightly "as God gives us to see the right." The general who rends his garments overmuch must retire from the field. Professor Mendelson failed to subject Frankfurter's understanding to critical analysis. To say that the latter is a "humilitarian"[60] is to say what the subject has already said. It has the felicity of a freshly-coined word but it deprives us of the fruits of study and reflection on the costs of judicial humility. Miss Thomas, on the matter of restraint, which, as we have said, is in action what humility is in mood, has gone further in that she approvingly quotes Professor Pritchett's critique.[61] But her approval of Pritchett and consequent disapproval of Frankfurter on this point runs far less than one page and amounts to no more than a mere assertion of disapproval. The doctrine is not stretched to show its full meaning and consequences. While Mendelson does the service of reduction of Frankfurter to the doctrine of restraint, Thomas, for the most part, does not go beyond the classification of doctrines. There is no ordering and relating, no reduction and resolution, and therefore no subjection of the fewest most comprehensive doctrines to vigorous and constructive criticism. As secondary literature it does not *add* much to an understanding of Frankfurter.

Miss Thomas offers a number of fairly sophisticated words and phrases as descriptions of what Frankfurter does and says. We are told that Frankfurter adheres to a "twentieth century variant natural law position"[62] but this turns out to be mere label, for there is no argument, properly speaking, explaining *what* natural law is supposed to be, how the twentieth-century variant varies, or why Frankfurter deserves the label. Further mention of "natural law"[63] displays grave shortcomings in her understanding of it, though it must be stated that her usage of the modifiers "traditional" and "twentieth-century" shows an awareness, not spread universally among constitutional lawyers, that there is an historical problem connected with natural law. But that the problem of the connection between history and nature—between nations and eternity—escapes her is shown by her uncritical usage of the phrase "'eternal verities' of English-speaking peoples."[64] One looks in vain for explicit recognition on her part that that phrase is internally contradictory: what belongs to a nation, by definition, does not belong to eternity.

The problem of history and nature is troublesome for her because the problem of history is troublesome. The whole of Part Three is devoted to it,[65] but we never find out what it is. The first sentence on the last page of the section elicits some hope from the reader: "Judgment is necessary to make history intelligible."[66] But a few lines below we learn that Frankfurter "turns to history for aid in making a choice" between two possible meanings of a term in law: Judgment makes history intelligible; history is the basis of judgment; we need not say what history is because everyone knows—or we dare not because no one knows. The chapter ends with a quotation from Professor Muller's *Uses of the Past*[67] which described the *study* of history as piety. Perhaps piety is only directed at what is unknowable but it does not follow that *whatever* is unknowable must elicit piety. Nor will reliance upon the authority of Professor Muller persuade us that study and piety are the same. Piety may induce scholarship and societies for the preservation of community antiquities may patronize scholars but if the scholar does not rise above his piety and tell the patron some things he does not want to hear he does not give fair value for his money. He gives only what is desired, not what is wanting.

There are other uncritical uses of terms in Thomas. Frankfurter is described as "pragmatic"[68] but comparison will show that, while Frankfurter has used the term "pragmatic" he has done so in the course of discussing a particular and practical legislative attempt. It is one thing to say that the resolution of certain problems involves "pragmatic considerations"; it is quite another thing to call someone a "pragmatic jurist."[69] Thomas' usage of the term "pragmatic" is as loose as her use of the term "natural law," and liberally sprinkling her text with it does not serve to refine our understanding of Frankfurter. Common terms are, of course, to be used as commonly understood. But when the terms are themselves fraught with philosophic difficulties it is better to avoid them than to make common, uncritical use of them. The word "philosophy" illustrates the problem.

> Perhaps the overriding distinguishing characteristic of Justice Frankfurter's opinions is the amount of space he gives to speculation on the nature of the judicial function after the particular points at issue have been decided. Of all the justices since Cardozo he typifies the deepest philosophic approach to the problem. Others may use Supreme Court opinions as tracts for the propagation of political theories; he uses them as vehicles of expression for the distillation of a lifetime's preoccupation with the essence of a judge's role and tasks. His observations on this topic are provocative and profound. Being included in official writings, they have the aura of having been pronounced from the bench and thus psychologically seem to carry more weight. If the function of an opinion is to communicate and educate on the technical points of the law, it is no less important to Justice Frankfurter as the means to familiarize the lower courts and bar with the agony of judging, an agony that is at the core of the judicial function for him.[70]

What this paragraph says is that *other* justices employ opinions for the propagation of political theories but Justice Frankfurter is head-and-shoulders above them for *he* employs opinions for the propagation of political theories. It could only mean something else if philosophizing about "the judge's role and tasks" had nothing to do with politics,[71] or if familiarizing courts and bar with the fruits of one's philosophizing is not "propagating" or if "philosophy" and "theory" dealt with different subjects or were of different rank (which for Miss Thomas, as examination of the passages cited for comparison will show, they are not).

Frankfurter teaches us that the judicial task is not mechanical, it involves the judge in the activity of judgment. Statutes must be construed and we see that they must sometimes be tested by the Constitution. This raises great difficulties because the Constitution itself is subject to construction. We are thus led necessarily to a concern with the problem of the judge's self-conception of the proper performance of his task. Miss Thomas tells us that Frankfurter turns to "federalism"[72] or that he employs "history"[73] or that he is half composed of "sociological jurisprudence"[74] or that he eschews "absolute" solutions[75] and scrupulously avoids "subjectivity."[76] But these words are offered as descriptive and explanatory phrases without any apparent awareness that they are at least as problematic as the words of the Constitution. One last example of the failure of Thomas to improve our understanding will have to do: "It is unfortunate that he feels constrained to recant his fo[r]mer comparison between due process and natural law, for candidness would surely require admission that 'notions of justice of English-speaking peoples' comes very close to being a modern statement of a very old theme."[77] But *how* close it comes and how worthy the "old theme" are precisely the problems and we do not see how that closeness can be affirmed and approved by elsewhere approving Frankfurter on the grounds that the "judiciary demands tough-minded relativists, not soft-hearted absolutists."[78] Is there no third possibility? It is failure to appreciate the possibility of a third alternative (which failure is based on the faulty and relativistic view that the only alternative to relativism is "absolutism"), and not lack of formal drill in torts and admiralty that prevents Thomas' book from fulfilling a useful scholarly task.

The other of the two recent works which is a full-scale book devoted exclusively to the intention of describing and explaining Frankfurter's judicial doctrines or a portion of them is *Justice Frankfurter and Civil Liberties* by Professor Jacobs.[79] It seems superior to that by Thomas for it is not as diffuse. Like Mendelson, Jacobs orders and reduces the data somewhat better. That is, he drives the analysis closer to the point where what might be called the "engine" of Frankfurter's thought is revealed and explained. That engine, or underlying principle, would be that which renders the diverse apparent strands of doctrine mutually consistent. If it is not what, to use Merrill's phrase, makes the judge "tick," it is what makes his several hundred judicial opinions "hang together." Somewhere around or between Mendelson's emphasis upon Frankfurter's concern with "humility" and Jacobs' emphasis upon Frankfurter's concern with the "living" character of the law lies an adequate understanding of what the whole of Frankfurter's contribution to the law means.

Frankfurter has argued that legislation ought not to be construed "pedantically,"[80] that "oversubtle" distinctions should not be made between criminal and "remedial" (i.e., civil *qui tam*) actions[81] and that the Court is not "imprisoned" in a "formal rule" governing its reviewing power.[82] We are told that "equity judges . . . have always escaped the imprisonment of reason and fairness within mechanical concepts of the common law." They are not "balked by the kind of considerations that seemed controlling to a Baron Parke."[83] The Court need not be imprisoned in technicalities because technicalities are simply instrumental to courts' doing their work well and "courts are, after all, in the service of justice."[84] But, on the other hand: "Law is essentially legalistic in the sense that observance of well-recognized procedure is, on balance, socially desirable."[85] And it requires no citations of proof to state that Frankfurter is not surpassed as an exegete of legislative intent, nor to say that "restraint" is inseparable from the avoidance of decision by way of the technical niceties of justicabililty and jurisdiction and deference to legislatures at the expense of substantive concern with their legislation. But, if a decision *is* to be rendered, it must be by "an empiric process, on case to case determinations. Abstract propositions and unquestioned generalities do not furnish answers."[86]

> Particularly in dealing with claims under broad provisions of the Constitution, which derive content by an interpretive process of inclusion and exclusion, it is imperative that generalizations, based on and qualified by the concrete situations that give rise to them, must not be applied out of context in disregard of variant controlling facts.[87]

But when should the judge be restrained and technical and when should he break from the bondage of technicalities and concern himself with "reason and fairness"? Having broken from that bondage and thrown himself into the freer but harder life of the judicial "agony," when the judge ponders the generalizations of past decisions in the factual context which fostered them, how does he know what the "facts" are? In the light of what does he know a fact for a fact and understand its meaning that he might understand the generalization it fostered? We are told that "laws are not abstract propositions,"[88] that "adjusting remedy to policy" is "an empiric process."[89] Even the interpretation and application of laws follows the same process, for, with respect to the judicial task, Frankfurter remarks that "experience counsels empiricism."[90]

In the course of showing that Frankfurter is "pragmatic"[91] Professor Jacobs explains:

> The justice's insistence on rigorous observance of seemingly technical rules regarding ripeness and standing and his disposition to avoid constitutional adjudication wherever a rationally tenable statutory ground for decision is available, are important manifestations of his strong feeling against judicial consideration of abstract constitutional questions—against decision making in a factual vacuum. . . .
> Facts alone are not, of course, enough. Constitutional adjudication [when reached] presupposes reference to those principles and values from which American society takes its bearings, but the facts of a specific case determine what principles are relevant to judgment. Moreover, the dimensions of each relevant principle, for Frankfurter, must be discovered in a factual context. Civil liberties are not self-defining abstractions; rather they are *functions* of life in a free but

ordered society. With respect to some, most notably the specific procedural safeguards, their dimensions are defined with relative clarity by history, and judicial discretion in making adjustments is accordingly limited. But as to the scope and meaning of others, including the freedoms of the First Amendment, history is more ambiguous, although it amply attests to their vital importance in an open society. With respect to them, Frankfurter's approach is empirical. These liberties, whether viewed as principles or values, are not absolutes but relatives originating in human experience and providing direction for the solution of present and future social problems.[92]

Apparently in a "free but ordered society," certain liberties will be kept safe. Some of the things which guard their safety are explained by past history, others by current history. That is, in some cases we are to be guided by the experience of our predecessors and in others by that and our own experience. And experience counsels that we be not only guided but directed by experience. If anything directs the experience it is liberty and order. But everyone knows that the "clash" of liberties sometimes threatens order. Jacobs seems to say that in the interest of the *principle* of liberty, actual liberties must be ordered. The "clash" presents a "social problem." The "solution" of such problems is to be directed by experience, including experience yet-to-be. But this seems to us inadequate. Let us speculate on the future for a moment, calling forth a vision of a "parade of the horribles."[93]

Everyone except the blindest of well-wishers recognizes that the existence of the negro in America presents a difficult social problem. Various opportunities have presented themselves for the solution of that problem, the problem having been bequeathed to the nation before it came into being as a nation-state. Various elements in the country pressed for solution between, say, 1819 and 1861. Some of these elements were more, some less, sensible; some more, some less, generous. Other elements in the country objected to interference with their liberty—liberty of property in slaves. Still other elements thought eventual solution desirable, but all proposals "too expensive." The Civil War was hardly an "economical" solution, but it was nonetheless fought. The *present* difficulty with respect to the negro in America presents interesting similarities. Various elements offer proposals—more or less sensible and more or less generous. Various other elements object to all the proposals as encroachments upon *their* liberties. Some feel free to ride in buses contrary to one set of laws. Others feel free to *burn* buses contrary to any set of laws. Still others feel free to prosecute one but not the other of these freedom-loving people. Other elements like some or all of the proposals but are sure we can't afford any of them. Taxes, it is said in a country sick with money, are "too high." The "government" must not "do too much." Especially, it ought not to hamper our liberty or property with excessive taxes. If we are very lucky, the problem might solve itself.

Nobody in his right mind really expects the "South to rise again," but no one can be so prophetic as to assure us that the Russians will leave us alone to solve our problems, or that the passionate rise of colored peoples throughout the world will not have sudden and radical effects within the United States, or that the continued urbanization, industrialization, and mobility of America will not reach such proportions as to aggravate the problem in question. It must be remembered that we are now talking about "luck" as well as about statesmanship and judgment; not simply about what *might* happen but about what we ought to *make* happen, if we can. The experiences yet-to-be, within which that making must take place include an indefinite number of potential aggravations, both domestic and foreign and both accidental and provoked. Professor Jacobs speaks of "the solution of present and future social problems" but he does not tell us what is true and what false solution. What experience teaches is itself a problem. If our present corps of historians is right what we ought to have learned from the Civil War is that our mistake was to try *any* solution to the then existing problem. Should we let "present and future social problems" solve themselves? Or, if not, when we attempt "solutions" in the light of what do we choose one experience, or something yet-to-be experienced, in preference to another experience? Can experience guide experience? In our reliance upon experience for the "solution" of "social problems" in the "future" we cannot but be struck with terror in reflecting upon a recent experience, elsewhere, with the attempted "final solution of the Jewish problem." And yet Jacobs tells us:

Men and society take their bearings not from a single star but
from a constellation, and whatever may be the immediate goal,
the ultimate destination, if any, remains unknown.[94]

Jacobs reports approvingly that Frankfurter found nothing
contrary to due process in electrocuting someone after a first attempt
to execute him had ended in failure,[95] but that it *does* so offend due
process to execute an insane man.[96] Why is the one thing "out" and
the other "in"?

> For Frankfurter [due process and equal protection] have an
> historic content, which is conceived broadly as running back to
> Magna Charta and as possessing contemporary relevance. But
> the meaning of these provisions is not exhausted by their historic
> content. Frankfurter perceives a dynamic society in which the
> struggle for justice and freedom continues: these provisions
> contemplate the enduring residue of that struggle.[97]

Jacobs tells us that Frankfurter "has sought external, impersonal
standards for guidance in due process cases."[98]

> Due process, as conceived by Frankfurter, is both a historical
> and a "generative" principle. As a product of history due
> process reflects the more or less enduring residue of the
> Anglo-American struggle for liberty, and as a generative
> principle it takes into account the possibility of further
> progress.[99]

"Enduring residue of the Anglo-American struggle for liberty" is a
handsome phrase but the usage Jacobs gives it does not promote
clarity of understanding. Due process is divided into "history" and a
"generative principle" and in one instance we are told that the
"historical" part is the "residue"[100] but in another it would appear
that the "generative" part, or perhaps the two parts together,
constitute that "residue."[101] What Jacobs says, of course, does not
conclude the question as to what Frankfurter says or means. But that
the attempt by Jacobs to explain Frankfurter culminates in a vague
felicity may be an indication of the true explanation of Frankfurter.
The latter does look to tradition for the content of due process and he
does maintain that the tradition is a continuing one. Jacobs, while
clearer and more direct than Thomas, does not help us to understand

Frankfurter for, at best, he simply restates him. He does not expose to understanding the meaning of that reliance upon tradition. If Jacobs' restatement is fully accurate, then Frankfurter himself culminates in a vague felicity.

Frankfurter admonishes us that Supreme Court justices may not prevent Louisiana's making a second attempt to execute Willie Francis "no matter how strong one's personal feeling of revulsion against a State's insistence on its pound of flesh."[102] No matter *how* strong? Apparently this is the case, for it is not the "personal" conscience of the judge that matters; it is something "impersonal" called "the conscience of mankind,"[103] or "our historic heritage," which *does* forbid executing the insane.[104] In other words, what is forbidden is what has always revolted everybody, or at least all Englishmen, or at the very least all Englishmen in America—or, anyhow, somebody other than or in addition to the judge doing the forbidding. But have "we" *been*, or are "we" now, more revolted by the execution of the insane than by the execution of someone whom we have tried once before, unsuccessfully, to execute? Would a public opinion poll help here?

Frankfurter cites Hale and Blackstone against executing those who have gone insane after conviction and sentence on the grounds that "'the law knows not but he might have offered some reason, if in his senses, to have stayed these respective proceedings.'"[105] But such an argument is nearly as good against the death penalty, as such, as it is against infliction of the death penalty on the insane, for the law knows not but that someone whose execution is set for three months after conviction and who until the last moment excitedly and passionately protests his innocence might, after, say, six months calm down, rethink the criminative evidence presented against him, rereason what it would take to refute it and, generally, "see through" the problem so as to prove his innocence or extenuate his guilt. If it be answered that he ought to have done that prior to the trial, we are at a loss to know why rehearings are permitted for the introduction of new evidence, and we must note that what is true of new evidence situations here is also true of cases of supervening insanity. If allowing *no* post-conviction opportunity appears unjust and *some* time is to be provided, and it be said that those who go insane ought to have the benefit of that time equally with those who do not go insane, we must ask whether there is any criterion by which we might set the time between conviction and execution. Suppose in one instance a fully sane man is executed thirty days after conviction and in another instance a man is committed to psychiatric care eighty-eight days after conviction and two days before his scheduled time for execution. Suppose sheer terror drives a man mad on "the last mile." Should *he* be spared?

The time elapsed between conviction and falling mad apparently does not matter, for Frankfurter cites another authority to the effect that it is "'against Christian Charity to send a great Offender . . . into another World, when he is not of a capacity to fit himself for it.'"[106] Now, "Christian Charity" is a "term of art"—that is, it is not to be understood according to the "plain meaning of the words" but according to church authority—and we strongly doubt that it is the duty of the Supreme Court to compel the Georgia courts to conform to it in passing on the administrative procedure employed to test allegations of supervening insanity. But even if we were charitable in our application of terms and transmuted "Christian Charity" into "the conscience of mankind" which is not revolted by the second attempt to execute Francis and, by *that* measure test Georgia's sending Solesbee "into another World" without allowing him an adversary proceeding in which to prove that he was "not of a capacity to fit himself for it," we would still face some difficulties. It is not impertinent to our argument to suggest that the corps of teachers of Constitutional Law in America (and we do not exclude teachers in colleges and universities wholly or partly supported by Christian funds) might supply expert testimony on what the present "conscience" of American "mankind" thinks about the proposition that we ought not to execute someone who is not fit to meet his maker. Not a few students laugh aloud and, enlightened and emancipated, dismiss all such talk as "medieval."

The authority against sending the mentally incapacitated into the other world whom Frankfurter quotes is Sir John Hawles. Hawles made these comments in the House of Commons in 1689. The comments were made in criticism of a series of trials conducted in the reign of James II, between whose reign and William's the "Glorious Revolution" had intervened. The comments concerned several trials. Those comments are cut up and parcelled out among the volumes of

State Trials, appropriate parts being appended to the respective trials. One of the trials was that of Bateman in 1685 and it is to the report of this trial that the passage quoted by Frankfurter is appended. Another of the trials criticized in Hawles' speech in the House of Commons was that of Stephen Colledge.[107] Hawles had been Colledge's assigned counsel.[108]

According to Frankfurter, "However quaint these ancient authorities of our law may sound to our ears, the Twentieth Century has not so far progressed as to outmode their reasoning."[109] We cannot but agree that authorities are not to be dismissed on account of quaintness. But what makes one an authority, and how authoritative are authorities? Frankfurter quotes approvingly Hawles' contention that sentence ought not to be executed upon a man gone mad, but Hawles' comments were made after the Bateman case and after the revolution that displaced the regime which had tried Bateman, and the reports show that *the sentence was executed*.[110] Why does Frankfurter take Hawles as an authority and ignore the authority of the court Hawles censures? Why does he quote approvingly Hawles' censure of the Bateman trial[111] and describe Hawles as an authority while ignoring what Hawles himself said—a few lines after his censure—about authorities?

> But I think it is fit for me to make some apology for the thing, and for myself, for taking on me to censure the opinions and actions of persons whose characters carried authority with them. I confess I never thought that either the great seal or a garment added to a man's sense, learning or honesty. . . .[112]

Perhaps Frankfurter ignores this part of Hawles' remarks because it is not particularly relevant to the question of executing the insane. But that Hawles *said* this reminds us of the fact that Frankfurter has stated, contrary to Hawles, that the gown *does* change the man—"if he is any good."[113] This draws the "authority" of Hawles into question. Of course in the passage on seals and garments, a portion of which we quoted, Hawles goes on to indicate that the particular wearers of seals and garments he is censuring were pretty *bad* and so he and Frankfurter may be in agreement. But if authorities are to be dismissed because they are bad it cannot be the *authority* of authorities which makes them authoritative; it must be their goodness.

Why does Frankfurter prefer the authority of Hawles to that of the court Hawles censures? We cannot suppose that Frankfurter is tinged with partisan feelings respecting the revolution of 1688 and favors Hawles because he was on the right side—who in turn perhaps censured the 1685 court for executing Bateman for plotting against James simply because he, Hawles, was in sympathy with the plot. Can it be because Hawles' authority is four years later than the censured court's? No. For if that were the reason then Mr. Justice Black (who wrote the Court opinion from which Frankfurter dissented in the *Solesbee* case) would have every right to regard Hawles as "quaint" 261 years after his censure.

Can it be because the court which sentenced Bateman made an erratic departure from an established tradition and Hawles is the true spokesman of, the restorer of, the tradition? Is, then, the tradition itself the authority? But every schoolboy *does* know that if one goes back far enough in the English tradition looking for standards as to what does not revolt the conscience there comes a point of diminishing returns. If not 1688 what is the point? 1485? 1066? 1832?

If the *tradition* is the authority and Hawles' censure of the Bateman trial is simply a restoration and vindication of it then the tradition must be examined. One thing of particular interest to students of due process stands out in that tradition. It is a thing which Frankfurter does not speak of. It is the *sentence* which was executed upon Bateman:

> That he should return to the place from whence he came, from thence to be drawn to the place of execution, there to be hanged by the neck, and whilst alive be cut down, and his bowels to be taken out and burnt; his head to be severed from his body, and his body divided into four parts, and that his head and quarters be disposed at the pleasure of the king.[114]

We have no doubt that "disposed at the pleasure of the king" is a "term of art" meaning simply that the five parts of Bateman might be displayed about town wherever the king liked. But the rest of the sentence is plain talk and requires no rules of construction to be understood. Whatever may be the guilt or innocence, sanity or insanity of Charles Bateman, we are bound to wonder whether a fully sane, manifestly guilty man who has committed a grave offense should be drawn, hanged until half dead, disemboweled, beheaded and quartered and then displayed in five different places at once. If what falls below the demands of due process is what revolts not just this or that hyper-sensitive judge, but the "conscience" of mankind," how does one establish what that conscience is and what it forbids? Bateman's sentence was not unique. It was standard fare for high treason, and high treason was standard fare for English courts. If Georgia or Alaska should choose to draw, disembowel and quarter fully sane and manifestly guilty doers of great crimes would the due process clause bar their choice? Could something be "downright fraud[ulent]"[115] and yet nothing be "downright" revolting? Can the "land" make *anything* due process of law "by its mere will"? Is it simply absurd to speak of a land or a tradition as being replete with or marred by revolting processes? Surely, revulsion is in the viscera of the revolted, but does the fact that almost any process one could imagine has found approval by some tradition somewhere mean that there is *nothing* which is, in itself, revolting?

The Court has to "thread" its way, term after term, through particular cases to determine due process.[116] For the "standards of justice" imposed by due process are, contrary to Black's interpretation of the intention of the framers of the Fourteenth Amendment, "not authoritatively formulated anywhere as though they were prescriptions in a pharmacopoeia."[117] Perhaps this imposes a great burden on the judges who must thread the way, but there "is no escape" from an appeal to due process.[118] And, while due process is not a technical formula, not an authoritative prescription, neither is it personal whim,[119] but "respect enforced by law for that feeling of just treatment which has been evolved through centuries of Anglo-American constitutional history and civilization,"[120] and so one must inquire into what is just treatment—unless there is a difference between that and a *"feeling"* of just treatment—and into evolution, history, civilization and, particularly, Anglo-American civilization.

But to speak of history is to speak of a very dark thing. It is, in a way, everything that ever happened. But that cannot be what is meant, for almost everything imaginable *has* happened and, on the other hand, all that has happened is not open to us. Maybe "history" is what has been written about what has happened but that, too, is unsatisfactory for the record is nearly as bulky and just as enigmatic as the series of events it imperfectly records. Perhaps "history" is the "stream" of history—the direction in which the events ineluctably move—but then that is not history but something which it is said is seen within it. But it must be something more like the last-named than like the former two, for much of what has happened is irrelevant. That on a particular Tuesday in Springfield Mrs. Moriarity was so angered by her husband's drinking that she failed to pick up Judge Brown's laundry cannot concern us unless Judge Brown was so distracted by having to wear a soiled shirt that he gave short shrift to defense counsel's objections to the prosecutor's intemperate badgering of witnesses. Even in that case we are only peripherally concerned, for the *significant* historical data are not Moriarity's thirst and his wife's anger but the prosecutor's intemperance, the judge's childish preoccupation, and the adequacy of post-conviction remedies fashioned. But to know what are significant data means to assign limits to what we will consider. These limits may be classifications of actions or of actors or they may exclude on the basis of geography or time or they may take into account that this or that event is a violent and transitory aberration and therefore to be excluded. But to draw such limits means to have regard for what is wanted and what is wanted is due process and we are back at the beginning. Why, for example, *Anglo-American* history? Frankfurter does not hesitate to cite an Indian case[121] when he picks his way along the "slippery slope of due process."[122] But, obviously, Anglo-Indian law inextricably marries what is Anglo to what is Indian. Will not what is Indian then make its way through what is Anglo-Indian and, thence, through the Anglo-American to affect what is American? In the "gradual process of exclusion and inclusion" should the Indian be let in or kept out? Whichever way, why?

Whatever may be the classificatory, spatial, or temporal limits marking the significance of data, a number of special problems occur within one of the universally accepted classes. Obviously, within the temporal and spatial limits set, what former judges have opined—precedent—will count, as will "legislative history"—i.e., what legislators said in debate over proposals and what they did not say but what must have been in their minds[123]—and a complete record of previous attempts to deal with similar mischief as well as a complete record of the mischief itself. The darkness of the legislative history of the Fourteenth Amendment with which we earlier dealt[124] and which Frankfurter notes[125] is only illustrative of the darkness of all legislative history. That darkness is in large measure imposed by the shadow of the debatability of and consequent debate over what is and what is not mischief.

But an exhaustive treatise on the problematic character of history is thankfully not requisite here. An indication of the difficulties posed by one part of history—precedent—will serve as an example sufficient for the present purpose. In one instance Frankfurter spoke of the "whole Philosophy of our law" as being "based on precedent."[126] Even when constitutional questions are involved the Court "should not be unmindful . . . of the principle of *stare decisis* by whose circumspect observance the wisdom of this Court as an institution transcending the moment can alone" be effective.[127] Special explanation is called for "when an important shift in constitutional doctrine is announced after a reconstruction in the membership of the Court. Such shifts of opinion . . . must be duly mindful of the necessary demands of continuity in a civilized society."[128]

> We recognize that *stare decisis* embodies an important social policy. It represents an element of continuity in law, and is rooted in the psychological need to satisfy reasonable expectations.[129]

Professor Mendelson advises us that judges are mediators between continuity and change[130] but he does not adequately explain the standard of mediation. Earlier in the same work he states:

> For Mr. Justice Black, plainly the essence of law is Justice—as he sees it. . . . In contrast, the essence of law for Mr. Justice Frankfurter is regularity and uniformity.[131]

It is proper to say that the essence of law for Frankfurter (and, as we now customarily use the term "law," for everybody else, too) is regularity and uniformity. But the implication that regularity is *preferable* to justice, or that Frankfurter so believes, overlooks the fact "that courts of law are, after all, in the service of justice."[132] As we suggested above[133] an essential element of law is the principle of expectation, or stability. A man must know what is expected of him and what he, in turn, has a right to expect. It must be noted that what *stare decisis* embodies, according to Frankfurter, is not law itself, but an *element* in law. It is—one might say *merely*—"an important social policy," and it is concerned not with *any* expectation, but only with *"reasonable* expectations." What may a man reasonably expect? That is, once again, the whole problem of due process. Surely judges do participate in the mediation between continuity and change and if the choice were presented in such a way, devoid of all other consider-ations, any sober judge would *always* prefer continuity, but of course the choice is *never* presented in such a way to any judge. It is always rather that some claimed thing calls for a change and another claimed thing relies on continuity. It is between the *claims* that the judge mediates. Because continuity, as such, is preferable to change, as such, the sober judge would, if he could, continue the law as it had been rather than change it. This is not because judicial sobriety is the equivalent of a kind of hardening of the moral arteries. In a day when prevalent opinion regards novelty as a merit in a thing it is difficult to appreciate that there have been days when novelty was considered a defect. Our preoccupation with "breakthroughs" and "frontiers" clouds the fact that in public matters the burden is upon change to prove that it is change for the better. Continuity need not bear such a burden. It is, in itself a human good. Law, as such, is a rule or standard of action. While it is true that one can "change the rules" it is no less true that "change" and "rules" are contradictory terms.

It is not that regularity or continuity is preferable to justice. It is a *part* of justice. It is so because justice is the greatest benefit to men and men are incapable of benefiting or being benefited if they cannot know what to expect or what is expected. Professor Thomas describes Frankfurter's position on precedent and continuity better than Mendelson does[134] but she seems to draw back from the task of going beyond description.[135] It may be that her use of the word "organic"[136] or Professor Jacobs' use of the word "empiric"[137] in this context at least puts the capstone on the description. But, once again, there is no critique of the "organic" or "empiricist" view.

So important is continuity—law, in a sense, *being* continuity—that Frankfurter wisely affirms, by contrasting Hohenzollern with Nazi

Germany, that even relatively bad law is superior to lawlessness.[138] Once again, this is not because law, or continuity, is enough. It is not enough because the continuity of law extends in two dimensions. Not only does it run in time, against the course of changing circumstances, but, at any one time it extends to all men with respect to classes of circumstance and it ignores the shadings of men and circumstances. That is, an attribute of law akin to its continuity is its universality. More even than continuity is universality "the essence" of law. There is a fixity about law. This is what it is good for. This is its excellence. But its very excellence is at once its fault. At least since Aristotle, equity has been understood to be that which mends the rigors of law in the name of justice.[139] If one immortal being who always knew what benefited each man and always willed that each man be benefited were to be recognized as such by all men and were to concern himself immediately with all the affairs of all men, then it would be silly vanity to speak of powers, of liberty, or of law. Justice would lie in that being having absolute discretion and in all men giving absolute obedience to it. And to speak of such a thing as justice is at once to speak, at least allegorically, of such a being. But to speak of such a "thing" as justice, as opposed to speaking of just actions or just men (that is, of justice relative to men and circumstances, and therefore to speak relatively of justice) is to theorize about justice or to speak of justice-in-theory. The practical problem arises in practice. That is, the problem of the relation between justice and law is precisely that of the relation between theory and practice. That relation is in the nature of compromise. Frankfurter, in discussing the relation between theory and practice, recognizes this by the use of the expression "a world of compromise."[140]

There are two senses in which one may use the expression "good lawyer." On the one hand, the word "good" may be relative to the word lawyer. One the other hand, it may be used to modify "lawyer" with "goodness." That is, while one may speak metaphorically of a "good thief," the term "good thief" is, in the other sense, a contradiction in terms. If one is to speak of the merely good lawyer he cannot thus be speaking of the truly good lawyer. If we are to measure, then, the excellence of a judge, it will not do to stop at the question of his view of the "role of the judge in a democracy" or even at that of the "role of the judge," for the answer to that question depends upon the answer to the question of the relation between theory and practice. For if "courts of law are, after all, in the service of justice," and law is to justice what practice is to theory and the one is related to the other by compromise, then how "good" a lawyer or a judge is will depend on how he understands the character of that compromise. The judge may have a faulty view of the character of the compromise because he is "out of touch" with actualities. He may be "living in the past" and may thus ignore the needs of the present. But what is presently needful does not arise simply out of the present. How the judge understands the compromise depends also on how he understands that which is being compromised. The true measure of the judge's worth depends in part, then, upon the measure of his understanding of justice.

To speak of "history" in speaking of justice is to suggest that justice is somehow immanent in some stream of things; in the actualities. But if justice is not—to turn one of Frankfurter's favorite Holmesian phrases about—a "brooding omnipresence" in the actualities, it must reside elsewhere. If practice is somehow a compromise of theory, then the theoretical is at least not obviously an extrusion of the practical. Justice is not obviously an arithmetic mean or least common denominator of laws. Frankfurter's concept of the relation between practice and theory is identical to what we have called his conception of the relation between the personal and the impersonal.[141] As compared to the measurement of a judge's views on the personal, or practical, measurement of his views on the impersonal, or theoretical—on justice as such—is very difficult. But it is the crucial measure. To speak of "humility" with respect to one's views of justice is not enough. Humility and consequent taciturnity explain little. No matter how humbly the judge may restrain himself from expressing views on the subject of justice, we must know those views if we are to measure his worth. Because a judge's understanding of the actualities is fairly easy to measure it is not so difficult to notice those judges who, like some on the pre-1937 Court, do not "believe in" the twentieth century. It does not oversimplify the matter to say that the remedy is relatively simple. One may "put the fear of God" in the judges as Frankfurter tells us the first Roosevelt did, or one may "pack" the Court with friends of the present as the second Roosevelt tried to do sooner and did do eventually. But a court may believe wholeheartedly in the twentieth century, as the present Court does, and not know what to do with it.

Continuity is, in itself, a good thing and change, while inconvenient, is necessary. Whenever changes are necessary, they are to be made with the least inconvenience to continuity which is possible. That is, continuity is to be preserved whenever possible. But that change is allowed *at all* demonstrates that continuity is not the ultimate measure.

> But considerations pertaining to *stare decisis* do raise a serious question for me. That principle is a vital ingredient of law, for it "embodies an important social policy." *Helvering* v. *Hallock*, 309 U.S. 106, 119. It would disregard the principle for a judge stubbornly to persist in his views . . . after the contrary had become part of the tissue of the law. Until then, full respect for *stare decisis* does not require a judge to forego his own convictions promptly after his brethren have rejected them.[142]

How long does it take for a view to become "part of the tissue of the law"?

> As one swallow does not make a summer . . . one ruling hardly establishes a practice . . .[143]

How many swallows make a summer? Apparently four swallows make a summer, for in an opinion rendered one week after the one from which the last quotation came we are told that four uniform decisions make law that should not be overruled.[144] But the comfort derived from such mathematical neatness is short-lived for, while it may not be necessary "to burn the house to roast the pig"[145] it may be necessary to kill a whole flock of swallows to give the house a new coat of paint for in disposing of a case which revolved around the legal status of women, Frankfurter dismissed Blackstone's views on the subject as "self-deluding romanticism" and overturned six centuries of precedent.

> The true significance of [a particular] decision . . . is not to be found in the Court's failure to respect *stare decisis*. The extent to which judges should feel in duty bound not to innovate is a perennial problem, and the pull of the past is different among different judges as it is in the same judge about different aspects of the past.[146]

The example afforded by the problem of precedent may serve to illustrate the problem of history in general and some summary comment on the general problem will carry the argument to its next step. The "pull of the past" in Frankfurter is fairly conclusive with respect to several specific provisions of the Constitution. In the treatment of such provisions, he is fond of quoting Holmes' admonition that "'a page of history is worth a volume of logic,'"[147] and in such cases, as in the case of statutory construction, one cannot justify a "novel view" in the "face of consistent and compelling inferences to be drawn from history and policy" by "empty logic, reflecting a formal syllogism."[148] Such confinement of provisions not only keeps a claimant from expecting more from them than he has a right to expect; it also assures him that he will not get less than he has a right to expect, for the "winds of logic" must not detract from constitutional limitations what the "depth and toughness of their roots in the past" assure.[149]

But not only are the specific provisions construed in the light of history. Even the "vague contours" of the due process clause are filled in by historical research. If a state "arbitrarily curtails one of those liberties of the individual, now enshrined in the Due Process Clause of the Fourteenth Amendment, that history has attested as the indispensable conditions for the maintenance and progress of a free society," that curtailment must be reversed.[150] Of course, that a particular "liberty" has been "enshrined in the Due Process Clause" says nothing about what constitutes a due taking of it. But the enshrined liberty in this particular case is that of the press, protected by the First Amendment from abridgment by the United States, and, while the "'liberty' secured by the Fourteenth Amendment summarizes the experience of history,"[151] the nature of that liberty and what constitutes its abridgment is also disclosed by history. That is, while it may be that the enshrinement in the Fourteenth Amendment of the First Amendment by history does not show what a due taking of its parts would be, since the character of the protection of the First Amendment is itself historically resolved, so due taking, in the Fourteenth Amendment sense, is also resolved historically, and so, for example:

> Our whole history repels the view that it is an exercise of one
> of the civil liberties secured by the Bill of Rights for a leader of a

large following or for a powerful metropolitan newspaper to attempt to overawe a judge in a matter immediately pending before him.[152]

All would be constrained to agree that if a particular activity has always been curtailed in a particular way and no objection to that curtailment has ever been credited, an essentially identical manifestation of that activity cannot claim that a constitutional provision protecting the activity, which provision has always stood side by side with repeated instances of the particular curtailment, prohibits the curtailment. The actors in the past have never expected immunity from such curtailment and therefore such immunity cannot be one of the expectations held out by the protection and therefore a present actor has no right to expect such immunity. But history is seldom so unambiguous. If it were, there would be no problem in the relation between continuity and change. If a claimant tries, by "empty logic," to say that the words of a law promise him that which the law, having stood for a very long time, has never given, it makes sense to refute him with the "empty logic" of history. History *is* empty logic here because all it says is that what is unchanged is unchanged. There will always be such claimants and so it will frequently be necessary to offer renewed refutations. But things do change.

> Mere age may establish due process, but due process does not preclude new ends of government or new means for achieving them.[153]

New governmental ends and means inevitably involve new deprivations of life, liberty, and property[154] and inevitably raise new expectations. Due process promises not only that continuity will continue—a matter of empty logic—and that change will only occur if it is necessary—a matter of "social policy." It also promises that when changes *are* necessary, whatever the changes, a man will be able to expect what he has a right to expect. And while "history" may appear to solve some problems under the due process clause, Frankfurter explicitly states that history is not enough, that due process is more than or different from an historical matter.[155]

NOTES TO CHAPTER V

[1]See Henry M. Hart, Jr., "The Time Chart of the Justices," Foreword to "The Supreme Court, 1958 Term," *Harvard Law Review*, LXXIII (November, 1959), 84.

[2]*The American Commonwealth* I (New York: Macmillan, 1888), pp. 340-41.

[3]See Frankfurter's article on "The Supreme Court of the United States," in the *Encyclopedia of the Social Sciences*, XIV (1934), 424. Reprinted in Felix Frankfurter, *Law and Politics: Occasional Papers of Felix Frankfurter 1913-1938*, ed. Archibald MacLeish and E.F. Prichard (New York: Capricorn Books, 1962), pp. 22-23. (The pagination in the 1962 paperback is identical with that in the 1939 Harcourt-Brace edition.) (Hereinafter cited as *L and P.*) See also his "Child Labor and the Court," *ibid.*, pp. 206-07.

[4]*United States* v. *Butler*, 297 U.S. 1 at 62.

[5]*Op. cit.*, p. 130.

[6]*Op. cit.*, I, 329.

[7]1 Cr. 137.

[8]8 S.&R. 330 at 344-58.

[9]*Ibid.*, p. 348.

[10]John Locke, *Two Treatises of Government*, ed. P. Laslett (Cambridge: Cambridge University Press, 1960), chapters xi-xii.

[11]*Federalist*, #49, the last two paragraphs.

[12]Bryce, *op. cit.*, I, 335.

[13]*Ibid.*, p. 336.

[14]*Ibid.*, p. 337.

[15]*Ibid.*, p. 328.

[16]"Suppose, however," someone may say, "that the Court should go beyond its duty and import its own views of what ought to be the law into its decisions as to what is the law. This would be an exercise of judicial will." Doubtless it would, but it would be a breach of duty, would expose the court to the distrust of the people, and might, if repeated or persisted in in a serious matter, provoke resistance to the law as laid down by the court. See chapter xxxiii, *post*. (Footnote by Bryce.)

[17]". . . The doctrine of the *Dred Scott* case . . . was set aside by the fourteenth amendment, but that amendment was intended to effect much more than merely to correct the courts." (Footnote, of which the relevant parts are reproduced, by Bryce.)

[18]Bryce, *op. cit.*, pp. 337-39. Also in the paperback edition, ed. Louis Hacker (New York: Capricorn Books, 1959), I, 60-61.

[19]*Ibid.*, pp. 486-87. Bryce's note omitted. This passage is not reproduced in the paperback edition.

[20]*West Virginia State Board of Education* v. *Barnette*, 319 U.S. 624. Frankfurter dissenting, at 666.

[21]Joseph Alsop and Turner Catledge, *The 168 Days* (Garden City, N.Y.: Doubleday, 1938), p. 76.

[22]See an article by Morton J. Frisch on the struggle over Roosevelt's judiciary bill soon to be published (early 1963) in the *Journal of Politics*.

[23]See a discussion of this matter in Thomas, *op. cit.*, chapter xii, especially pp. 286-89. And see Mendelson, *op. cit.*, p. 47 and chapter v.

[24]Dissenting in *United States ex rel Knauff* v. *Shaugnessy*, 338 U.S. 537 at 548 and again at 550 (1950).

[25]*Pope* v. *Atlantic Coast Line R. Co.*, 345 U.S. 379, Frankfurter dissenting, at 392.

[26]*San Diego Union* v. *Garmon*, 359 U.S. 236, Frankfurter for the Court, at 243.

[27]357 U.S. 371 at 378.

[28]343 U.S. 579.

[29]*I.C.C.* v. *J-T Transport Co.*, 368 U.S. 81 (1961), Frankfurter dissenting, at 107.

[30]Berns, *op. cit.*, pp. 178-79.

[31]An item in the *New Republic* entitled "The Red Terror of Judicial Reform," reprinted in *L and P*, p. 16.

[32]Concurring in *Joint Anti-Fascist Refugee Committee* v. *McGrath*, 341 U.S. 123 at 174. And see Frankfurter's "Talk to Members of the Council and the Faculty," in *Proceedings in Honor of Mr. Justice Frankfurter and Distinguished Alumni*, Harvard Law School Occasional Pamphlet No. 3, 1960, p. 43.

[33]To say that it was "not the 'same man' who spoke in 1951 as the one who had spoken in 1924" does not suggest "evolution" for, except for the literary inhibitions which realization of the embarrassment involved in so stark and rapid a change might impose, we can imagine the change from vigorous advocate to dutiful judge not only in twenty-seven years, but in twenty-seven days. Every lawyer who has moved from private practice to public office—and such moves occur overnight—can appreciate this.

[34]See the discussion of this matter in Thomas, *op. cit.*, p. 282, and see the last sentence of the first of Frankfurter's pieces (1912), reprinted in *L and P*, p. 9. The last word of that first piece is, significantly, "democracy." See also, *L and M*, p. 18.

[35]Evidence of his irony can be seen in his reversal, in *Mishawaka Mfg. Co.* v. *S.S. Kresge Co.*, 316 U.S. 203, 208, of a dime store's defense against a trademark infringement suit by a heel manufacturer, which defense argued that the trademark holder had to prove not only that the mark had been copied but also that the profit accruing to the copier was the result of the psychological effect of the mark on the purchaser, on the grounds that "the shoe is on the other foot."

[36]"The Supreme Court of the United States," reprinted in *L and P*, pp. 21-33.

[37]*Ibid.*, p. 32.

[38]*Ibid.*, p. 29.

[39]"The Red Terror of Judicial Reform," *ibid.*, p. 16.

[40]*Ibid.*, p. 8.

[41]*Ibid.*, pp. 7-8.

[42]*Ibid.*, p. 15. Compare his 1955 refutation of the prevalent notion that the 1937 hearkening had been due to such fear. *L and M*, pp. 204, 206-12.

[43]*L and P*, p. 15.

[44]*Ibid.*, p. 16. Cf. Wallace Mendelson, "Foreign Reactions to American Experience With 'Due Process of Law,'" *Virginia Law Review*, XLI (May, 1955), 493.

[45]*L and P*, p. 13.

[46]*Moore* v. *Dempsey*, 261 U.S. 86.

[47]268 U.S. 652.

[48]283 U.S. 697.

[49]The "Scottsboro" case, 287 U.S. 45.

[50]302 U.S. 319.

[51]"The Supreme Court Writes a Chapter on Man's Rights," reprinted in *L and P*, pp. 189-94.

[52]Reprinted in *L and M,* pp. 196-203. See especially pp. 202-03. Cardozo's *Palko* opinion does not appear to us to be superior to Matthews' *Hurtado* or Moody's *Twining* opinion in explicating due process, but it may be that Frankfurter was not thoroughly familiar with the latter two opinions in 1924. That is, it may be that his energies and attention were turned so much in other directions that, although he no doubt knew of the cases and of the reasoning of the opinions in them, he had not gotten the "feel" of them.

[53]See *infra,* pp. 197, 225-26.

[54]Thomas, *op. cit.*

[55]Book Review, *Oklahoma Law Review,* XIII (November, 1960), 476.

[56]See Miss Thomas' observations on the question raised by Merrill. Thomas, p. 345. And see also Frankfurter, "Social Issues Before the Supreme Court," in *L and P,* p. 52, and "The Zeitgeist and the Judiciary," *ibid.,* p. 3.

[57]Merrill, *op. cit.*

[58]Frankfurter dissenting in *First Iowa Hydro-Electric Corp.* v. *Commissioner,* 328 U.S. 152 at 187.

[59]H. Jaffa, *Crisis of the House Divided* (New York: Doubleday, 1959), chapter ix, and especially pp. 218 and 222.

[60]Mendelson, *op. cit.,* p. 124.

[61]Thomas, *op. cit.,* p. 288, quoting C. Herman Pritchett, *Civil Liberties and the Vinson Court* (Chicago: University of Chicago Press, 1954), p. 245.

[62]Thomas, *op. cit.,* p. 161.

[63]*Ibid.,* p. 172. Cf. pp. 153, 162, 231, 362.

[64]*Ibid.* Some hesitancy is implied by her use of quotation marks around the phrase "eternal verities" but the hesitancy does not ripen into criticism.

[65]*Ibid.,* pp. 121-93.

[66]*Ibid.,* p. 193.

[67](New York, 1952), pp. 372-73 are cited.

[68]See Thomas, *op. cit.,* pp. 171, 221, 225, 234, 235, 317, 322, 333 and 364.

[69]See Frankfurter's usage in *Cassell* v. *Texas,* 339 U.S. 282, 292 and in *Brock* v. *North Carolina,* 344 U.S. 424, 428. Compare Mendelson's usage, *op. cit.,* pp. 13, 40, 47, 61, 67, 73 and 115.

[70]Thomas, *op. cit.,* p. 347. Cf. other uses of the term "philosophy" at pp. 15, 109, 114, 176, 283 and 333, and of related terms at 216 and 363.

[71]But see pp. 97-100, *supra, and* pp. 143, 167-168, and 189-190 *infra.*

[72]Thomas, *op. cit.,* pp. 62-63.

[73]*Ibid.,* see pp. 129, 170, 171, 173, 178, 191, 362.

[74]*Ibid.,* pp. 15, 171, 350.

[75]*Ibid.,* p. 30.

[76]*Ibid.,* pp. 151, 203, 224. Cf. pp. 272, 287, 328.

[77]*Ibid.,* p. 162.

[78]*Ibid.,* p. 225.

[79]Clyde Jacobs, *Justice Frankfurter and Civil Liberties* ("University of California Publications in Political Science," Vol. XII; Berkeley and Los Angeles: University of California Press, 1961).

[80]*U.S.* v. *Turley,* 352 U.S. 407, Frankfurter dissenting, at 417-18.

[81]*United States ex rel Marcus* v. *Hess,* 317 U.S. 537, Frankfurter concurring, at 553-54.

[82]*Ferguson* v. *Georgia,* 365 U.S. 570, Frankfurter concurring, at 600.

[83]*Addison* v. *Holly Hill Co.,* 320 U.S. 607, Frankfurter for the court, at 620. According to the *Dictionary of National Biography,* Parke's weakness was an "almost superstitious reverence for the dark technicalities of special pleading." The reforms of the Common Law Procedures Acts of 1854-55 caused him to resign from the bench.

[84]Frankfurter dissenting in *Elkins* v. *United States,* 364 U.S. 207 at 235 (1960).

[85]*Uveges* v. *Pennsylvania,* 335 U.S. 437, Frankfurter dissenting, at 449.

[86]*UMW* v. *Arkansas Oak Flooring Co.,* 351 U.S. 62, Frankfurter dissenting, at 76.

[87]*Gomillion* v. *Lightfoot,* 364 U.S. 339, Frankfurter for the Court, at 343.

[88]*Tigner* v. *Texas,* 310 U.S. 141, Frankfurter for the Court, at 147.

[89]*Ibid.,* p. 148.

[90]*United States* v. *Toronto, H.&B. Navigation Co.,* 338 U.S. 396, Frankfurter concurring, at 408.

[91]That Jacobs, *op. cit.,* uses the word "pragmatic" more self-consciously and, we believe, more instructively than Thomas is indicated by the fact that the word merits an entry in his index, which see at p. 264 for direction to those passages where he employs the term.

[92]*Ibid.,* pp. 213-14.

[93]Frankfurter tells us that constitutional adjudication does not thrive on such visions in his opinion (judgment of the Court) in *New York* v. *United States,* 326 U.S. 572 at 583 (1946).

[94]Jacobs, *op. cit.,* p. 211. Emphasis not in the original.

[95]*Ibid.,* p. 194, concerning *Louisiana ex rel Francis* v. *Resweber,* 329 U.S. 459.

[96]*Ibid.,* p. 201, concerning *Solesbee* v. *Balkcom,* 339 U.S. 9.

[97]*Ibid.,* p. 194.

[98]*Ibid.,* p. 207.

[99]*Ibid.,* p. 208.

[100]*Ibid.*

[101]*Ibid.,* p. 194.

[102]*Louisiana ex rel Francis* v. *Resweber,* 329 U.S. 459, Frankfurter concurring, at 471.

[103]*Ibid.,* pp. 470, 471-72.

[104]See *Solesbee* v. *Balkcom,* 339 U.S. 9, Frankfurter dissenting, at 16.

[105]*Ibid.,* p. 19, citing Blackstone, *Commentaries,* IV, 388-89. Our Blackstone has it at pp. 395-96.

[106]*Ibid.,* p. 18. Frankfurter cites as follows: "Remarks on the Tryal of Charles Bateman by Sir John Hawles, Solicitor-General in the reign of King William III, 3 State-Tryals 651, 652-53 (1719.)" Our copy of *State Trials* (London, 1811) appends Sir John's remarks immediately after the Bateman trial. Trial of Charles Bateman for High Treason, *State Trials, op. cit.,* XI, 467 (1 James II, 1685). Remarks, etc., at *ibid.,* pp. 473-80. The passage quoted by Frankfurter is at column 477.

[107]See *State Trials,* VIII, 723.

[108]*Ibid.,* p. 561.

[109]*Solesbee* v. *Balkcom,* 339 U.S. 9 at 19.

[110]*State Trials, op. cit.,* XI, 474.

[111]*Ibid.,* p. 477.

[112]*Ibid.,* column 478.

[113]*L and M,* p. 133, and see *ibid.,* pp. 40-41.

[114]*State Trials, op. cit.,* XI, 474.
[115]Frankfurter's dissent in *United States* v. *Bethlehem Steel Corp.,* 315 U.S. 289, 326.
[116]Frankfurter concurring in the result in *Kingsley Pictures* v. *Regents,* 360 U.S. 684 at 696.
[117]Separate opinion of Frankfurter in *Malinski* v. *New York,* 324 U.S. 401 at 417.
[118]Judgment of the Court in an opinion by Frankfurter joined by Justices Murphy and Rutledge, in *Watts* v. *Indiana,* 338 U.S. 49 at 50.
[119]"The vague contours of the Due Process Clause do not leave judges at large. We may not draw on our merely personal and private notions. . . ." Opinion of the Court by Frankfurter in *Rochin* v. *California,* 342 U.S. 165 at 171.
[120]Frankfurter concurring in *Joint Anti-Fascist Refugee Committee* v. *McGrath,* 341 U.S. 123 at 162.
[121]*L and M,* p. 16.
[122]*Ibid.,* p. 15.
[123]"Legislators" is here intended to include the founding fathers of both constitutions and statutes.
[124]Chapter ii, *supra.*
[125]See *L and M,* p. 17.
[126]Dissenting in *Milanovich* v. *United States,* 365 U.S. 551 at 562.
[127]*Green* v. *United States,* 355 U.S. 184, Frankfurter dissenting, at 215.
[128]Frankfurter concurring in *Graves* v. *New York ex rel O'Keefe,* 306 U.S. 466 at 487.
[129]Frankfurter for the Court in *Helvering* v. *Hallock,* 309 U.S. 106 at 119.
[130]*Justices Black and Frankfurter,* pp. 114-15.
[131]*Ibid.,* p. 41.
[132]Frankfurter dissenting in *Elkins* v. *United States,* 364 U.S. 207, at 235.
[133]See chapter iv, *supra.*
[134]See Thomas, *op. cit.,* especially pp. 174-76.
[135]*Ibid.,* pp. 178-81.
[136]*Ibid.,* p. 179.
[137]Jacobs, *op. cit.,* p. 214.
[138]In a 1945 testimonial to Thomas Mann, *L and M,* p. 347. This is one of the few encomia gathered in the Elman collection in which the criticism, or at least reservation, interleaved with the praise, is near the surface.
[139]*Eth. Nich.,* 1137a31-38a4.
[140]"The Conditions for, and the Aims and Methods of, Legal Research," reprinted in *L and P,* pp. 292-93.
[141]See *supra,* p. 121 and *infra,* p. 167.
[142]Frankfurter dissenting in *Radovich* v. *National Football League,* 352 U.S. 445 at 455.
[143]Frankfurter dissenting in *Commissioner* v. *Wodehouse,* 337 U.S. 369 at 415.
[144]*United States* v. *I.C.C.,* 337 U.S. 426, Frankfurter dissenting, at 446.
[145]Frankfurter for the Court in *Butler* v. *Michigan,* 352 U.S. 380 at 383. The context of the phrase quoted is not immediately related to the present discussion.
[146]Frankfurter dissenting in *Commissioner* v. *Estate of Church,* 335 U.S. 633, at 677.
[147]Holmes for the Court in *New York Trust Co.* v. *Eisner,* 256 U.S. 345, 349, quoted by Frankfurter, dissenting in *Bridges* v. *California,* 314 U.S. 252 at 292 and

for the Court in *Ullman* v. *U.S.*, 350 U.S. 422 at 438, as well as elsewhere. He sometimes varies Holmes' phrase by substituting "rhetoric" for "logic." See his opinion for the Court in *Ludecke* v. *Watkins,* 335 U.S. 160, 173.

[148]Frankfurter for the Court in *Romero* v. *International Terminal Co., 358 U.S.* 354 at 377.

[149]Frankfurter dissenting in *Davis* v. *United States,* 328 U.S. 582, 616, quoting L. Hand in *United States* v. *Kirschenblatt,* 16 F.2d 202, 203.

[150]Frankfurter for the Court in *Butler* v. *Michigan,* 352 U.S. 380, 384.

[151]Frankfurter dissenting in *Bridges* v. *California,* 314 U.S. 252 at 284.

[152]*Ibid.,* p. 279.

[153]Frankfurter concurring in the result in *Hannah* v. *Larche,* 363 U.S. 420, 493.

[154]Perhaps properly speaking government has no new ends; only new means. But the terms here are acceptable for the sake of argument.

[155]See his opinions for the Court in *Ullman* v. *United States,* 350 U.S. 422 at 438 and *Gore* v. *United States,* 357 U.S. 386 at 392 and his dissent in *United States* v. *Union Pacific Railroad Co.,* 353 U.S. 112 at 122.

CHAPTER VI

REASON

The dilemma which Adamson faced was presented to the Court so as to invite it to overthrow its traditional stand on the relation between the Fourteenth Amendment and the first eight Amendments. The Court, instead, reaffirmed that traditional stand. Black's dissenting opinion accused the traditional view of putting the Court in the position of applying a discredited doctrine of natural law. That doctrine, it was said, was merely a cover for personal whim. But Frankfurter, despite earlier disapproval of the due process clauses on the ground that they allowed or perhaps compelled judges to rule by such whims, defended the clause and the Court's stand with regard to it in the *Adamson* case. Judges were not, he there said, compelled by the due process clause to rule by whim. Black's view, we are told, reduces the clause to a "pharmacopoeia" of prohibitions. The clause, rightly understood, calls upon the judge to engage in the practice of judgment. Judgment, as we have seen, is not a mechanical thing. If it be supposed that the choice is between mechanism and whim we are reminded that the judgment judges exercise is *judicial* judgment and that is protected from whimsical abuse by an understanding of the judicial role. There are, then, standards other than mechanical standards to which a judge may turn. He is not compelled, in the exercise of judgment, to look within himself to subjective things. He can turn outward to external measures even though they be not neat, mechanical, external measures.

Where, then, does the judge turn? For one thing, it is said, he may turn to history. But the problem of history is illustrated by the problem of precedent, which is a kind of or a sub-class of history. Quite obviously, to rely upon precedent simply is to engage in a merely more entertaining version of mechanical jurisprudence for to do so amounts to saying that judgment consists in asking what some other judge at some other time has ruled without asking what was the basis of his ruling.

Despite Frankfurter's frequent mention of history, we have seen that the manner of his reliance upon precedent raises problems. For if precedent, as such, were enough, it would make no sense to distinguish between incidents which hearken to *one* precedent and those which hearken to four or more. We have even seen Frankfurter oppose himself to numberless precedents accumulated over several centuries. The difficulty posed by precedent shows itself upon some reflection and analysis. In the first place, when one speaks of precedent he necessarily means precedent in like or analogous cases. But what is a like case? It is all very well for lawyers and judges to bear themselves loftily and speak with derision of the "abstract arguments" and "generalizations" of laymen and of other and backsliding lawyers and judges but can one *decide* a case without being decisive? Can one make a ruling without having in mind a rule?[1]

> The court does not now over-rule *Rock* but says that it "must be limited to its precise facts." I take it this statement refers to the facts relevant to the result in that case; it does not mean that the plaintiff must be named Rock.[2]

If a fact is *relevant* it is so with respect to the question presented, and the question, to be intelligible as such, must be capable of being asked without reference to the names of the parties. To say the contrary would be to deny to the law and to the rule of law that impersonality in favor of which lawyers are bound to prefer it to the rule of men. Although Frankfurter can tell us on one occasion that it is "not a juristic requirement that decisions be carried to their logical consequences,"[3] a decision the consequences of which are manifestly untenable is a manifestly untenable decision, and so we are told on another occasion that "episodic" instances in the law must from time to time be "harmonized."[4] Lawyers may be justified in their impatience with social scientists who frequently pay insufficient attention to the particularities of the case in their sweeping pronouncements about principles. This will be especially true if one has regard to social scientists—but, to some lawyers and judges as well—whose attention is fixed on a single, partial principle which is mistakenly seen as the comprehensive principle. Such would be the problem, for example, in the case of a practitioner or analyst who measures all things by liberty, believing liberty to be the one comprehensive principle of society. But it may be that the problem here is *not* that the practitioner or analyst involved has erred in generalizing, but rather that a generalization which is partial is stretched to encompass more than it can manage. It is true that anyone who is in jail is without his liberty, and if he applies for release, one can say that he has made a claim for "civil liberties." If judge A favors his application and judge B rejects it, it is certainly true that the former has here evidenced a greater regard for liberty than has the latter. We can well see how the applicant would prefer judge A to judge B, but even if in ten such applications the former favors all ten and the latter rejects all of them, proving that A is vastly more favorable to liberty than B, we cannot yet see that the one or the other ought to be commended to us. Nor can we see that B is to be regarded as "against" liberty. We cannot see *anything* of significance without an examination of the merits of the particular cases. It may be that judge B favors liberty *among other things*, and that in the sample here suggested there has simply been a run of frivolous applications. But to say all this is not to say that principles are for "romantics" or "absolutists" and that particulars appeal to the "tough-minded" or to "realists," for to speak of the *merits* of a case is simply to speak of some *other* generalizations, some other principles in the light of which the application for liberty is weighed. Those who remind us of the importance of the case, as opposed to principles, or "abstractions," must themselves be reminded that case law is, after all, law. There is a massive contradiction in fondly remarking the beauties of the common law in order to make a case for cases and against principles, and yet there is no lack of lawyers who will say that it is proper for the Court to decide between Brown and Topeka because the case between them was pressed upon it but that it is usurpation for the same Court to point to the *consequences* of its decision in favor of Brown, declaring what is the *law* for others and how, conveniently, they may fulfill it.

To appreciate the contradiction, it is only necessary to reflect upon the distinction between decision and opinion. The Anglo-American or common-law system is composed of two essential ingredients: adversaries and precedents. Perhaps the latter follows of necessity from the former. Even in constitutional cases the Court is essentially and necessarily engaged in a common-law kind of activity. The case between Brown and Topeka begins not with an inquisition but with an accusation, and the Court, at first, is in the posture of a non-involved referee over the dispute which ensues from the accusation. Even if the Court faced this dispute with an empty slate behind it, that it *is* a dispute between two parties who get the Court's attention because each deserves that attention means that the Court cannot decide for one or the other without explaining the *grounds* of its decision. It is this which calls forth the suggestion that the system of precedents follows from the fact of adversaries. For that explanation, or opinion, which accompanies the decision is the Court's *justification*. Its constant reminder that it is a *court of law* is tantamount to a declaration that it has come to such and such a decision because it was *compelled* to, could come to no other; its *opinion* is, as it were, an attempt to persuade the losing party that were it to find itself in the court's place *it* would have been compelled to come to the *same* decision. Once having rendered the opinion in support of the decision, the Court cannot then pretend it has *not* rendered it. The moment it goes beyond decision and enters into the writing of *opinions*, every case which follows is necessarily involved in precedent.

It would be possible, in theory, for a court to confine itself to rendering one- or two-word decisions: it could say "guilty" or "not-guilty"; or, on appeal, it could say "reversed" or "affirmed." Similar short declarations could be found for all manner of cases and perhaps nothing would call for a judgment longer than, "The defendant shall pay to the plaintiff the sum of $10,000.00 and costs."

The instant a court goes beyond such a terse declaration, the instant it offers to *support* its decision with an opinion, or explanation, or justification, that instant it goes beyond the case at hand. It is then no longer concerned with these parties or this case but with principles, or generalizations—with what some are prone slightingly to call "abstractions." It may be that a generalization, expressed as it is within certain confines, may not appear relevant in this or that subsequent case. That is, what a court says in support of its decision to let a conviction stand in a rape case may not appear helpful in the decision of an admiralty dispute involving the seaworthiness of a vessel in the service of which a seaman has fed on spoiled rations. But if the latter case is decided in *defiance* of what is said in the former decision, it must be because the decision in the admiralty case is wrong or the opinion in the criminal case faulty, for, in a way, *every* decision—even one pronounced without a supporting opinion—rests ultimately upon some principle, be it express or implied, which is applicable to *every* case. In practical affairs, judges may seldom or never get around to an exposition of those underlying principles but this does not mean that they are not efficacious in the decision of cases and relevant to the issue of all other cases. The neat division of subject matters in a law school curriculum is as deceiving as are the artificialities in all university administration. There is something satisfyingly solid about a heavy book entitled "Cases on Contract" or "Cases on Tort," but whether a case is in fact one in tort or one in contract may depend upon what course seems most profitable to counsel for the plaintiff. Indeed, even the distinction between civil and criminal law depends upon what the public chooses to regard as falling within its concerns and what it chooses to leave to private parties. It cannot be forgotten that what is now regarded here as the crime of murder was once regarded there as a cause for the family of the deceased to go against the killer for money damages.

What else could a "harmony" of "episodes" mean? Those who speak of cases in derogation of "abstractions" must know that if two ladies glare at each other because each feels some discomfort in the other's presence and, one of them, going to law for consolation, is told she has "no case," it must be that some principle which is independent of the several cases is the root of that consideration which says what shall be and what shall not be a case. That is, that a case *is* a case is dependent upon a prior general principle.

There is in the *Harvard Law Review* for June, 1909, a book review signed "F.F.," which we suppose was done by Frankfurter, which, praising enthusiastically the book reviewed, says, "The great mass of decisions that have poured from the courts is here passed through the sieve of legal principles. . . ."[5] And Judge Augustus Hand, writing a

foreword to Professor Jaffe's article on Frankfurter in an issue of the
Harvard Law Review dedicated to the latter forty years after that
review tells us that Frankfurter, as a professor, "had a rare capacity
for abstract reasoning. . . ."[6]

While Frankfurter has told us that decisions need not be carried to
their logical consequences and, in dealing with the troublesome
business of domicile, he has told us that "legal doctrines have, in an
odd kind of way, the faculty of self-generating extension,"[7] we do
not see the oddness in the extension nor an escape from the
consequences of a decision. In an opinion delivered six months after
Judge Hand's remarks on Frankfurter's professorial capacity for
abstract reasoning, Frankfurter, now a judge for ten years, taught as
follows:

> Case-by-case adjudication gives to the judicial process the
> impact of actuality and thereby saves it from the hazards of
> generalizations insufficiently nourished by experience. There is,
> however, an attendant weakness to a system that purports to
> pass merely on what are deemed to be the particular
> circumstances of a case. Consciously or unconsciously the
> pronouncements in an opinion too often exceed the justification
> of the circumstances on which they are based, or, contrariwise,
> judicial preoccupation with the claims of the immediate leads to
> a succession of *ad hoc* determinations making for eventual
> confusion and conflict. There comes a time when the general
> considerations underlying each specific situation must be
> exposed in order to bring the too unruly instances into more
> fruitful harmony. The case before us presents one of those
> problems for the rational solution of which it becomes
> necessary, as a matter of judicial self-respect, to take soundings
> in order to know where we are and whither we are going.[8]

What is the relation between "judicial self-respect" and judicial
"humility" and between the "rational solution" of problems and
"history"? The doubt regarding "whither we are going" suggests
that choice is open and raises the question as to the grounds of choice.
In the quoted passage Frankfurter affirms that "cases" involve,
rather than oppose themselves to, "principles" and that, because
precedent cases may involve insufficient principles, the fundamental
question is over principle rather than over precedent. This reaffirms

what our earlier inquiry indicated, that precedent is merely "social policy" rather than that which commands social policy.

> The evolution of judge-made law is a process of accretion and erosion. We are told by a great master that law is civilized to the extent that it is purposefully conscious. Conversely, if law just "grow'd" like Topsy, unreflectively and without conscious design, it is irrational. When it appears that a challenged doctrine has been uncritically accepted as a matter of course by the inertia of repetition—has just "grow'd" like Topsy—the Court owes it to the demands of reason, on which judicial law-making power ultimately rests for its authority, to examine its foundations and validity in order appropriately to assess claims for its extension.[9]

"History," then, cannot be left to its aimless meanderings. It must be guided. "Whither we are going" is up to lawmakers, and judges, protestations of humility to the contrary notwithstanding, *do* sometimes make law. And, since "law" means principles or generalizations and not just the law of the case, the law-making of judges is in part, or at times, indistinguishable in product from the law-making of legislators. If the law judges make, because of the "episodic" character of its making, lacks "harmony," judges must sometimes establish harmony by seeking the principles which are at the root of the several episodes and, since a disharmony among the episodes suggests a disharmony among the principles, presumably judges must prefer one principle to another. The choice of principle depends upon the *purpose* of the judge. To what is the purpose answerable? In the light of what is his purpose formed? It cannot be "the law" for it is the law that the judge is *making*. Since the most interesting case is that of constitutional adjudication, we cannot say that the judge's purpose is guided by the Constitution for, in this case what is wanted is guidance in the making of the Constitution itself. We are back again to Bryce's question: American judges do just what English judges do, they interpret the laws; but the laws include the Constitution and the Constitution is brief and vague and so the judge's bounds are loose. What intrinsic thing narrows those bounds? Frankfurter tells us that a proper understanding of the "role" of the judge answers that question. But the answer turns in on itself, for the admission that judges "make" law defies the notion of a neat division of roles between judges and others. We are back yet once more to the same question: what narrows the bounds of judicial law-making? What keeps judges from imposing mere whim upon the country? To this question—the question as to what guides the purpose of judges when they harmonize the Topsy-grown accretion of judge-made law—Frankfurter's answer is "reason." All we need to know is what that means.

What Frankfurter means by "reason" is, in fact, the measure of him. All the talk about history, judgment, pragmatism, empiricism, restraint, humility, subjectivity, federalism and the clash of interests becomes intelligible, if at all, only after his use of the word "reason" is understood.

While we would seem to be pointed in one direction by his admission, in a speech honoring Jefferson, that we ought not "to float unthinkingly on the stream of history,"[10] our movement in that direction is checked by his reference in an article on Roberts, to the "coral-reef fabric which is law,"[11] for one cannot help remembering what a coral reef is made of and how unthinkingly it comes into being. It is with enthusiasm that Frankfurter tells us in the *Guaranty Trust Co.* case that *Erie* "did not merely overrule a venerable case. It overruled a particular way of looking at law which dominated the judicial process long after its inadequacies had been laid bare."[12] That the older way of looking at law, whatever its inadequacies, might be superior to the newer way suggests itself when we see that Frankfurter goes on to tell us that, according to the old way, "Law was conceived as a 'brooding omnipresence' of Reason, of which decisions were merely evidence and not themselves the controlling formulations."[13] It is small consolation that the "reason" which Frankfurter's exposition of the due process clause claims to retain is spelled with a lower-case initial and that which he jettisons with sarcasm in *Guaranty Trust* is capitalized, for, in the second *Dennis* case he emphatically cautions that there is a disjunction between wisdom and constitutionality.[14] If the Constitution commands "reason" but judgment as to constitutionality does not include judgment as to "wisdom" then it must be that reason and wisdom are separable. Can this be? The disjunction of reason and wisdom is more clearly, not to say starkly, revealed in Frankfurter's dissent in the later flag-salute case.

> It can never be emphasized too much that one's own opinion
> about the wisdom or evil of a law should be excluded altogether
> when one is doing one's duty on the bench. The only opinion of
> our own even looking in that direction that is material is our
> opinion whether legislators could in reason have enacted such a
> law.[15]

Apparently legislators can be *altogether* bad and altogether foolish
and still be quite reasonable.

Had he never used the word "reason" in any of his opinions we
would still need to know what Frankfurter thought reason was. That
he frequently turns explicitly to "reason," and in a great variety of
cases[16] merely emphasizes the necessity, to which our inquiry has
driven us, to know what he means by the use of the word. In a 1947
opinion he quotes approvingly Dean Pound's remark of ten years
earlier that, "Civilization involves subjection of force to reason, and
the agency of this subjection is law."[17] With this statement one can
warmly agree, but it is still necessary to know what he *and* Pound
mean. Six terms later he referred to the Rules of Civil Procedure as
"rational instruments for doing justice between man and man."[18]
The burden of his dissent in this case was his contention that the
majority had frozen the Rules into the same sort of formalism which
delighted Baron Parke and which the Rules were supposed to reform.
That the Rules should be seen as "rational" rather than "lifeless
formality" reminds us of his distinction between "mechanical
jurisprudence" and "judgment." In support of his construction of
the Rules he quotes a 1909 comment by Pound to the effect that
procedure is merely a means to the ends of substantive law.[19] Once
again one can agree readily with Pound as well as with Frankfurter's
application of the spirit of the Rules which, no doubt, *were* intended
to overthrow the cumulative idiocies of common-law pleading and
practice and the cumulative inconveniences of what had come to be a
near-meaningless distinction between law and equity. But, once
again, agreement must wait upon understanding.

Frankfurter's reference on these two occasions to Pound leads to
the supposition that finding out what *Pound* means by "reason" will
help in finding out what Frankfurter means. There could not be a
better place to look than to Pound's latest book, devoted, as it is, to
the same general question as this study. It would be presumptuous to
purport to dispose of someone of Pound's eminence as a mere

incident to an exposition of Frankfurter but confession of an unripe appraisal of Pound's view is not avoidable in this instance. He begins the last chapter of that latest book, a chapter entitled "Reason and Reasoning in Law Finding," with a short quotation from Coke to the effect that the common law "is nothing else but reason" and follows the quotation with the query, "But what did Coke mean by 'reason?'"[20] Whatever Coke meant by it, Pound promises his own definition[21] and this is what would concern us. It begins with the assertion that, "reason and reasoning are not the same thing,"[22] by which we take it he means that reason is something more than mathematical syllogisms. But the hoped for definition soon fades into a repetition of the word itself. The title of the book is *Law Finding Through Experience and Reason* which raises the hope that *both* reason and experience will be defined and the two distinguished one from the other, but early in the first chapter we are told:

> Experience teaches decisions that prove to satisfy demands of justice. Reason shapes and orders and develops decisions to ideals of justice and so into principles of law. I repeat: We must not underestimate the role of ideals in the development of the law.[23]

Reason, then, serves a ministerial function in the service of "ideals of justice" the importance of which must not be underestimated. "Ideals of justice" are to be understood etymologically:

> Ideal gets its name from a Greek word meaning picture. An ideal of a thing is a picture of it to which we fit our conception of it as we think it is or ought to be. The ideals of the social order, however, which become authoritative guides to determination of controversies and ordering of conduct, are not photographs or photographically retouched drawings of the social order of the time and place. They are largely pictures of a social order of the past, drawn to it at its best, undergoing retouching as to details in order to fit exigencies of the present. Ideals of law and ideals of principles and rules of law, are pictures made to conform to an ethical-philosophical juristic picture of the legal order, intended to guide judges and legislators and administrative agencies toward making the means afforded by the legal order achieve its postulated ends.

> Understanding and exposition of the ideal element in law, and
> of law as guided in its development by ideals, is the task of
> philosophy of law.[24]

Experience, then, supplies the incidents of law. These are molded
and guided by reason which, it appears, is the right arm not of justice
nor even of what the wisest men have said about justice but rather of
"ideals" of justice. From the context it is clear that the "we" who do
the thinking about what "it is or ought to be" is the communal
"we"—i.e., the folk. The important "ideals" then are not those of
wise men like Pound, but those of the folk who, it must be pointed
out, have at best a watered-down version of the teachings of Pound
and the other philosophers of law. Reason, then, is the handmaid of
public opinion about justice. But public opinion, which is always a
little late in forming, is molded by what? Obviously, it is molded by
experience, or at best, by Johnny-come-lately appreciations of what
those who might here be called "opinion leaders" have said about
experiences. And, of course, the opinion leaders would include, in an
important way, philosophers of law and their business is
"understanding and exposition of the ideal element in law."

Philosophy of law is, then, a little like a movie about show
business, and, conversely, just as common men begin to behave as
movies portray them as behaving, so the folk think about justice as
philosophers tell them folks think about justice. Judges and
legislators and administrators are not guided by justice but by what
folks think, and what folks think, though a little behind the times,
just grows like Topsy—bent this way and that by experiences guided
by that which is itself the product of experiences. Reason, then, loses
its independent potency. It fades into the experience it is supposed to
guide and, therefore, into thin air.

But, of course, that Frankfurter quotes Pound approvingly from
time to time does not mean that their views on this or any other
subject are identical. The former has, in fact, implicitly rejected the
jurisprudence of the latter by explicitly referring to his scholarship as
"largely spoiled" by his having been Dean,[25] and so the
disintegration of reason in Pound is to be taken not as evidence
respecting Frankfurter's views but simply as an illustrative warning as
to what sort of problems to look for. But, on the other hand, one

need not look far. A strong hint that the disjunction of wisdom and reason in the *Barnette* case is occasioned by a grave difficulty with reason itself is indicated by his opinion for the Court rendered three months before the *Barnette* opinion in a case involving the admissibility into evidence of statements made to police by defendants in a United States case prior to their arraignment. At one point in the opinion, the Court says through Frankfurter's pen:

> The history of liberty has largely been the history of observance of procedural safeguards. And the effective administration of criminal justice hardly requires disregard of fair procedures imposed by law.[26]

Reminded as we are that due process means "essential fairness"[27] and that the search for what is "fair" involves recourse to "reason" and that, "Reason and fairness demand . . . procedural safeguards within which the needs for the effective administration of justice can be amply satisfied while at the same time the reach of so drastic a power is kept within limits that will minimize abuse,"[28] we are confused when we read, earlier in the *McNabb* case:

> In the view we take of the case, however, it becomes unnecessary to reach the Constitutional issue pressed upon us. For, while the power of this Court to undo convictions in state courts is limited to the enforcement of those "fundamental principles of liberty and justice," *Hebert* v. *Louisiana*, 272 U.S. 312, 316, which are secured by the Fourteenth Amendment, the scope of our reviewing power over convictions brought here from the federal courts is not confined to ascertainment of Constitutional validity. Judicial supervision of the administration of criminal justice in the federal courts implies the duty of establishing and maintaining civilized standards of procedure and evidence. Such standards are not satisfied merely by observance of those minimal historic safeguards for securing trial by reason which are summarized as "due process of law" and below which we reach what is really trial by force. Moreover, review by this Court of state action expressing its notion of what will best further its own security in the administration of criminal justice demands appropriate respect for the deliberative judgment of a state in so basic an exercise of its jurisdiction. Considerations of large policy in making the necessary accommodations in our federal system are wholly irrelevant to the formulation and application of proper standards for the enforcement of the federal criminal law in the federal courts.[29]

It is almost embarrassing to enter into a long explication of this passage for such an explication can only end in the charge that the passage is "double-talk." It must be done, however. First, it is necessary to remember that judges are to be restrained; they are not to usurp the legislative function. The court is a court of law, not of justice. Next, Congress has not commanded reversal in this case by fixing a rule of evidence which the trial court defied in convicting the McNabbs. The McNabbs had complained, on *certiorari*, that statements made by them to police investigating a murder of a federal officer had been used as evidence against them in a trial which convicted them of that murder. A distinction exists between the impropriety of the police interrogation without arraignment in the face of Congressional command of such arraignment, on the one hand, and admissibility into evidence of matter secured in that interrogation, on the other. A sensible argument could be, and often has been, made to the effect that it just doesn't make sense for the government—through the mouth of Congress—to say that federal officers may not get evidence by such and such means and then for the government—through the mouth of one of its judges—to say that, well, the officers shouldn't have done so, but, having done so, there is no point in ignoring the fruits of their forbidden action. We can readily concede such an argument, for it appears to us that the contrary would be just the sort of procedural nicety that would put sparkle into the gaunt eye of Baron Parke's ghost. But the point is that Frankfurter has *made the contrary argument* in a state case.[30] Our question is, what is the principle of distinction between state and federal cases? It may be that what is good for the goose is *not* good for the gander—or, perhaps one should say, what is good for the flock is not good for the goose—but the difference must be *explained*.

Throughout this study we have warmly agreed with Frankfurter and with the traditional stand of the Court that the first eight Amendments impose numerous and detailed restraints upon United States courts, while the Fourteenth Amendment imposes a comprehensive and very general restraint upon the states. The generality of that restraint permits actions on the part of the states that are forbidden, in terms, to the United States. It makes perfect sense, therefore, for the Court to say that it must be more stringent in the review of the United States trials than it is in the review of state trials. It might, for example, permit Colorado to convict Wolf in a trial to which has been admitted evidence got illegally and yet *forbid* the United States so to convict the McNabbs. It might do so by citing in the *McNabb* case the search and seizure, the self-incrimination, or the right to counsel provisions of the Fourth, Fifth and Sixth Amendments, respectively. But it didn't do so in *McNabb*. It explicitly refused to rely upon the Constitution. Blinking the fact that for the Supreme Court to apply a principle found *neither* in a statute nor in the Constitution is contrary to Frankfurter's own doctrine of restraint, we ask again, what principle of distinction *permits* the conviction in *Wolf* and forbids it in *McNabb*? We defy any United States District Judge to read the passage from *McNabb* quoted above and to derive any instruction from it. Does that passage not somehow add up to the proposition that state trials need be merely civilized, that is, reasonable and fair, but United States trials, on the other hand, need to be civilized, that is, reasonable and fair?

The *McNabb* ruling might have been made on the basis of an intersection of the appellate power provision in Article III and the due process clause of the Fifth Amendment but, since all agree that "due process" in the Fifth means exactly the same as "due process" in the Fourteenth and since it has been settled, and rightly, since *Martin* v. *Hunter's Lessee*[31] that the Supreme Court's appellate power extends to criminal trials in state courts, so to rule would be to overthrow the principle of the *Wolf* case. In *McNabb* we learn that due process means "those minimal historic safeguards for securing trial by reason" but we do not know yet what "reason" is and, if the *McNabb* ruling is to be understood by United States trial judges—*as it must*—"reason," as it is used there *must* be understandable to them. It must, of course, *also* be intelligible to state trial judges. It would not do, for example, for the Court to say, well, such and such is permissible in a Colorado court but not in a United States court and we can't *really* say why, but we just feel we ought to be a bit stiffer on United States judges and policemen and that's all there is to it. So to say would be to exercise that visceral, or personal judgment which Frankfurter denies the justices engage in.

Courts can fulfill their responsibility in a democratic society only to the extent that they succeed in shaping their judgments by rational standards, and rational standards are both impersonal and communicable.[32]

We suggested above that justice-in-practice, or the law, is to be understood as a compromise of justice-in-theory, or, justice simply, and that the compromise is necessitated by the exigencies or relativities of the moment and that a judge, to practice well, must be abreast of the things of the moment, but, that the crucial measure of the Supreme Court Justice is not his practice—as important as that obviously is—but his theory, his understanding of justice, simply.[33] This means that reduction of the measure of the judge to the problem of his conception of the judge's role is inadequate, for it tends to emphasize *practice*—how the judge *applies* himself, as it were—whereas the root question is *theory*—what it is that he applies. For, if one emphasizes "role" he is emphasizing the *judge* in the scheme of things and he is led, almost by grammatical necessity, to see the problem of application, or practice, as the problem of how the judge applies *himself* and, of course, the decent judge will draw back from the specter of "personal" jurisprudence, or judicial fiat, and, if the problem is so conceived, the only way to draw back is for the judge to apply himself as little as possible—hence the doctrines of "restraint" and "humility." That is why we suggested also that understanding Frankfurter's view of the relation between theory and practice is identical with understanding his distinction between "personal" and "impersonal."[34]

Now, a goodly portion of the law is plain enough, and plainly enough acceptable, so as to leave little leeway to courts. Another and goodly portion of judicial labor is answerable to the superior law of the Constitution, and a portion of that is plain and plainly acceptable. But there is a remainder which is not so plain. These are the hard cases. It may be that "hard cases make bad law,"[35] but that is only because it is easy to make law in easy cases. The hard cases are the crucial cases. They are the only cases which *make* law in any appreciable degree. How they are resolved *points* the law, and the resolution of the easy cases falls in with that direction. One could say that the only cases fit for the supreme judgment of the Supreme Court are the hard cases. That a great proportion of the Court's time each year is devoted to cases involving due process questions and that the proportion tends to increase through the years is testimony to the proposition that what the Court thinks is due process points out the direction in which the Court's whole understanding of the relation between theory and practice moves—points out, that is, the Court's whole understanding of the law and its application.

We have argued, early in this inquiry, that the view of due process taken by Black and what during Frankfurter's tenure was the minority of the Court was clearly defective and that the traditional, or Frankfurter, or majority view has been superior. That much may be said to have been the "easy" case. But the *hard* case is the question of the sufficiency of Frankfurter's view. It *is* a hard case simply because it is not easy. That is, the resolution of the question is difficult because Frankfurter's view, unlike Black's rather transparent doctrine, is very complex. But it is a hard case in another sense. For if Frankfurter's view of due process—the best available contemporary view of the most crucial question—is not sufficient, then contemporary American law as such is found wanting.

Frankfurter teaches that due process is essential fairness and, in the light of his defense against Black's charge that such a view reintroduces natural law, we have been seeking an understanding of what Frankfurter means by "essential fairness." In a 1954 talk before the American Philosophical Society, to which we have previously referred, he said:

> Representing a profound attitude of fairness between man and man, and more particularly between the individual and government, "due process" is compounded of history, reason, the past course of decisions, and stout confidence in the strength of the democratic faith which we profess. Due process is not a mechanical instrument. It is not a yardstick. It is a process. It is a delicate process of adjustment inescapably involving the exercise of judgment by those whom the Constitution entrusted with the unfolding of the process.[36]

It seems to us that it confounds the problem to say that the due process against which the Court is supposed to test the taking of life, liberty, or property is identical with the process of testing. It begins to sound as though the "due" is "*in* the process," which is reminiscent of the doctrines of Hegel and so far from being a kind of "twentieth century variant natural law" position, as Miss Thomas suggested,[37] it is more like a twentieth-century historicist position. But for the moment we can pass this to note simply that the Court is entrusted with the process of "unfolding" the meaning of due process and that due process is "compounded" of history, reason, precedent, and democracy.

To be precise, we suppose that precedent must be distinguished from history in that the former involves *particular* commands of the law and the latter involves *general* and instructive advice on the law. But, at bottom, it appears that one is a sub-class of the other, or they are both sub-classes of a more general thing or term, experience. And we have treated them as such herein. We are left, then, with history, reason, and democracy and, by the logic of our discussion, in the last chapter, of "continuity and change," it appears that the "unfolding" consists in deciding *when* to *depart* from history and so, as we have been arguing, the cutting edge of due process remains and to this Frankfurter gives the names "reason" and "democracy."

Just after quoting his *Joint Anti-Fascist Refugee Committee* concurrence in his American Philosophical Society talk, Frankfurter explains that when the process unfolds—that is, when there is a shift from what has been the history of the law—"a merely private judgment that the time has come for a shift of opinion regarding law does not justify such a shift."[38] What *does* justify such a shift, then, will not be private, but will be the opposite of private, or "personal," or "subjective," and this would appear to be the "reason" and the "democracy" mentioned in the analysis of the "compound."[39] In the later portions of our inquiry we have been trying to find out what Frankfurter means by use of the word "reason" and we have had some difficulty in our search. That search moved to a point, a few pages above, where we quoted Frankfurter as indicating that the role of judges "in a democratic society" was to "shape their judgments by rational standards."[40] Here then are two instances where a connection is made between democracy and reason, or the rational. What is rational is said to be "impersonal and communicable."[41] That which is "rational" would then appear to be identical with that which is "impersonal," or "communicable." The ultimate guide of judges, then, the crux of due process, is "reason." It is "impersonal" and, as we have said, knowing what that means involves understanding the distinction between "personal" and "impersonal," so that the worth of Frankfurter's answer to Black that judges aren't offered a simple choice between mechanical jurisprudence and personal whim may be measured. Our clue so far is that what is "impersonal" or "rational" is "communicable."

It would be possible to ask at this point what "communicable" means and to stop there with the conclusion that it is all a word game and that Frankfurter has been teasing us all along—that his opinions are like the pieces of a treasure map in a child's game which, when put together, leads to home and spells out in an anagram "Happiness is in your own back yard." But we need not stop here, for the question can be put another way so as to take us a step nearer, and perhaps the last step toward, understanding. We can ask: Communicable to whom? And, obviously, the juxtaposition of "democracy" and "rational" is the clue to the answer.

The problem of the relation between democracy and reason is illustrated by Frankfurter's comments on Jefferson.

> The popular will can steer a proper course only when sufficiently enlightened to know what is the proper course to steer. No one was more conscious than [Jefferson] that democracy is not remotely an automatic device for a good society. Democracy, he well knew, is dependent on knowledge and wisdom beyond all other forms of government. The grandeur of the aims of democracy is matched by the difficulties of their achievement. For democracy is the reign of reason and justice on the most extensive scale. . . . And now we also know how slender a reed is reason—how recent its emergence in men, how deep the countervailing instincts and passions, how treacherous the whole rational process.[42]

We pass the difficulties raised by the assertion that we know how recent is the emergence of reason in men without first knowing what reason is, in order to point to two other aspects of the passage. In the first place, is the statement that reason is a slender reed and the rational process treacherous an argument for democracy or against reason or what? Does it simply equate the two? Or does it subordinate the one to the other, and, if so, which to which? In the second place, and following upon the first question, does it promote the well-being of democracy—can democracy *be* the reign of reason and justice—if one expects knowledge and wisdom to become democratic commodities? To put it another way, if democracy is the reign of reason and justice, and reason and justice are the fruits of or kin of knowledge and wisdom, *where* in a democracy do knowledge and wisdom reside? Can democracy be saved by reliance on democracy?

In his testimonial to Thomas Mann, Frankfurter points to the correlation of the rise of Nazism and the weakening in Western nations of "faith in democracy."[43] But these phenomena were accompanied by lowering of regard for reason, also, and simply to note their coincidence is not the same as explaining them. He goes on to speak of citizenship as the "most important office in a democracy" and then to say that "no citizen exercises a more important function in a democracy than does a poet."[44] But this raises certain problems in any attempt to see the relation between democracy and reason, for poets are not champions of reason. Certainly the raising of patriotic sentiment in the breasts of the ruled is indispensable to the maintenance of any rule, and certainly poets are charged with raising and maintaining such sentiments. Especially in a democracy would it be difficult to have such sentiment without employment of the poetic art. But it is not for nothing that Plato has Socrates banish the poets early in his account of the *Republic* only to let them back in after they have become chastened and have discovered that there *are* officers of higher rank than they, and the ludicrous business of the Soviets demoting their poets for "counter-revolutionary" or "bourgeois" output rests on a crazy approximation to the truth that the office of raising sentiments must be subordinated to the office of deciding *which* sentiments are to be raised. Poetry rests on inspiration and, as Socrates is made to show in the *Ion*, inspiration, as such, cannot be the ultimate guide. In the same year (1945) as his testimonial to Mann, Frankfurter wrote the foreword to a study in criminology[45] in which he points out that "the imaginative insight of a Shakespeare is no substitute for the systematic, scientific pursuits of a Freud."[46] While we cannot agree with the relative ranks he assigns to Shakespeare and Freud, we think that the subordination of poetry, properly understood, to science, properly understood, is right.

Reason, or science, or some such thing, then, may be said to be the chief-of-staff and poets are merely the colonels of society. But, while Frankfurter and Plato may appear to be in agreement on the relative ranking of science or reason and poetry, they differ greatly in that there is in the Platonic *corpus* a clear indication of the nature of reason. In the case of Frankfurter, one must winnow a great deal in order to see what it is that he thinks reason is. Thus far we have only shown that it is somehow related to democracy in his view. Poetry, too, is left undefined by him and, in fact, he states explicitly that it need not be defined.

> It is not for this Court to formulate with particularity the terms of a permit system which would satisfy the Fourteenth Amendment. No doubt finding a want of such standards presupposes some conception of what is necessary to meet the constitutional requirement we draw from the Fourteenth Amendment. But many a decision of this Court rests on some inarticulate major premise and is none the worse for it. A standard may be found inadequate without the necessity of explicit delineation of the standards that would be adequate, just as doggerel may be felt not to be poetry without the need of writing an essay on what poetry is.[47]

Very good! But to distinguish between poetry and doggerel requires some *taste* or *discrimination*, and taste is the preserve of the few, which is the same as to say that the many are notoriously fond of doggerel.

Is reason, then, more widespread than taste? Will most everybody know what standards satisfy the Fourteenth Amendment or only most everybody who reads the *United States Reports*? Why didn't the Circuit Court of Harford County, Maryland know, in the case from which we just quoted? Frankfurter tells us that the "public conscience must be satisfied that fairness dominates the administration of justice."[48] This is an agreeable statement as far as it goes, but it does not go very far. It goes only as far as to say that the many are the seat of a rough quantum of sense and sensibility and, in the long run, if they are not corrupted, they will not abide manifest breaches of common sense and common justice. But it does not say whether justice is or is not identical with common justice. And it does not say how much the many may be corrupted and how such corruption may be warded off. Most important, in the context of our present inquiry, it is a mere tautology, for it says nothing at all about the satisfaction of fair standards in the *hard* cases—the due process cases. In a larger sense, however, it is not tautology for to say that the many *may* be sufficiently uncorrupted as to recognize and reject manifest injustice is to say that popular governments may be relatively just, and that is to say no small thing.

History, reason, and democracy are said to be the guides of due process, and we have seen the great difficulty with history and so have turned to reason and democracy, but we have encountered resistance to our efforts to disentangle the two. Some light is thrown on the problem by a case involving such an ignominious matter as the sale of black pepper. In 1944 the War Department requisitioned from Commodities Trading Corporation a quantity of pepper which the latter had been withholding from the market, and paid it the O.P.A. ceiling price of 6.63 cents per pound. Commodities Trading sued for "just compensation" which, according to is calculations was 22 cents per pound. The Court of Claims awarded 15 cents and the government got a review by the Supreme Court which by a five to two vote, speaking through Mr. Justice Black, reversed the Court of Claims and directed it, on remand, to rule in favor of the government's ceiling-price stand. Frankfurter, dissenting in part, agreed that the Court of Claims had ruled by inadequate standards, but contended that just compensation might well be above the ceiling price. What *would* be just? "The owner should be requited by that which satisfies prevailing standards of justice."[49]

"Prevailing standards of justice" do not equate perfectly with "market value," according to Frankfurter but it seems they are cousin to it. The difference may be explained in this way: For a particular commodity—especially one which, like pepper, makes up a tiny proportion of the household budget—the individual members of society may be willing to pay an "outrageous price," and such a price may be the "market value"; but, acting together through a government, the same society may use some rough measure of what the price of the commodity *ought* to be and would, at market, be, if the market were not bent by some irregular condition, and that is the "prevailing standard of justice" with respect, at least, to the price of pepper. How they are related may be explained thus: the one is the working of the market place of commodities and the other is the working of what may be called the "market place of opinion." That is, both are simply a function of "what folks think" about pepper and about money.

That one could look high and low and not find anyone willing to equate the price of a pound of pepper and the price of a medium bomber indicates that there is some connection between "prevailing standards" and justice—that is to say, that there is such a thing as common sense or common decency. But that the market price of a singer of popular songs may be, say, fifty times the market price of a commanding general suggests the limited validity of those prevailing standards. The limitations become more pressingly apparent when one inquires into the relation between "just compensation" and justice; between a fair price and a fair trial.[50] Can one look to the same sources for an answer? Is the taking of private property for public use without just compensation the same as, or different from, the taking of life or liberty without due process of law? There is the strongest indication that, for Frankfurter, the answers to the two questions are to be found in the same source.

In his concurring opinion in the faulty electric chair case we are told that the standards are not:

> personal standards but the impersonal standards of society which alone judges, as the organs of law, are empowered to enforce. . . . One must be on guard against finding in personal disapproval a reflection of more or less prevailing condemnation. Strongly drawn as I am to some of the sentiments expressed by my brother Burton, I cannot rid myself of the conviction that were I to hold that Louisiana would transgress the Due Process Clause if the State were allowed, in the precise circumstances before us, to carry out the death sentence, I would be enforcing my private view rather than that consensus of society's opinion which, for purposes of due process, is the standard enjoined by the Constitution. . . . Since I cannot say that it would be "repugnant to the conscience of mankind" . . . for Louisiana to exercise the power on which she here stands, I cannot say that the Constitution withholds it.[51]

For the Court, with Black, Warren, Douglas and Brennan dissenting, in a case upholding the propriety of a conviction in an Illinois court on evidence which failed to get a conviction in a United

States District Court in Illinois for a single act which was said to constitute two offenses—one against the state and one against the United States—he again quoted the *Palko* reference to "the conscience of mankind."[52]

> The Anglo-American system of law is based not upon transcendental revelation but upon the conscience of society ascertained as best it may be by a tribunal disciplined for the task and environed by the best safeguards for disinterestedness and detachment.[53]

Is this, then, the answer to our question "communicable to whom?" Is that which is "impersonal" and therefore not "subjective" that which is *public*? Is the public or communicable thing the popular thing? Are there no other choices beside that which is dismissed with the phrases "transcendental revelation" and that which is lauded as "the conscience of society?" Is the "Brooding omnipresence of Reason" cast out in favor of the brooding omnipresence of the *Zeitgeist* or the *Volksgeist*? Where does "mankind"—a thing quite as "abstract" as the transcendent—get *its* revelation, or is the "conscience" answerable to nothing? Can the land make anything due process of law by its mere will, or is the "will of the people" appreciably different from "the conscience of mankind?" Is what is revealed to mankind obviously superior to what is revealed to the few? Won't this be true only of the easy cases, and, if so, is the ultimate standard of right and wrong forged in the easy cases?

Time and again we are told that due process is "respect enforced by law for that feeling of just treatment which has been evolved through centuries of Anglo-American constitutional history and civilization,"[54] or is composed of "standards of decency deeply felt and widely recognized in Anglo-American jurisdictions."[55] So pervasive and so compelling is his deference to the "conscience of mankind" that he has been willing to override his deference to state powers, the words of the Eleventh Amendment, his abhorrence of "judicial legislation," his restraint in the face of Congressional action, and even "history" in order to find governmental immunity from suit an "anachronistic survival of monarchical privilege."[56]

The conclusion is inescapable that when Frankfurter denies Black's taunt that judgment at all means judgment by personal whim, his denial takes the form of equating private or individual judgment with personal whim. For the judge to look outside himself means to Frankfurter *not* to look to external standards which are right despite personal opinion but which may be understandable only to a few, for to look to such standards appears to him to be to look to something which deserves to be dismissed with sarcasm as "transcendental" or as a "brooding omnipresence." To look outside oneself, according to Frankfurter means to look to dominant opinion. The most astounding of his statements on this matter occurs in a case which reversed the conviction of a fifteen year old negro in a trial to which was admitted in evidence a confession secured after a five-hour interrogation begun at midnight:

Subtle and elusive as [are the criteria of due process], we cannot escape that duty of judicial review. The nature of the duty, however, makes it especially important to be humble in exercising it. Humility in this context means an alert self-scrutiny so as to avoid infusing into the vagueness of a Constitutional command one's merely private notions. Like other mortals, judges though unaware, may be in the grip of prepossessions. The only way to relax such a grip, the only way to avoid finding in the Constitution the personal bias one has placed in it, is to explore the influences that have shaped one's unanalyzed views in order to lay bare prepossessions.

A lifetime's preoccupation with criminal justice, as prosecutor, defender of Civil liberties and scientific student, naturally leaves one with views.[57]

The "views" he is left with, including disapproval of capital punishment as such and disapproval of trying boys of fifteen by the same mode as trials of men, are then mentioned and dismissed. It is not that the legislative judgment of Ohio or the judicial judgment of its Supreme Court is not to be opposed. It is that *if* they are to be opposed it must be by the "deep, even if inarticulate, feelings of our society" which judges "must divine."[58]

But is this not absurd? Does it not defy the very proposition that the rational is the communicable, for can one communicate if words have lost their meaning? Can *anything* mean *anything* to *anybody*, if the distinction between judgment and pre-judgment, between considered judgment and prejudice, is destroyed by equating the views one is left with after what then amounted to forty years of preoccupation, roughly divided between theoretical inquiry and practice at bar and bench, with "prepossessions" and "bias?"

If the conclusion of long study is no better than a "prepossession" it must be that there is no such thing as truth, including true justice, or at least that long study will not bring one a whit closer to it than he was to begin with. Every opinion is as good as every other, and opinion is indistinguishable from feeling. The only alternative to visceral jurisprudence is the "conscience of mankind" and the conscience is informed by the viscera of mankind. This is why Frankfurter takes refuge, in all humility, in the dominant view, and why he often refers to that view not as opinion, but as "feeling." The dominant feeling is a sanctuary to which judges may turn for safety. If it is followed there is less trouble and less trouble is to be sought because civil peace is preferable to civil war. But, no! This would only be true when civil peace obtained, for nothing is true, simply, and, quite obviously, when civil war is in progress the "dominant feeling" favors civil war over civil peace, else there would be no war. Self-restraint becomes a kind of selfishness, a kind of dereliction. "Dominating humility" in the face of dominant opinion overlooks the fact that something may be right *in spite of* the fact that the judge, after long study, has concluded that it is right.[59]

Frankfurter, though a democrat, is not a simple democrat. *Salus populi suprema lex* is not transmuted simply into *vox populi, vox Dei*. It is more that *viscera populi, salus populi* with a recognition that, often enough, the *vox* and the *viscera* are not identical. The majority can be wrong. It is more that after the manner of Burke, one looks to the "views and feelings that may fairly be deemed representative of the community as a continuing society."[60] But that sends us back around the circle to history. "Reason" is not subsumed by democracy; it is simply ground between the millstones of democracy and history. As in the case of Pound, it loses its independent potency. In place of a Reason derided as a "brooding omnipresence in the sky" we have a reason which flits from behind the cloud of history to behind the cloud of democracy, teasing us as a bird does a cat, now swooping almost within reach, now careening off and out of sight with enticing but maddening, and finally fading, chatter.

One cannot look to the "conscience of the community" or the "conscience of mankind" as a check upon legislative action, for the "community," or "mankind," *has* no conscience in the sense in which a man may be said to have one. Insofar as a community *has* a conscience it is expressed by the legislature more often than by anything else, and this fact is the basis of Frankfurter's doctrine of restraint. But to say this need not drive one to identify conscience and will and it is precisely legislative willfulness that is to be checked.

Nor can one look to the "continuing" aspects of the community, for it is precisely the mediation between the what was of continuity and the what-has-just-come-to-be of the legislature which the due process clause demands of the Court. Either one would have to rule out *all* change as inconsistent with the what was of continuity or one would have to discern those "trends" or "processes" of history upon the stream of which Frankfurter has rightly told us we must not unthinkingly float. History, or continuity, cannot be the ultimate judge. History is a thing to be judged. If one looks to history for "due process" he sees that it is characterized by a kaleidoscopic array of processes. In the name of what does the judge prefer this process to that? It is useful here to repeat what has elsewhere been said on the judge's problem in selecting some and excluding other processes:

> Why does he prefer, say, an adversary proceeding to ordeal by fire? It cannot be because ordeal by fire is older and adversary proceedings newer—that is, it cannot be what has "evolved"—because then the latest process to be adopted would be due process and reliance upon that history which antedates breakfast would be mere reaction. It cannot be because ordeal by fire "shocks the sensibilities" because, quite obviously, whatever has been adopted by the voice of the people does not shock the people's sensibilities. If the people choose ordeal by fire it is due process. It will not do to turn to what "English-speaking peoples" consider due, for so to turn would be to deprive the several jurisdictions among English-speaking peoples of their freedom to adopt and abandon processes. Or, to put it another way, the several jurisdictions *are* the English-speaking peoples and to look to those peoples for a standard means to look also to the jurisdiction which has elected ordeal by fire as its process. . . . Stability *is* an essential element of the law, and change there *will* be, and courts as well as legislatures *are* concerned with striking a balance. But life, liberty or property may not be taken without due process of law, and what is due is not immanent in what has been nor in what is coming to be.[61]

It would seem that the Court's difficulty in dealing with the due process clause of the Fourteenth Amendment and with the phrase "essential fairness" which, and no more than which, the due process clause of the Fourteenth Amendment is said to require of the states is capable of resolution only by restoring to reason its independent status.

NOTES TO CHAPTER VI

[1]L.L. Jaffe, "The Judicial Universe of Mr. Justice Frankfurter," *Harvard Law Review,* LXII (January 1949), 357.

[2]Frankfurter concurring in the judgment in *Still* v. *Norfolk and Western R. Co.,* 368 U.S. 35 at 47 (1961).

[3]Dissenting in *Reed* v. *Pennsylvania R. Co.,* 351 U.S. 502, 509 (1956).

[4]Frankfurter dissenting in *Public Service Commission of Utah* v. *United States,* 356 U.S. 421, 429 (1958).

[5]Review of A.W. Machen, Jr., *A Treatise of the Modern Law of Corporations* (Boston: Little Brown, 1908), in *Harvard Law Review,* XII (June, 1909), 618-19.

[6]A.N. Hand, "Mr. Justice Frankfurter," *Harvard Law Review,* LXII (January, 1949), 353.

[7]Separate opinion by Frankfurter in *Texas* v. *Florida,* 306 U.S. 398 at 434 (1939), and compare his dissent in *Connecticut Life Ins. Co.* v. *Moore,* 333 U.S. 541 at 555 (1948), and his dissent in *Johnson* v. *United States,* 333 U.S. 46 at 56 (1948).

[8]Dissenting in *Larson* v. *Domestic & Foreign Commerce Corp.,* 337 U.S. 682 at 705-06. Cf. Frankfurter's opinion (judgment of the Court) in *New York* v. *U.S.,* 326 U.S. 572 at 575.

[9]Frankfurter dissenting in *Mitchell* v. *Trawler Racer, Inc.,* 362 U.S. 539 at 550-51 (1960).

[10]"The Permanence of Jefferson," in *L and M,* p. 229.

[11]"Mr. Justice Roberts," *ibid.,* p. 212.

[12]For the Court in *Guaranty Trust Co.* v. *York,* 326 U.S. 99 at 101 (1945).

[13]*Ibid.,* p. 102.

[14]*Dennis* v. *United States,* 341 U.S. 494. Concurring in affirmance of the judgment at 555-56.

[15]*West Virginia State Board of Education* v. *Barnette,* 319 U.S. 624 at 647. Cf. Berns, *op. cit.,* p. 180. "The Court will exercise its powers only when legislators are idiots. But [not even then, really.]"

[16]*Dennis* v. *United States* (the first Dennis case), 339 U.S. 162, in dissent with respect to a Fifth Amendment impartial jury question, at 184-85; *Sacher* v. *United States,* 343 U.S. 1, in dissent with respect to the summary judicial power to find contempt, at 24; *United States* v. *Rabinowitz,* 339 U.S. 56, in dissent with respect to a Fourth Amendment search and seizure question, at 79; *Baltimore & Ohio R. Co.*

v. *Kepner,* 314 U.S. 44, in dissent with respect to a question of statutory construction, at 62; *Czaplicki* v. *The Hoegh Silvercloud,* 351 U.S. 525, concurring in a case involving the Longshoremen's and Harbor Workers' Compensation Act, at 535; *McNabb* v. *United States,* 318 U.S. 332 at 340, for the Court with respect to the admissibility of evidence.

[17]*United States* v. *United Mine Workers,* 330 U.S. 258, Frankfurter concurring in the judgment, at 308, citing Roscoe Pound, "The Future of Law," *Yale Law Journal,* XLVII (1937), 1, 13.

[18]*Johnson* v. *New York, N.H. & H.R. Co.,* 344 U.S. 48 (1952), dissenting at pp. 55-56.

[19]*Op. cit.,* p. 62, quoting Roscoe Pound, "The Etiquette of Justice," *Proceedings of the Nebraska State Bar Association,* III (1909), 231.

[20]Roscoe Pound, *Law Finding Through Experience and Reason* (Athens, Ga.: University of Georgia Press, 1960), p. 45.

[21]*Ibid.,* p. 46.

[22]*Ibid.*

[23]*Ibid.,* p. 7.

[24]*Ibid.*

[25]*Felix Frankfurter Reminisces,* p. 169.

[26]*McNabb* v. *United States,* 318 U.S. 332 at 347.

[27]See Frankfurter concurring in *Adamson* v. *California,* 332 U.S. 46 at 62; dissenting in *Penfield Co.* v. *S.E.C.,* 330 U.S. 585, 609.

[28]Frankfurter dissenting in *Sacher* v. *United States,* 343 U.S. 1 at 24. Presumably the "drastic power" here mentioned is either that of the instant sentence—the power of effective administration of justice, in general—or that of the case—the summary contempt power in particular.

[29]*McNabb* v. *United States,* 318 U.S. 332 at 340-41.

[30]For the Court in *Wolf* v. *Colorado,* 338 U.S. 25.

[31]1 *Wheat.* 304 (1816).

[32]Frankfurter concurring in *American Federation of Labor* v. *American Sash and Door Co.,* 335 U.S. 538, at 557.

[33]See *supra,* p. 143.

[34]*Ibid.,* and see also, *supra,* p. 121.

[35]*United States* v. *Rabinowitz,* 339 U.S. 56 (1950), Frankfurter dissenting at 68.

[36]*L and M,* p. 36. This is an exact quotation from his own concurring opinion in *Joint Anti-Fascist Refugee Committee* v. *McGrath,* 341 U.S. 123, 162-63.

[37]See *supra,* p. 126.

[38]*L and M,* p. 37.

[39]Why something which is not a "pharmacopoeia," Frankfurter's opinion in *Malinski* v. *New York,* 324 U.S. 401 at 417, should be described by a word most at home in a pharmacy is not explained.

[40]335 U.S. 538, 557. See *supra,* p. 166.

[41]*Ibid.*

[42]"The Permanence of Jefferson," in *L and M,* p. 235. Cf. Frankfurter's concurring opinion in *Pennekamp* v. *Florida,* 328 U.S. 331 at 350.

[43]*L and M,* p. 348.

[44]*Ibid.,* p. 349.

[45]Sheldon and Eleanor Glueck, *After-Conduct of Discharged Offenders* (New York: St. Martin's Press, 1945). Foreword reprinted in *L and M,* p. 72.

⁴⁶*Ibid.*, p. 74.

⁴⁷*Niemotko* v. *Maryland*, 340 U.S. 268, Frankfurter concurring in the result, at 285.

⁴⁸For the Court in *Adams* v. *United States ex rel McCann*, 317 U.S. 269 at 279.

⁴⁹Frankfurter, dissenting in part in *United States* v. *Commodities Trading Corp.*, 339 U.S. 121, 134.

⁵⁰The equation here of justice and a fair trial is in agreement with the views of Frankfurter. Of course a perfect equation of justice-in-theory and justice-in-practice would mean that all the guilty would be apprehended and punished in exact proportion to their crimes and that no innocent person would ever be punished. Or, better, it would mean the absence of all punishment because of an absence of all guilt. To equate justice and a fair trial is not to suppose that such a perfect equation of justice-in-theory and justice-in-practice would ever come to pass. It is only to suggest that the nearest we may come, humanly speaking, to justice is to adhere rigorously to standards of fairness in trials. A country which is just-in-practice is not one in which everyone ''gets what is coming to him'' in the sense of divine justice. But an unjust country is one that does not give everyone the process which is due him. The inquiry we have been pursuing is directed to determining where one looks to see what process is due.

⁵¹*Louisiana ex rel Francis* v. *Resweber*, 329 U.S. 459 at 470-72.

⁵²*Bartkus* v. *Illinois*, 359 U.S. 121 at 127, quoting *Palko* v. *Connecticut*, 302 U.S. 319 at 323.

⁵³359 U.S. at 128.

⁵⁴*Joint Anti-Fascist Refugee Committee* v. *McGrath*, 341 U.S. 123, Frankfurter concurring at 162.

⁵⁵Dissenting in *Stein* v. *New York*, 346 U.S. 156 at 199. Cf. his opinion for the Court in *National City Bank of New York* v. *Republic of China*, 348 U.S. 356 at 360, and see his opinions for the Court in *Wolf* v. *Colorado*, 338 U.S. 25 and *Rochin* v. *California*, 342, U.S. 165 in their entireties.

⁵⁶Dissenting in *Kennecott Copper Corp.* v. *Tax Commission*, 327 U.S. 573 and compare the *National City Bank* case cited in the preceding note and his dissent in *Great Northern Insurance Co.* v. *Read*, 323 U.S. 47 at 59 and his opinions for the Court in *Keifer and Keifer* v. *R.F.C.*, 305 U.S. 381 at 389 and 396, and in *Indian Towing Co.* v. *United States*, 350 U.S. 61 at 65. The Keifer case may have been the first case he heard argued, for it was argued on January 31, 1931, and he took his seat the day before, a Monday on which at least seventeen decisions involving full scale opinions were rendered. See 59 *S. Ct.* 366-447 and 456-58.

⁵⁷Joining in reversal of the judgment in *Haley* v. *Ohio*, 332 U.S. 596 at 602.

⁵⁸*Ibid.*, p. 603.

⁵⁹The best critique we have seen of Frankfurter's doctrine of restraint is that in Clyde Summers, ''Frankfurter, Labor Law and the Judge's Function'' which is part of a *Festschrift* to Frankfurter to which Vol. LXVII, No. 2 of the *Yale Law Journal* is devoted. See especially pp. 281-82, 290, 292 and 302-03. That critique is based on other grounds: namely, that deference to the legislature ignores the fact that the legislature often does not do its work and seldom does it neatly and well.

⁶⁰Frankfurter, ''The Judicial Process and the Supreme Court,'' *L and M*, p. 40. Compare E. Burke, *Reflections on the Revolution in France*, ''Each contract of each particular state is but a clause in the great primeval contract of eternal society. . . .'' Burke's *Political Writings*, ed. J. Buchan (London: Thomas Nelson,

n.d.), p. 306. Also in *Selected Writings of Edmund Burke,* ed. W.J. Bate (New York: Modern Library, 1960), p. 407.

  [61]Stevens (1961), *op. cit.,* pp. 216-17.

CHAPTER VII

FRANKFURTER'S TEACHING

Frankfurter admonishes us that, since "the significance of every expression of thought derives from the circumstances evoking it, results reached rather than language employed give the vital meaning."[1] In the face of this admonition, lawyers might not look with approval upon a study of the law which begins with a detailed account of a case but proceeds to treat principally of the character of Frankfurter's reasoning almost to the exclusion of consideration of the results in that case. It must be admitted that the present study concentrates almost entirely upon the "language employed." But our purpose is to criticize the law as such and this cannot be done by pious adherence to the modes of analysis most congenial to lawyers.

The present concern is not so much with the results in specific cases as with the character of Frankfurter's teaching. But, lest the forest be said to hide the trees, the connection between language employed and individual results may be illustrated. Under the provisions of the Nationality Act of 1940[2] a native-born citizen of the United States named Trop was deprived of his citizenship for desertion from the army in wartime. A split majority reversed that deprivation on the grounds that the portion of the Nationality Act involved[3] was unconstitutional in that it inflicted "cruel and unusual punishment" forbidden by the Eighth Amendment.[4] Frankfurter, writing a dissent joined by Justices Burton, Clark and Harlan, restrained himself despite his admission that it "is not easy to stand aloof and allow want of wisdom to prevail, to disregard one's own strongly held view of what is wise in the conduct of affairs."[5] In the course of his dissent he asks:

> Is constitutional dialectic so empty of reason that it can be
> seriously urged that loss of citizenship is a fate worse than
> death?[6]

Several difficulties suggest themselves. First the mention of
"dialectic" reminds us of Socrates, who, by Frankfurter's rules, must
have been empty of reason—a soft, old fool. It cannot be forgotten
that he preferred death to exile. Can "reason" have any meaning at
all if the life and death of Socrates are kept out? In the second place,
can the doctrine of restraint be so empty of reason as to declare that
the notion that loss of citizenship is a fate worse than death is
unreasonable while overlooking the fact that *the entire rationale of
section 401(g) of the Nationality Act is the supposition that the threat
of the loss of citizenship will be sufficient in most cases to inhibit
desertion from exposure to fire*. It may be that Frankfurter's result in
this case is the right one, for it may be that loss of citizenship is not
worse than death for a coward. Alternatively, it may be that a fate
worse than death is a fate appropriate to cowards according to the
highest wisdom, but, on the other hand, it may be that the
Constitution, in its restraint, forbears to award it. Maybe the
Constitution does not think it appropriate to confront all men with a
problem only a Socrates could resolve. Is there not a certain boldness
in preferring one's own restraint *from* laying hands on the legislature
to the Constitution's laying of restraining hands *on* the legislature?

The result in the individual case, however, seems to us, as academic
commentator, less important than the result *of* the case upon the
law,[7] and the result of the case upon the law, seems to us, contrary to
Frankfurter's preference in *Dennis* for results as opposed to
language, to depend more upon the language than upon the result.
This is, in fact, not out of keeping with what he has said elsewhere:

> The disposition of a case is of prime importance to the parties.
> How a result is reached concerns the rational development of the
> law.[8]

How a result is reached, what the *reasoning* of the case is—that is,
the language employed—is important in the development of the law
in two senses. On the one hand, the whole understanding of bench
and bar regarding the nature of the law is fashioned by the

explanation of the Supreme Court more than by anything else.[9] On the other hand, despite Frankfurter's telling us, as we noted, in the last chapter,[10] that poets were the great officers of democracy and his telling us in another place that teachers are the "priests of democracy,"[11] we believe that statesmen—and, among them, judges—are vastly important as teachers in a democracy. What else could *Cooper* v. *Aaron*[12] and its militant unanimity import? Judges are important as teachers in a democracy both in that they teach what the law is and—and this may be the crucial matter in a democracy because it guards what is by nature democracy's weakest flank—in that they teach the habit of law-abidingness without which a democracy can be the most brutal of tyrannies. It requires no citation of proofs to assert that Frankfurter is fully aware of the Jacobin danger to democracy and busier than any of his colleagues in an earnest effort to teach lawfulness to the country.

But the question is, has his teaching been salutary? He reminds us from time to time that courts are to construe so as to save legislation.[13] We have been arguing throughout this study that just as statutes are to be "saved"—i.e., rendered constitutional if they may be—so the Constitution, which must also be "construed," should be construed so as to render it just rather than the contrary. It is not possible to construe legislation without regard to its "wisdom or evil." Nor is it possible to construe the Constitution without regard to its "spirit" or "plan and purpose." Since it must be construed it ought to be construed so as to save rather than destroy.

The juridical teaching of the law and of lawfulness operates through the media of both results and reasoning. Our mention of *Trop* v. *Dulles* suggests—or, rather, states the obvious—connections between reasoning and results within the case. Before turning to concluding remarks on the connection between Frankfurter's reasons, or theory—which in his case shows itself at first as a theory of reason—we must offer an illustration of the connection between his results-in-the-case and the result upon law and lawfulness.

In a divorce case involving a full-faith-and-credit question Frankfurter's dissent offers what is to our mind an excellent teaching about the special interest which society has in the well-being of the marriage contract. It is, we believe, a "conservative" counsel in the best sense of that much-abused word. In the course of his opinion he indulges himself in moral outrage because the practical result of the Vinson decision from which he dissents is:

> to offer new inducements for conduct by parties and counsel, which, in any other type of litigation, would be regarded as perjury, but which is not so regarded where divorce is involved because ladies and gentlemen indulge in it.[14]

Quite aside from the fact that his stand in this case is questionable when measured by his own criteria—for it would be hard to deny that the "dominant feeling" is, and has for some time been in this country, one of permissiveness toward both divorce and the lying that is done in order to circumvent ancient and conflicting laws to get it—we would assert that the stand is salutary in its vigorous refusal to contribute to the country's delinquency by ruling so as to promote lying. But, if it is wrong in Frankfurter's view for the Court to rule in such a way as to encourage "ladies and gentlemen" to commit perjury, what can one say of his judgment for the Court in the recent attempt to test the Connecticut laws forbidding the giving of advice on contraceptive methods?

That judgment, carried in an opinion joined by Justices Clark and Whittaker and the Chief Justice, with Justice Brennan writing a concurring opinion to make up the majority, presses the doctrine of restraint to its uttermost limits. Connecticut law forbids the use of contraceptives.[15] It also promises that any "person who . . . counsels . . . another to commit any offense may be prosecuted and punished as if he were the principal offender."[15] The State's construction of the confluence of these two provisions is that it is a criminal offense for anyone—even a licensed physician—to counsel anyone— regardless of physical condition or marital status—respecting the use of contraceptives. In the instant case, a physician wished to counsel one of his patients, a woman who had a history of stillborn offspring and whose life was said to be endangered by the possibility of subsequent pregnancy, respecting contraceptive devices and methods. A previous Supreme Court decision having ruled that a *physician* had no "standing" as a real "adversary" to the law in such a problem[16] and therefore did not present the Court with a "justiciable" question, the parties in *this* instance were the *patient* and the state. The Court's ruling this time was that the patient did not present a "real" case to the Court because prosecution was very unlikely. It said, in effect: Go out and get yourself arrested and then come back and see us![17]

Now, the doctrine of restraint as pressed by Frankfurter goes further than the express limits of the Constitution in its hold on Court action. As his dissent in the apportionment case[18] shows, it is based on a general understanding of how the Court can best apply its qualities to the well-being of the country. But what does *Poe* v. *Ullman* do? Even if we grant *arguendo*, that Dr. Buxton and his fictitiously named patient had been for some time defying Connecticut law, is the result in the *Poe* case not calculated to teach all men that when they find themselves conscientiously to believe that the law unconstitutionally forbids their doing what they believe themselves to have every right to do, their proper course of action is to *defy* the law—to take the law in their own hands? Frankfurter dismisses this problem by referring to Dr. Buxton's "personal sensitiveness."[19] Is that *all* it is? With Mr. Justice Harlan, in dissent, "I find it difficult to believe . . . that high-minded members of the profession would . . . deem themselves warranted in disrespecting this law so long as it is on the books."[20]

Much of our law is the product of litigation pressed by low-minded men. Admiral Dewey Adamson was not a pillar of Los Angeles society. Perhaps much law must be made in such litigation, but must it be the law of the land that high-minded professional men are forbidden to contribute? Is it "good law" to teach Americans that they ought to be lawful only when they are in agreement with the law—that they ought to defy the law every time they think a good chance exists of "beating" it in the courts? In 1941 Frankfurter said, "Litigation is, as it were, the pathological aspect of society."[21] But this is simply pious antiquarianism if the underlying principle of the *Poe* case—that the law is made by everyone living as he pleases and telling the law to come and get him if it likes—is to be the law of the land. Litigation is pathological only if the healthy state is seen as one in which the whole apparatus of the law teaches the citizen to abide by the spirit of the law—to *aim* at what the law aims at. But *Poe* teaches the citizen to skate as close to criminality as he dares and to cross the line whenever in his judgment the law is defective, just as Frankfurter's opinion for the Court in *Atlantic Coast Line Railroad*

Company v. *Phillips* teaches that the citizen's duty is to pay as little taxes as he can get away with paying.[22] We cannot have it both ways. We cannot have a law based fundamentally upon individual freedom as the highest good and then speak of that law in terms which, outside of the traditional understanding that the law is pointed toward human excellence, amounts to no more than a rhetorical flourish. Rhetorical flourishes cannot shore up the law, they only trick it up. They make desirable adornments to, but cannot be adequate substitutes for, sound teaching.

Sound teaching is composed not of rhetorical flourishes but of what might be called the "noble rhetoric." It is addressed by the wise to those who lack wisdom, and the latter group is composed of a small number who may be said to be not yet wise and a great number who will never be wise. Of course, the largest and most immediate share of this didactic burden falls upon politicians who command the ear of the many from day to day. In the United States this task of necessity falls like a great and full sack upon the shoulders of the President. But it cannot on account thereof be supposed that the judge's burden is small, or can be done poorly, or can be avoided.

Frankfurter has admitted that judges exercise "a profound task of statecraft,"[23] and has recognized that judges make law.[24] But lawmaking is said by him to be confined by the "judicial function" and by "democracy."[25] But that judges should be judicial cannot mean that when they make law they don't make law and yet that is the mood of all such sayings by Frankfurter. Nor can harmony with democracy—unless it be complete submission to democracy which, ultimately, is the denial of the "judicial function"—mean that the judge must not do what he must do. In one place, Frankfurter has told us that:

> however limited the area of adjudication may be, the standards of what is fair and just set by courts in controversies appropriate for their adjudication are perhaps the single most powerful influence in promoting the spirit of law throughout government. These standards also help shape the dominant civic habits and attitudes which ultimately determine the ethos of a society.
>
> In exercising their technical jurisdiction, courts thus release contagious consequences.[26]

There can be no quarrel with Frankfurter's assertion that judges ought to do what judges ought to do. This limitation involves a disinclination to leap to the decision of cases not yet "ripe," a disinclination to leap to a contest with other governors. It even involves what the Declaration calls a "decent respect for the opinions of mankind." Thus far "judicial restraint" make sense and one would expect in the normal course of events for judges who agree thereon to engage from case to case in respectably lawyer-like disputes over when and how it comes into play. But the hard cases—the due process cases—drive judges to say what is "fair and just." Frankfurter's shortcoming is the *extent* to which his doctrine of restraint leads him to draw back from judgment and the fact that when he says what is fair and just he does not say it well and he therefore releases in society a contagion that requires a cure. In the last analysis, Frankfurter's view of the "role of the judge" is identical with his view of what is "fair and just." Both views rest upon the same underlying notion and that is why we have contended[27] that the measure of a judge *cannot* be the measure of his view of the role of the judge.

Frankfurter has admitted that "the quality of society is largely determined by a few people,"[28] and he knows that judges are among the few. But he draws back from the consequences of that knowledge. We must repeat what has been elsewhere urged, in order to press this argument to its conclusion:

> There is a sense in which one may speak of the "conscience of the community." That is, there is a wish common to men in society that somehow justice be done. The Constitution leaves it largely to the legislature to declare what belongs to whom. But certain limits are set upon the legislature . . . and one of the limitations in the law of the Constitution points beyond law proper to law in the largest sense: that is the due process clause. It commands that legislative innovations shall not run counter to what is, by nature, right. To know what is by nature right is to be very wise, and wisdom is the preserve of the few. . . .
>
> The "conscience of the community" is a vague undefined wish for justice and its expression in the due process clause refers its specific application to the wisdom and expertise of judges. . . .
>
> [W]hen Mr. Justice Frankfurter refers to the "conscience of the community" to find due process he simply returns to the

arbitrament of a vague wish what that wish had referred to him.
He is our hired conscience. . . .

What justifies the community in vesting such a duty and the
judge in accepting it? Well, the judge is a student of the law. The
law does not present the final answer, for, in the hard cases—the
due process cases—the law is the very thing to be judged. But the
law everywhere *points* to justice, and a life spent in its study
prepares the ground for an understanding of justice. If that
understanding were to be reached it could not be reduced to a
plain formula to be conveyed like a title to real property, for the
admission that it is the product of life-long study is a denial that
it can be so conveyed. The "conscience" of the many require it;
the wisdom of only a few can apply it. The law cannot judge
itself. It points beyond itself to that by which it is judged. The
law stands in need of something, and . . . we would suggest that
the thing by which the law is judged and to which judges may
apply themselves is political philosophy.[29]

We noted above[30] that Frankfurter in one place admitted that the
view of judicial role was dependent upon the "judge's philosophy,
conscious or implicit, regarding the nature of society." But, while
Frankfurter is regarded by many as the most philosophic of recent
justices, we are not so sure that his philosophy is adequate. Merely to
be highly literate, to read a lot of good books, is not to philosophize
about the highest things, unless "read" and "good books" are very
precisely defined. Perhaps Frankfurter's difficulty is not a lack of
philosophy, broadly speaking. Perhaps it is the *wrong* philosophy.
But the defect may be all the same, for the problem may be the
character of present-day philosophical orthodoxies, and Frankfurter's failure to transcend them. These orthodoxies deny the
existence of the truth their adherents claim by their labels to seek.

The Constitution *demands* construction and despite Frankfurter's
prohibition against construing it according to its "spirit" we find him
construing it in the light of his view of judicial role which view is itself
a *construction* of the spirit of the Constitution. "Separation of
powers," "federalism" and "the wall of separation of church and
state" nowhere appear in the Constitution. Even if it be
conceded—and our understanding of the Constitution refuses to
concede it—that these "glosses" on the text are all in keeping with its
spirit, the glosses *themselves* require construction and that
construction is dependent upon one's view of the nature of society

which is dependent upon or identical with one's view of the nature of man. A sensible understanding, for example, of the compelling need for healthy, local self-government need not settle for the merely dominant view of "federalism."[31] Nor need the "separation of powers" drive judges from the vigorous employment of their powers in the public good as they are given to see that good.[32] Nor need a thirst for liberty drive one to see society as a "clash of interests"[33] nor read into the establishment clause a "wall of separation."[34]

The identity of Frankfurter's "restraintist" view of the "role of the judge" and his looking to "dominant feelings" for what is "fair and just" amounts to this: His "philosophy . . . regarding the nature of society" compels him to look for fairness and justice not to philosophy—not to the difficult choice from among the contending statements of the wisest few in all times—but to the "community"—to the many who *have no* philosophy and who are, in fact the antithesis of philosophy. *Salus populi is*, for him, ultimately, *vox populi*. Where Justice Black seems to us to *make* judgments without using judgment often enough, Frankfurter's answer is not to counter it with an appeal to better judgment but with an appeal *from* judgment. Judicial restraint is pressed to the point of judicial dereliction. Frankfurter's view amounts to a highly sophisticated moral relativism. Like all sophisticated things it has a certain merit. It certainly softens the blow of immediate popular opinion. Just as the friction between House and Senate and between Congress and President and between Nation and States has often done us good service, as Madison hoped it would, so the friction between the lawyer's love of continuity and the legislator's passion for change has also dulled the edge of present passions. But opposing present passions merely by reference to continuity systematically promotes the view, indistinguishable at base from a submission to passion or will or public opinion, that ultimately, behind the continuity and the change and the contest between the two there is no *reason* to prefer now the one and now the other for, ultimately, there *is no such thing* as fairness and justice by which the contention can be resolved.

There is no reason because reason itself dissolves in a compound of history and democracy—of continuity and present passion. The conclusion cannot be avoided that to Frankfurter "reason" means

nothing other than what it meant to Justice Stone and it meant
nothing of independent potency to Stone.[35] Twenty-five years ago it
was common to charge Hitler with the accusation that for him "the
ends justified the means." But, in our Kantian attachment to good
means we had not paid sufficient attention to the badness of Hitler's
ends and we had forgotten that truly good ends are achieved only by
good means. The "popular philosophy of the day"—a contradiction
in terms—is not concerned with ends. It is enamored of "process."
As long as judges play the approved "role," or engage in the
approved judicial "process" they will insure "*due* process," but the
"approved process" according to Frankfurter is to defer to the
democratic and historical processes. What is "due" to a person is
what the history of democracy chooses to give to him. The land may
not make anything due process of law by its mere will but it may by its
fairly sustained will or by the "process" through which its will is
played out.

To sum up, then, what the framers intended by the phrase "due
process of law" is not precisely clear and the words themselves clearly
do not provide a precise catalog of commands and prohibitions. The
traditional interpretation of the clause, which Frankfurter continues,
is that the clause means "essential fairness" or that which is "implicit
in the concept of ordered liberty." But Black charges that that means
natural law and that natural law means just what the justices like it to
mean. But Frankfurter answers that it does not mean that—it does
not mean individual, or personal, or subjective judgment. There are,
he says, external criteria to which judges may turn. These criteria
appear to be history and reason and democracy. But upon
examination it appears that neither history nor democracy is an
adequate standard for they are precisely the things *to be judged*. It
further appears that "reason" evaporates in the presence of history
and democracy and, so the ultimate standard by which Frankfurter
finds what process is due to a person is the process of democratic
history or the history of democratic process.

American democracy is, we believe, at a critical stage. Frankfurter
is aware of this and his response seems to be to recall previous
instances where the Court has interfered with the country's attempts
at solutions of its problems, and to believe that the Court's proper
"role" is to stand aside and let the country have its reins. But the

Court is a *part* of the country and we believe that the opposite of hindrance is help, not aloofness. The "role of the judge in a democracy" is not to contribute to the narcissism toward which democracy, by its nature, tends. The judge must, no doubt, teach that democracy is good, but he must do so as much by concern for and teaching about the good as by concern for and teaching about democracy. The way, that is, to keep democracy good is not simply to keep it democratic. Thus, while Black's view of the meaning of due process is wooden and historically false, and Frankfurter's view is both truer and more salutary, and is, in fact, the best available contemporary view, it, too, is defective.

Complete reconstruction of an alternative to Frankfurter's view would be a very great task and we are reminded that to indicate the difficulties in the best available view may, in itself, be useful.[36] But we are also reminded that at least a sketch of where the argument would go from this point is desirable.[37]

The Constitution aims at a "more perfect union" and is established with a view to justice, tranquility, defense, welfare, and liberty. It is perhaps not by accident that union and justice take precedence over liberty. It ordains a legislature, an executive and a judiciary for the furtherance of these ends of the union. Out of a fear of the evils of centralization, a group of amendments was soon added. One of this group assures that whatever the states had been doing they should continue to do unless the Constitution forbade their doing it, or gave the doing over to the union. But what *was* given over included a vast proportion of governmental activity, which it has taken the greater part of two centuries to put to practice. Neither the Tenth Amendment nor any other clause in the Constitution guarantees "states' rights," for the Constitution recognizes that the dangers of centralization are not best checked by recourse to the states as states. The states did not come into being by nature but by historical accident and many were in 1787 far too extended in size to be a refuge from centralization.

Except, however, for a few specific limitations in Art. I, sec. 10 and a few commands in Art. IV (and perhaps by implication, the *habeas corpus* clause in Art. I, sec. 9) the Constitution did leave the ordinary administration of justice to the states. This was not because the states, as states, had by nature a peculiar capacity for justice. It was simply because they were there. But the restrictions in the Constitution do show a concern on the part of the union that the aims of the union be not foreclosed by the fact of the continuation of the states. During the four-score years subsequent to the adoption of the Constitution, however, partisan interests and narrow passions did, in fact, set awry the ordinary administration of justice. And so the Reconstruction, while still leaving that ordinary administration of justice where it had been, tightened the restrictions upon it. After 1868, not only must the states not cross the specific prohibitions of Art. I, sec. 10, but they were also forbidden to deny justice to litigants by any arbitrary administration of their systems of justice.

What the Fourteenth Amendment promises is that the power of the union shall be brought to bear to set things aright whenever a state's system of administration of justice goes wrong. This is no insult to the state. Is it an insult if, when a man's worse gets the better of his better part, his friends, in concert, restrain him? This is no usurpation by the union; it is what the union is for.[38]

All this is not to say that the union will see to it that justice be done in every case. That is not only not feasible as a matter of work-load; it is not within the reach of human ingenuity. Even if a perfectly righteous Supreme Court could give adequate attention to all cases now tried in all courts in the country, and were to try them all *de novo*, it would *at least* be beset with the same difficulty in resolving issues of fact which besets any trial court. But it does say that the union will see to it that justice be *attempted* in every case. No constitution can promise that, in practice, every man will get his due, but a constitution can, and ours does, promise that courts will *try* to give what is due and that promise is tantamount to the promise of a due trial—to the due process of law. Neither life, nor liberty, nor property shall be taken without process nor by improper process.

Of course what one has a right to expect is partly explained by what one has been used to expect. Of course one cannot talk about process, as such, without talking of examples and those examples are bound to be historical examples. And, of course, *our* history will be more understandable and more relevant than somebody else's. And, also, of course, our history is a democratic history in the context of a complicated structure we call "federal." But due process cannot be lost in this forest. It is a tree among trees. The Constitution provides that the history of our federal democracy shall provide due process and due process is not democratic process, nor historical process, nor federalistic process. It is due process.

Due process, as the Court has often said, is essentially fair process. To know what is essentially fair is to have a view of justice, for "due process" is, as Professor Sutherland has neatly said, "that curious phrase we self-consciously use in place of 'justice' or 'right'"[39] The full meaning of justice is to be sought by philosophy. Philosophical truth, like justice, and like due process, is not anywhere laid out "in a pharmacopoeia." Neither is it exuded by history nor stored by the folk. It is philosophized. This means that, at bottom, the judge must have recourse to philosophy.

The judge, we admit, is a practical man concerned day in and day out with affairs, and some of these affairs are petty—say, the price of black pepper—or disgusting—say, what happened to the Los Angeles widow for whose murder Admiral Dewey Adamson was convicted. But concern for affairs great and petty, noble and base, cannot free the judge from concern for that in the light of which affairs are understandable, and the judge may not drive off examination by the use of such epithets as "abstraction" and "transcendental." No one asks him to eschew concern for the things of the moment, the practicalities of the day, the "caseness" of cases, in order to turn to an ivory tower. But Felix Frankfurter was fifty-seven years of age when he went to the Supreme Court. Almost half his life, up to that point, had been spent in Austin Hall at the Harvard Law School. He was not all that time concerned with affairs and with cases.

The difficulty with Frankfurter's view of due process is not that judges have no time for philosophy. Nor is it that he was too busy before his coming to the Court. He came to the Court with a full-blown view as to the order of things. That view is perhaps as well expressed by a statement in a 1931 article he and Nathan Greene wrote as by anything.

> The law must not be asked to be a pioneer in ethics, but it ought
> not to lag behind the common feelings of justice.[40]

This statement is congenial to his doctrine of restraint. It adds up to the popular statement, "You can't legislate morality." The

counterpart of that statement among the current orthodoxies of
political science is the sociological, as opposed to philosophical,
doctrine that theory emanates from practice, that the highest things in
society are simply excrescences upon the lower, that the connection
between "law" and "values" is a one-way street. That connection is
a one-way street because there *are* no higher values. Justice is for
Frankfurter indistinguishable from "common feelings of justice."

So far is he from eschewing the "spirit" of the Constitution that he
is willing to dance close to the edge of a scheme for reading out of the
Constitution those clauses—like the diversity clause and the due
process clause—he does not feel are consistent with its spirit. He does
this by construing them as narrowly as he can. There is nothing in the
Constitution that calls for their narrow construction. His view of the
"spirit of the Constitution" is, then, identical with his view of the
right ordering of society, and that view is identical with the view that
judges ought to be "restrained." All of these sides of the same view
demand that justice be found by recourse to democracy and history,
for, if there is no such thing as justice it certainly is not to be found
elsewhere.

Reconstruction of the due process clause from the posture in which
Frankfurter leaves it would require turning his doctrines of restraint,
democracy, history, and federalism upon their sides. We do not say
"upon their backs," for they are approximations to the right view.
Since the Constitution allows for construction in the light of
Frankfurter's view, it also allows for construction in the light of the
alternative view. That view would see democracy as permitted by the
Constitution, as one of the possible alternative orderings of society
toward justice, tranquility, defense, welfare, and liberty, and as
demanded by the exigencies of the times. But it would also see it as
demanding the guidance of a vigorous judiciary. That guidance and
that vigor would be employed to point democracy upward, rather
than inward. And, that view would call for judicial restraint no less
than Frankfurter's view does, but where the Constitution imposes the
power of the union to check the injustices of the states, that power
would not be turned wrong-side-out by refuge in vague felicities. It
would not be so turned for, were Frankfurter's federalism turned on
its side it would give encouragement to the legitimate preservation of
local self-government without giving strength to those who rely on

wooden and historically specious formulae for the maintenance of narrow and illegal purposes nowhere condoned by the Constitution. That reconstruction would rest upon a view of the judicial role which understood the nature of man and the nature of the political as pointed toward a justice which is not dependent upon the accidents of history nor the will of the multitude.

There is nothing in the Constitution to forbid its construction in the light, say, of an Aristotelian understanding of the nature of man and the nature of the political. For Aristotle a democracy was good or bad depending upon whether it was good or bad. It was good if its laws made men better, for he understood that the relation between "values" and laws is reciprocal. For him "reason" had an independent potency. It is reason which renders man man and not brute, but this is not to say that men are equal in their rationality. Some men are manlier, one might say. They are more reasonable than others. This suggests, to shift to a Platonic figure, that men are better or worse, that is, more or less men, to the extent that they participate in reason. It is for this reason that large portions of Plato's *Republic* and Aristotle's *Politics* are given over to the subject of education. It is also for this reason that the words "citizen" and "Athenian" were not interchangeable expressions for either Plato or Aristotle. Public affairs, according to Aristotle, were best left to those who, having the native capacities, were prepared by and within the country to care for them. These are reasonable men, or men of perfected self-mastery. That self-mastery pertains to a minority of the whole people and it is characterized not by humility, but by self-recognition. Neither humility nor altruism would cause the man of self-mastery to defer his judgment to that of the multitude.[41]

In a perfect city, about which one might speak for the sake of argument, if the wisest of men had mastered the element of change—if, that is to say, they had become as gods—any two of them would arrive at identical solutions to any given problem. To put it another way, if gods ran a perfect city it would *have no* problem. But, for Aristotle, for a man to be not a brute does not mean for him to be a god. In an actual city, two reasonable men might well arrive at different solutions to the same problem. That is, their judgments might differ. And that is why we have herein devoted ourselves to the relation between decisions and opinions, results and the reasons for them, and why, also, we have been more concerned with the latter than with the former.

That connection is interestingly displayed in a case decided on the last Monday of Frankfurter's last full term. His opinion there, representing the judgment of the Court, but, as opinion, joined only by Mr. Justice Stewart, is his last full-scale dissertation on the matter of fairness in state criminal prosecution.[42] Mr. Chief Justice Warren, concurring there, objects to a discussion of principles. He states that Frankfurter's treatment of the problem is "in the nature of an advisory opinion,"[43] and so he joins the separate concurring opinion of Mr. Justice Brennan. But what is Brennan's opinion? In its entirety it reads:

> It is my view that the facts stated in Part V of the opinion of my Brother Frankfurter require the conclusion that all and not alone the Wednesday confessions were coerced from the petitioner, and that under our cases none is admissible in evidence against him. See, e.g., *Fikes* v. *Alabama*, 352 U.S. 191, and cases there cited.[44]

In other words, the "facts" speak for themselves. But they *don't*. They *could* speak for themselves *only* if they were *plain* facts and then only if the principles in the light of which they were seen and measured were fully understood and agreed to. But not even then would they "speak for themselves" and that is why human judgment is what it is and not replaceable by the "subtlest of modern brain machines." Mr. Justice Harlan, in a dissenting opinion joined by Justices Clark and Whittaker, explains that he *agrees* with Frankfurter's *principles* but comes to a different conclusion when he applies them to the facts. Because men can agree in principle and disagree on application, the road to understanding cannot be through immersion in particularities but must rather lie in sustained argument over principle. Indeed, if one is to argue about the *Constitution* rather than about *Culombe*, principle is what there is to talk about. Admittedly, results are what count but one cannot "get at" them except through the principles underlying them. That is, if one objects to *results*, his options are to keep silent or to criticize principles.

A homely analogy may help here. If two heart specialists disagree in their proposed remedies and one, attempting surgery, fails, leading to the death of the patient, one may well continue to hail him as a great heart surgeon and commiserate as much with him over the loss as with the patient's bereaved family. A few failures amid a great many successes need not necessarily raise questions of principle. A few *more* failures, proportionately, begin to *suggest* a defect in principle. But as to the heart specialist who proposes dropping the patient out a fourth floor window to see if that might not jar the malfunction out of the heart, there is no question. He is wrong in principle.

So, even though an examination of the records and briefs in the *Adamson* case leads us to the same result Frankfurter comes to, we would prefer that that result be based upon an improved principle. If it were necessary to concur specially in that case, rather than remaining in silent agreement with Mr. Justice Reed's opinion, might he not have approached the problem after the following fashion?

> An elderly widow was found strangled in her Los Angeles apartment. Appellant's fingerprints were found on the door to the garbage disposal compartment beneath her sink. It appears that the door had been forced from its hinges. Some diamond rings which testimony showed the victim regularly wore were nowhere to be found and one witness, positively identifying the appellant, testified that she overheard him, less than two weeks after the murder, offering an unseen diamond ring for sale to an unidentified third person. It was shown that the victim's stockings had been removed and that the lower half of one of her stockings was near her when she was found. It was further shown that the upper halves of women's stockings were found in appellant's lodgings. None of the parts there found matched the part found near the murdered woman, however.
>
> Appellant did not take the stand in his own defense nor, in fact, were any witnesses presented on his side; the defense rested without making a case. Had he taken the stand, his former convictions, otherwise kept from the jury's knowledge, could have been revealed to the jury to impeach his testimony. He therefore faced an unhappy

choice: he might keep silent and allow the jury to draw conclusions as to his silence, or he might testify and allow it to draw conclusions as to the import of his former convictions. The prosecutor, in his closing argument, repeatedly called the jury's attention to the defendant's failure to testify.

Appellant was convicted of murder in the first degree and, lacking a jury recommendation for mercy, was sentenced to death. He comes here contending that execution of that sentence will deprive him of one of the privileges or immunities of national citizenship which states are forbidden to abridge and will deny him that due process of law without which the state may not take his life.

His chief complaint is against the prosecutor's comment to the jury upon his failure to testify and he comes at it from both the privileges and immunities and the due process vantage. But he cannot come at it from the privileges or immunities clause, for he contends that the prosecutor's comment negated the privilege against compulsory self-incrimination and that privilege is guaranteed him by the Fifth Amendment. This will not do, for *Barron* v. *Baltimore*, 7 Pet. 243 (1833), showed that what the Fifth Amendment guaranteed was immunity from testimonial compulsion *by the United States*. And so, if he is to come at it at all, it must be by way of the due process clause.

Appellant's due process claim covers two matters. It covers the matter of the prosecutor's comment on his failure to testify and it covers the matter of the introduction into evidence of the parts of women's stockings found in his lodgings. Since the latter is the easier question, it may be disposed of first. Appellant contends that the introduction of the stocking parts was improper for, it is said, the *only* reason for introducing them would be to inflame the jury by hinting that such stockings constitute a "fetish," that the accused was somehow perverse. But the record shows (p. 347) that the prosecutor, in his closing argument, suggested the possibility of a stocking-cap (i.e., a "hair trainer") and this is the only explicit suggestion as to the *why* of the possession of stockings made on the trial. Since appellant fails to show any attempt on the part of the prosecutor to impassion the jury by the introduction of the stockings, he must contend that the prosecutor could have had no other purpose, and such contention would fail. It would fail because the mere coincidence of there being parts of stockings near the murdered woman and other parts in the lodgings of the accused is a legitimate link in a chain of evidence tending to connect the person of the accused with the place of the crime.

The due process argument against the prosecutor's comment upon the failure of the accused to testify is a more difficult one to meet. Questions of the founders' intent, and of the high politics of the Civil War and Reconstruction, as well as general questions concerning the nature of justice, are raised. The dissenting opinions here contend that the prohibition against deprivation by a state of life, liberty or property without due process of law, contained in the Fourteenth Amendment, was intended by the framers of the Amendment to bar the states from doing any of the things which the first several amendments had theretofore barred the United States from doing. But the historical record of the adoption of that Amendment shows no such intention on the part of its framers. If that record is fully and rightly read it shows rather an intention to leave as it had been the division of labor between nation and states concerning the administration of criminal justice, but to protect the individual citizen from the improprieties into which some states had sometimes fallen by providing ameliorative recourse to the union if such improprieties should again occur. The standards by which states were to be judged were not to be the catalogue of specific standards imposed upon the United States by the first eight amendments, but, rather, the general standard of due process.

The fundamental character of due process of law was well defined before the Civil War. See *Murray's Lessee* v. *Hoboken Land and Improvement Co.*, 18 How. 272

(1856). That definition was embellished as recently as *Palko* v. *Connecticut*, 302 U.S. 319 (1937), but another word upon it here will be useful. There is no rigid list of processes which comprehends due process. Whether in fact it is lacking is to be determined in each case by an examination of the entire proceeding. Certain marks divide the easy from the difficult cases. Experience has shown some things—say, the opportunity to be heard—are so necessary, and others—say, extraction of confession by physical torture—are so objectionable that if the former are lacking or the latter are present, due process has been denied. Likewise, if the law of a state specifically promises one thing or another to the accused and, on the trial, he did not get what he was given to expect, then due process is also lacking. In short, nothing shall be done or omitted contrary to law, nor shall the law itself allow what is bound to infect the proceedings or withhold what is essential if they are to be fair proceedings. The law may not do so directly, nor may it do so indirectly, either by subtle artifice or by careless oversight.

It seems that in the present case appellant's contention, at its best, urges that the law of California promises immunity from self-incrimination and then denies the benefit of that immunity by indirection. If this were true, the conviction could not stand. But, is it true? The truth or falsity of the contention can only be ascertained by examining the whole record to see whether what California gave Adamson explicitly it took away implicitly.

Appellee, in his brief here, admits to seven instances where the prosecutor commented upon the defendant's faiure to testify. We find eleven such instances. (Record, pp. 343, 346, 348, 350, 357, 367, 368, 370, 372, 376 and 379.) In three, perhaps four, of these instances the prosecutor came near suggesting that Adamson's failure to testify is an admission of guilt. (*Ibid.*, pp. 350, 368, 370 and 379.) But he does not quite say so, and the whole burden of the eleven instances, within the context of the prosecutor's closing argument, is simply an emphasis upon the strength of the prosecution's case and the implications to be drawn by the fact that the defense must allow that case to stand for it cannot or will not counter it with any testimony by any witness. Of course, the defendant need not prove his innocence. It is up to the prosecution to prove his guilt. But if the prosecution presents what may well persuade a jury that the defendant is guilty, the fact that the tactics of the defense are that no case is the best case is a fact upon which the prosecutor may well remark without infecting an otherwise proper proceeding. Instructions to the jury concerning the matters of guilt beyond reasonable doubt and the presumption of innocence with which the accused is clothed were well and fully given by the trial court in this case.

Can a jury of ordinary, common-sensical people hear such comment as that made by the prosecutor on the trial and still weigh the evidence fairly? There is no neat answer to be found in the Constitution of the United States. Neither does experience supply a ready answer, for the several jurisdictions within which the adversary system obtains have come to various conclusions on the matter. And so, this Court, compelled as it is to measure California's practice, is compelled also to turn to its own reasoned judgment for an answer. It does not resolve the problem to say accusingly that so to turn is to turn to "natural law," for the confident denial that anything can be, by nature, right or wrong is at once a show of contempt for the Constitution itself. Was it out of a newfound chauvinism that we broke from English rule, or was it not rather a belief that English rule was unjust? Was it for the sake of bigness alone that the Constitution replaced the Articles of Confederation, or was it not rather, as the preamble states, that better union better provides justice and the other human goods there listed?

It has become the fashion recently to speak as though the Constitution were devoted solely to the rights of the accused. But what are those rights? They are, first of all, the rights granted by the constitutions and laws of the United States and of the states. Fundamentally, the accused has but one right by nature and that is the right to such rights as will insure justice. Within the current fashion, it often appears that justice is nothing more than tender mercy for the accused—for the "underdog" against whom the powerful forces of governmental prosecution have been brought to bear. Surely a harsh and cold disregard for the accused is not a hallmark of justice, but it must not be forgotten that justice is also concerned with the elderly widow who was strangled with malice aforethought and for the peace of the community which that strangulation breached. Nor can we forget what the first count of the information upon which Appellant was tried reminds us of, that that elderly widow was "a human being"; nor what the instructions to the jury remind us of, that malice aforethought involves an "abandoned and malignant heart." While passion for retribution must not be allowed to convict a man unfairly, neither should sympathy for the weaker side in a trial cause us to find injustice where it does not lie. Mercy is a civilized component of, but it is not a surrogate for justice.

NOTES TO CHAPTER VII

[1]Concurring in *Dennis* v. *United States,* 341 U.S. 494 at 528.
[2]54 Stat. 1168, 58 Stat. 4.
[3]Sec. 401(g).
[4]*Trop* v. *Dulles,* 356 U.S. 86.
[5]*Ibid.,* p. 120.
[6]*Ibid.,* p. 125.
[7]We are not far from agreeing even with Frankfurter's notion that it is appropriate for the *Court* to show disdain for the question of individual justice in order to conserve its energies for the task of purifying the *system* of justice. But maybe even that can be carried too far. See his opinion for the Court in *Rice* v. *Sioux City Memorial Park Cemetery,* 349 U.S. 70. For the facts in that case, see it below at 60 N.W. 2d. 110, 245 Iowa 147.

[8]Concurring in *Czaplicki* v. *Hoegh Silvercloud,* 351 U.S. 525 at 535.
[9]See Frankfurter's dissent in *Flournoy* v. *Weiner,* 321 U.S. 253 at 263.
[10]*Supra,* p. 171, citing *L and M,* p. 349.
[11]*Wieman* v. *Updegraff,* 344 U.S. 183 at 196.
[12]358 U.S. 1.
[13]See, for example, his opinion concurring in the judgment in *United States* v. *Raines,* 362 U.S. 17, 4 L.Ed.2d. 524 at 533.
[14]*Sherrer* v. *Sherrer,* 334 U.S. 343 at 367.
[15]Conn. Gen. Stat. Rev., 1958, §§53-32 and 54-196.
[16]*Tileston* v. *Ullman,* 318 U.S. 44.
[17]*Poe* v. *Ullman,* 367 U.S. 497, especially at 504-05.
[18]*Baker* v. *Carr,* 369 U.S. 186.
[19]367 U.S. at 508.
[20]*Ibid.,* p. 533.
[21]*L and M,* p. 237.
[22]332 U.S. 168 at 173. From the point of view of our study it is noteworthy that this opinion was handed down on the same day as that in *Adamson.*
[23]*L and M,* p. 149.
[24]See for example his dissent in *Mitchell* v. *Trawler Racer,* 362 U.S. 539 at 550 and compare his comments in *L and M,* p. 21.
[25]*Ibid.,* p. 53.
[26]*Ibid.,* p. 29.
[27]See above, pp. 97-100, 143, and 167-168.
[28]*L and M,* p. 323.
[29]Stevens (1961), *op. cit.,* pp. 217-18.
[30]*Supra,* p. 99.
[31]See Bryce, *op. cit.,* I, 342-47, and compare Diamond, "The Federalists' View of Federalism," in Benson, Diamond, *et al., op. cit.,* in its entirety.
[32]See Madison in *Federalist,* #47, and note that he merely *concedes* rather than introduces and promotes the doctrine. Madison was as much concerned that the *legislature* be divided in itself as he was that it be divided *from* executive and judiciary. His principle seems to us to be the desirability of introducing contending forces into a government rather than a wooden notion that the government is naturally divisible into clearly defined roles. To understand the "separation of powers" one would have to go back to its sources. The American Constitution speaks of legislative, executive and judicial powers, but it draws its understanding both from habits and practices and from Locke and Montesquieu. Locke spoke of legislative and *federative* powers. The last-named seemed to be concerned with treaties and the like, as the Latin source of the word would suggest. See Richard Cox, *Locke on War and Peace* (Oxford: Clarendon Press, 1960). Locke's executive power seemed to include what we call judicial power. Montesquieu's division was that there were in each state, *"trois sortes de pouvoirs: la puissance législative, la puissance exécutrice des choses qui dépendent du droit des gens, et la puissance exécutrice de celles qui dépendent du droit civil."* De L'Esprit Des Lois (Paris: Editions Garnier Freres, n.d.), Liv. XI, chapter vi, the first paragraph. Even if it be conceded that his *puissance legislative* is identical with our "legislative power," there is no easy answer to the relation between our executive and judicial powers and his two executive powers, one related to the *"droit des gens"* and the other to the *"droit civil."* One cannot even begin to understand these terms and what they

import without an understanding of the significance of the transformation of the traditional classification of kinds of law—*ius civile, ius gentium, ius naturae*—into the modern classification of kinds of powers, as well as Grotius' transformation of *ius gentium* into something out of which the term "international law" and Locke's term "federative power" could be fashioned. See H. Grotius, *Prolegomena to the Law of War and Peace,* trans. F.W. Kelsey (New York: Liberal Arts Press, 1957). All this is only to illustrate that construing the Constitution in order to uphold it necessitates not only a study of political philosophy and its history, but a deliberate *choice* from among contending philosophies for philosophers, like legislators, differ.

[33]See *supra*, p. 99.

[34]See Mr. Justice Stewart dissenting in *Engle v. Vitale,* 370 U.S. 421, the recent school prayer case in the decision of which Frankfurter took no part, being then in the hospital with the illness that led to his retirement.

[35]See "The Common Law in the United States" an address by Stone reprinted in *Harvard Law Review,* L (November, 1936), 4. See especially p. 25.

[36]See *L and M,* p. 293.

[37]See McG. Bundy, Book Review, *Yale Law Journal,* LXVII, No. 5 (April, 1958), 944, 946-47.

[38]See Madison, *Federalist,* #43, toward the middle.

[39]A.E. Sutherland, *The Law and One Man Among Many* (Madison: University of Wisconsin Press, 1956), p. 65.

[40]"Congressional Power over the Labor Injunction," *Columbia Law Review,* XXXI, (No. 3, (March, 1931), 385, 397.

[41]Aristotle, *Eth. Nich.,* 1140b8-42all, and *Politics,* 1276b16-77b33.

[42]*Culombe v. Connecticut,* 367 U.S. 568 (1961).

[43]*Ibid.,* p. 636.

[44]*Ibid.,* pp. 641-42.

A Composite of all the Entries for the Word "Right" in all the Editions of Bouvier's *Law Dictionary* from 1839 to 1914

Following is a composite of all the entries for the word "right" in the various editions of Bouvier's *Law Dictionary* from 1839 to 1914 inclusive. The entries for 1867 and 1914 are treated as identical for the only changes are two or three editorial revisions of individual words, such as reducing words not crucial to the problem discussed in chapter III of this text from the plural to the singular. It would be too burdensome to the copy to show these changes.

[Right. This word is used in various senses. 1. Sometimes it signifies a law, as when we say that natural right requires us to keep our promises, or that it commands restitution, or that it forbids murder. In our language it is seldom used in this sense. 2. It sometimes means that quality in our actions by which they are denominated just ones. This is usually denominated rectitude. 3. It is that quality in a person which he has to do certain actions, or to possess certain things which belong to him by virtue of some title. In this sense we use it when we say that a man has a right to his estate, or a right to defend himself. (cit. om.)]	*Deleted 1867*
[In this latter sense alone, will this word be considered. Right is the correlative of duty, for, wherever one has a right due to him, some other must owe him a duty. (cit. om.)]	*Added 1852 Deleted 1867*
[Right. A well-founded claim. If people believe that humanity itself establishes or proves certain	*Added 1867*

claims, either upon fellow-beings, or upon society
or government, they call these claims human
rights; if they believe that these claims inhere in
the very nature of man himself, they called them
inherent, inalienable rights; if people believe that
there inheres in monarchs a claim to rule over their
subjects by divine appointment, they call the claim
divine right, *jus divinum*; if the claim is founded
or given by law, it is a legal right. The ideas of
claim and that the claim must be well founded
always constitute the idea of right. Rights can only
inhere in and exist between moral beings; and no
moral beings can coexist without rights, conse-
quently without obligations. Right and obligations
are correlative ideas. The idea of a *well-founded*
claim becomes in law a claim founded in or
established by the law: so that we may say a right
in law is an *acknowledged* claim.

Men are by their inherent nature moral and social   *Added*
beings; they have, therefore, mutual claims upon   *1867*
one another. Every well-grounded claim on others
is called a right, and, since the social character of
man gives the element of mutuality to each claim,
every right conveys along with it the idea of
obligation. Right and obligation are correlative.
The consciousness of all constitutes the first
foundation of the right or makes the claim well
grounded. Its incipiency arises instinctively out of
the nature of man. Man feels that he has a right of
ownership over that which he has produced out of
appropriated matter, for instance, the bow he has
made of appropriated wood; he feels that he has a
right to exact obedience from his children, long
before laws formally acknowledge or protect these
rights; but he feels, too, that if he claims the bow
which he made as his own, he ought to
acknowledge (as correlative obligation) the same
right in another man to the bow which he may
have made; or if he, as father, has a right to the
obedience of his children, they have a correspon-
ding claim to him for protection as long as they
are incapable to protect themselves. The idea of
rights is coexistent with that of authority (or

government); both are inherent in man; but if we understand by government a coherent system of laws by which a state is ruled, and if we understand by state a sovereign society, with distinct authorities to make and execute laws, then rights precede government, or the establishment of states, which is expressed in the ancient law maxim: *Ne ex regula jus sumatur, sed ex jure quod est, regula fiat.* SEE GOVERNMENT. We cannot refrain from referring the reader to the noble passage of Sophocles Oedyp. Tyr. 876 et seq., and to the words of Cicero, in his oration for Milo: *Est enim haec, judices, non scripta sed nata lex; quam non didicimus, accepimus, legimus; verum ex natura ipsa arripuimus, hausimus, expressimus; ad quam non docti sed facti; non instituti sed imbuti sumus.*

As rights precede government, so we find that now rights are acknowledged above governments and their states, in the case of international law. International law is founded on rights, that is, well-grounded claims which civilized states, as individuals, make upon one another. As governments come to be more and more clearly established, rights are more clearly acknowledged and protected by the law. A legal right, a constitutional right, means a right protected by the law, by the constitution; but government does not create the idea of right or original rights; it acknowledges them; just as government does not create property or values and money, it acknowledges and regulates them. If it were otherwise, the question would present itself, whence does government come? Whence does it derive its own right to create rights? By compact? But whence did the contracting parties derive their right to create a government that is to make rights? We would be consistently led to adopt the idea of a government by *just divinum*,—that is, a government deriving its authority to introduce and establish rights (bestowed on it in particular) from a source wholly separate from human society and the ethical character of man, in the same manner in which we

Added 1867

acknowledge revelation to come from a source not
human.

Rights are claims of moral beings upon one
another: when we speak of rights to certain things,
they are, strictly speaking claims of persons on
persons,—in the case of property for instance, the
claim of excluding others from possessing it. The
idea of right indicates an ethical relation, and all
moral relations may be infringed; claims may be
made and established by law which are wrong in
themselves and destitute of a corollary obligation;
they are like every other wrong done by society or
government; they prove nothing concerning the
origin or essential character of rights. On the other
hand, claims are gradually more clearly acknowledged, and new ones, which were not
perceived in early periods, are for the first time
perceived, and surrounded with legislative protection, as civilization advances. Thus, original
rights, or the rights of man, are not meant to be
claims which man has always perceived or insisted
upon or protected, but those claims which,
according to the person who uses the term,
logically flow from the necessity of the physical
and moral existence of man; for man is born to be
a man,—that is, to lead a human existence. They
have been called inalienable rights; but they have
been alienated, and many of them are not
perceived for long periods. Lieber, in his Political
Ethics, calls them primordial rights: he means
right directly flowing from the nature of man,
developed by civilization, and always showing
themselves clearer and clearer as society advances.
He enumerates, as such especially the following:
the right of protection; the right of personal
freedom,—that is, the claim of unrestricted action
except so far as the same claim of others
necessitates restriction: these two rights involve
the right to have justice done by the public
administration of justice, the right of production
and exchange (the right of property), the right of
free locomotion and emigration, the right of
communion in speech, letter, print, the right of

Added
1867

worship, the right of influencing or sharing in the legislation. All political civilization steadily tends to bring out these rights clearer and clearer, while in the course of this civilization, from its incipiency, with its relapses, they appear more or less developed in different periods and frequently wholly in abeyance: nevertheless, they have their origin in the personality of man as a social being.

Publicists and jurists have made the following further distinction of rights:—]

Added 1867

Rights are *perfect and imperfect*. When the things which we have a right to possess, or the actions we have a right to do, are or may be fixed and determinate, the right is a perfect one; but when the thing or the actions are vague and indeterminate, the right is an imperfect one. If a man demand his property which is withheld from him, the right that supports his demand is a perfect one, because the thing demanded is or may be fixed and determinate; but if a poor man ask relief from those from whom he has reason to expect it, the right which supports his petition is an imperfect one, because the relief which he expects is a vague, indeterminate thing. Rutherforth, Inst. c.2, p. 4; Grotius, lib. 1. c. 1, p. 4.

[Rights are also *absolute* and *qualified*. A man has an absolute right to recover property which belongs to him; an agent has a qualified right to recover such property when it has been intrusted to his care and which has been unlawfully taken out of his possession.]

Added 1852

Rights might with propriety be also divided into *natural and civil rights*; but as all the rights which man has received from nature have been modified and acquired anew from the civil law, it is more proper, when considering their object, to divide them into political and civil rights.

Political rights consist in the power to participate, directly or indirectly, in the establish-

ment or management of government. These
political rights are fixed by the constitution. Every
citizen has the right of voting for public officers,
and of being elected; these are the political rights
which the humblest citizen possesses.

Civil rights are those which have no relation to
the establishment, support, or management of the
government. These consist in the power of
acquiring and enjoying property, of exercising the
paternal and marital powers, and the like. It will
be observed that every one, unless deproved of
them by a sentence of civil death, is in the
enjoyment of his civil rights,—which is not the
case with political rights; for an alien, for
example, has no political, although in the full
enjoyment of his civil, rights.

These latter rights are divided into *absolute and
relative*. The absolute rights of mankind may be
reduced to three principal or primary articles: the
right of personal security, which consists in a
person's legal and uninterrupted enjoyment of his
life, his limbs, his body, his health, and his
reputation; the right of *personal liberty*, which
consists in the power of locomotion, of changing
situation or removing one's person to whatsoever
place one's inclination may direct without any
restraint unless by due course of law; the right of
property, which consists in the free use, enjoyment, and disposal of all his acquisitions, without
any control or diminution save only by the laws of
the land. 1 Bla. Com. 124-139.

The *relative rights are public or private*: the first
are those which subsist between the people and the
government; as, the right of protection on the part
of the people, and the right of allegiance which is
due by the people to the government; the second
are the reciprocal rights of husband and wife,
parent and child, guardian and ward, master and
servant.

[Rights are also divided into *legal and equitable*.   *Added*
The former are those where the party has the legal   *1852*

title to a thing; and in that case his remedy for an infringement of it is by an action in a court of law. Although the person holding the legal title may have no actual interest, but hold only as trustee, the suit must be in his name, and not, in general, in that of the *cestui que trust*, 8 Term 332; 1 Saund. 158, n. 1; 2 Bing. 20. The latter, or equitable rights, are those which may be enforced in a court of equity by the *cestui que trust*.]

In summary: three substantive additions were made in 1852 to the 1839 edition text; the 1852, 1862 and 1864 tests are just alike; two deletions and a very large addition were made for the 1867 edition; the 1914 edition is virtually identical to the 1867 edition.

Mr. Justice Frankfurter's Concurring Opinion in *Adamson* v. *California*

ADAMSON v. *CALIFORNIA*
332 U.S. 46
June 23, 1947
Appeal from S.C. of California

Opinion of the Court by Reed, pp. 47-59
Dissent by Black, joined by Douglas, pp. 68-92
Appendix to Black's dissent, pp. 92-123
Dissent by Murphy, joined by Rutledge, pp. 123-25

Mr. Justice Frankfurter, concurring, pp. 59-68.

[59] Less than ten years ago, Mr. Justice Cardozo announced as settled constitutional law that while the Fifth Amendment, "which is not directed to the states, but solely to the federal government," provides that no person shall be compelled in any criminal case to be a witness against himself, the process of law assured by the Fourteenth Amendment does not require such immunity from self-crimination: "in prosecutions by a state, the exemption will fail if the state elects to end it." *Palko* v. *Connecticut*, 302 U.S. 319, 322, 324. Mr. Justice Cardozo spoke for the Court, consisting of Mr. Chief Justice Hughes, and McReynolds, Brandeis, Sutherland, Stone, Roberts, Black, JJ. (Mr. Justice Butler dissented). The matter no longer called for discussion; a reference to *Twining* v. *New Jersey*, 211 U.S. 78, decided thirty years before the Palko case, sufficed.

Decisions of this Court do not have equal intrinsic authority. The *Twining* case shows the judicial process at its best—comprehensive briefs and powerful arguments on both sides, followed by long deliberation, resulting in an opinion by Mr. Justice Moody which at once gained and has ever since retained recognition as one of the outstanding opinions in the history of the Court. After [60] enjoying unquestioned prestige for forty years, the *Twining* case should not now be diluted, even unwittingly, either in its judicial philosophy or in its particulars. As the surest way of keeping the *Twining* case intact, I would affirm this case on its authority.

The circumstances of this case present a minor variant from what was before the Court in *Twining* v. *New Jersey, supra.* The attempt to inflate the difference into constitutional significance was adequately dealt with by Mr. Justice Traynor in the court below. *People* v. *Adamson*, 27 Cal. 2d, 478, 165 P.2d 3. The matter lies within a very narrow compass. The point is made that a defendant who has a vulnerable record would, by taking the stand, subject himself to having his credibility impeached thereby. See *Raffel* v. *United States*, 271 U.S. 494, 496-97. Accordingly, under California law, he is confronted with the dilemma, whether to testify and per chance have his bad record prejudice him in the minds of the jury, or to subject himself to the unfavorable inference which the jury might draw from his silence. And so, it is argued, if he chooses the latter alternative, the jury ought not to be allowed to attribute his silence to a consciousness of guilt when it might be due merely to a desire to escape damaging cross-examination.

This does not create an issue different from that settled in the *Twining* case. Only a technical rule of law would exclude from consideration that which is relevant, as a matter of fair reasoning, to the solution of a problem. Sensible and just-minded men, in important affairs of life, deem it significant that a man remains silent when confronted with serious and responsible evidence against himself which it is within his power to contradict. The notion that to allow jurors to do that which sensible and right-minded men do every day violates the "immutable principles of justice" as conceived by a civilized society is to trivialize the importance of "due process." Nor does it [61] make any difference in drawing significance from silence under such circumstances that an accused may deem it more advantageous to remain silent than to speak, on the nice calculation that by taking the witness stand he may expose himself to having his credibility impugned by reason of his criminal record. Silence under such circumstances is still significant. A person in that situation may express to the jury, through appropriate requests to charge, why he prefers to keep silent. A man who has done one wrong may prove his innocence on a totally different charge. To deny that the jury can be trusted to make such discrimination is to show little confidence in the jury system. The prosecution is frequently compelled to rely on the testimony of shady characters whose credibility is bound to be the chief target of the defense. It is a common practice in criminal trials to draw out of a vulnerable witness' mouth his vulnerability, and then convince the jury that nevertheless he is telling the truth in this particular case. This is also a common experience for defendants.

For historical reasons a limited immunity from the common duty to testify was written into the Federal Bill of Rights, and I am prepared to agree that, as part of that immunity, comment on the failure of an accused to take the witness stand is forbidden in Federal prosecutions. It is so, of course, by explicit act of Congress. 20 Stat. 30; see *Bruno* v. *United States*, 308 U.S. 287. But to suggest that such a limitation can be drawn out of "due process" in its protection of ultimate decency in a civilized society is to suggest that the Due Process Clause fastened fetters of unreason upon the States. (This opinion is concerned solely with a discussion of the Due Process Clause of the Fourteenth Amendment. I put to one side the Privileges or Immunities Clause of that Amendment. For the mischievous uses to which that clause would lend itself if its scope were not confined to that given it by all but [62] one of the decisions beginning with the *Slaughter-House Cases*, 16 Wall. 36, see the deviation in *Colgate* v. *Harvey*, 296 U.S. 404, overruled by *Madden* v. *Kentucky*, 309 U.S. 83.)

Between the incorporation of the Fourteenth Amendment into the Constitution and the beginning of the present membership of the Court—a period of seventy years—the scope of that Amendment was passed upon by forty-three judges. Of all these judges, only one, who may respectfully be called an eccentric exception, ever indicated the belief that the Fourteenth Amendment was a short-hand summary of the first eight Amendments theretofore limiting only the Federal Government, and that due process incorporated those eight Amendments as restrictions upon the powers of the States. Among these judges were not only those who would have to be included among the greatest in the history of the Court, but—it is especially relevant to note—they included those whose services in the cause of human rights and the spirit of freedom are the most conspicuous in our history. It is not invidious to single out Miller, Davis, Bradley, Waite, Matthews, Gray, Fuller, Holmes, Brandeis, Stone and Cardozo (to speak only of the dead) as judges who were alert in safeguarding and promoting the interests of liberty and human dignity through law. But they were also judges mindful of the relation of our federal system to a progressively democratic society and therefore duly regardful of the scope of authority that was left to the States even after the Civil War. And so they did not find that the Fourteenth Amendment, concerned as it was with matters fundamental to the pursuit of justice, fastened upon the States procedural arrangements which, in the language of Mr. Justice Cardozo, only those who are "narrow or provincial" would deem essential to "a fair and enlightened system of justice." *Palko* v. *Connecticut*, 302 U.S. 319, 325. To suggest that it is inconsistent with a truly free [63] society to begin prosecutions without an indictment, to try petty civil cases without the paraphernalia of a common law jury, to take into consideration that one who has full opportunity to make a defense remains silent is, in de Tocqueville's phrase, to confound the familiar with the necessary.

The short answer to the suggestion that the provision of the Fourteenth Amendment, which ordains "nor shall any State deprive any person of life, liberty, or property, without due process of law," was a way of saying that every State must thereafter initiate prosecutions through indictment by a grand jury, must have a trial by a jury of twelve in criminal cases, and must have trial by such a jury in common law suits where the amount in controversy exceeds twenty dollars, is that it is a strange way of saying it. It would be extraordinarily strange for a Constitution to convey such specific commands in such a roundabout and inexplicit way. After all, an amendment to the Constitution should be read in a "'"sense most obvious to the common understanding at the time of its adoption.' . . . For it was for public adoption that it was proposed." See Mr. Justice Holmes in *Eisner* v. *Macomber*, 252 U.S. 189, 220. Those reading the English language with the meaning which it ordinarily conveys, those conversant with the political and legal history of the concept of due process, those sensitive to the relations of the States to the central government as well as the relation of some of the provisions of the Bill of Rights to the process of justice, would hardly recognize the Fourteenth Amendment as a cover for the various explicit provisions of the first eight Amendments. Some of these are enduring reflections of experience with human nature, while some express the restricted views of Eighteenth-Century England regarding the best methods for the ascertainment of facts. The notion that the Fourteenth Amendment was a covert way of imposing upon the [64] States all the rules which it seemed important to Eighteenth Century statesmen to write into the Federal Amendments was rejected by judges who were themselves witnesses of the process by which the Fourteenth Amendment became part of the Constitution. Arguments that may now be adduced to prove that the first eight Amendments were concealed within the historic phrasing* [footnote omitted] of the Fourteenth Amendment were not unknown at the time of its adoption. A surer estimate of their bearing was possible for judges at the time than distorting distance is likely to vouchsafe. Any evidence of design or purpose not contemporaneously known could hardly have influenced those who ratified the Amendment. Remarks of a particular proponent of the Amendment, no matter how influential, are not to be deemed part of the Amendment. What was submitted for ratification was his proposal, not his speech. Thus, at the time of the ratification of the Fourteenth Amendment the constitutions of nearly half of the ratifying States did not have the rigorous requirements of the Fifth Amendment for instituting criminal proceedings through a grand jury. It could hardly have occurred to these States that by ratifying the Amendment they uprooted their established methods for prosecuting crime and fastened upon themselves a new prosecutorial system.

Indeed, the suggestion that the Fourteenth Amendment incorporates the first eight Amendments as such is not unambiguously urged. Even the boldest innovator would shrink from suggesting to more than half the States that [65] they may no longer initiate prosecutions without indictment by grand jury, or that thereafter all the States of the Union must furnish a jury of twelve for every case involving a claim above twenty dollars. There is suggested merely a selective incorporation of the first eight Amendments into the Fourteenth Amendment. Some are in and some are out, but we are left in the dark as to which are in and which are out. Nor are we given the calculus for determining which go in and which stay out. If the basis of selection is merely that those provisions of the first eight Amendments are incorporated which commend themselves to individual justices as indispensable to the dignity and happiness of a free man, we are thrown back to a merely subjective test. The protection against unreasonable search and seizure might have primacy for one judge, while trial by a jury of twelve for every claim above twenty dollars might appear to another as an ultimate need in a free society. In the history of thought "natural law"has a much longer and much better founded meaning and justification than such subjective selection of the first eight Amendments for incorporation into the Fourteenth. If all that is meant is that due process contains within itself certain minimal standards which are "of the very essence of a scheme of ordered liberty," *Palko* v. *Connecticut*, 302 U.S. 319, 325, putting upon this Court the duty of applying these standards from time to time, then we have merely arrived at the insight which our predecessors long ago expressed. We are called upon to apply to the difficult issues of our own day the wisdom afforded by the great opinions in this field, such as those in *Davidson* v. *New Orleans*, 96 U.S. 97; *Missouri* v. *Lewis*, 101 U.S. 22; *Hurtado* v. *California*, 110 U.S. 516; *Holden* v. *Hardy*, 169 U.S. 366; *Twining* v. *New Jersey*, 211 U.S. 78, and *Palko* v. *Connecticut*, 302 U.S. 319. This guidance bids us to be duly mindful of the heritage of the past, with its great lessons of how liberties are won and [66] how they are lost. As judges charged with the delicate task of subjecting the government of a continent to the Rule of Law we must be particularly mindful that it is "a *constitution* we are expounding," so that it should not be imprisoned in what are merely legal forms even though they have the sanction of the Eighteenth Century.

It may not be amiss to restate the pervasive function of the Fourteenth Amendment in exacting from the States observance of basic liberties. See *Malinski* v. *New York*, 324 U.S. 401, 412 *et seq: Louisiana* v. *Resweber*, 329 U.S. 459, 466 *et seq*. The Amendment neither comprehends the specific provisions by which the founders deemed it appropriate to restrict the federal government nor is it confined to them. The Due Process Clause of the Fourteenth Amendment has an independent potency, precisely as does the Due Process Clause of the Fifth Amendment in relation to the Federal Government. It ought not to require argument to reject the notion that due process of law meant one thing in the Fifth Amendment and another in the

Fourteenth. The Fifth Amendment specifically prohibits prosecution of an "infamous crime" except upon indictment; it forbids double jeopardy; it bars compelling a person to be a witness against himself in any criminal case; it precludes deprivation of "life, liberty, or property, without due process of law. . . ." Are Madison and his contemporaries in the framing of the Bill of Rights to be charged with writing into it a meaningless clause? To consider "due process of law" as merely a shorthand statement of other specific clauses in the same amendment is to attribute to the authors and proponents of this Amendment ignorance of, or indifference to, a historic conception which was one of the great instruments in the arsenal of constitutional freedom which the Bill of Rights was to protect and strengthen.

[67] A construction which gives to due process no independent function but turns it into a summary of the specific provisions of the Bill of Rights would, as has been noted, tear up by the roots much of the fabric of law in the several States, and would deprive the States of opportunity for reform in legal process designed for extending the area of freedom. It would assume that no other abuses would reveal themselves in the course of time than those which had become manifest in 1791. Such a view not only disregards the historic meaning of "due process." It leads inevitably to a warped construction of specific provisions of the Bill of Rights to bring within their scope conduct clearly condemned by due process but not easily fitting into the pigeon-holes of the specific provisions. It seems pretty late in the day to suggest that a phrase so laden with historic meaning should be given an improvised content consisting of some but not all of the provisions of the first eight Amendments, selected on an undefined basis, with improvisation of content for the provisions so selected.

And so, when, as in a case like the present, a conviction in a State court is here for review under a claim that a right protected by the Due Process Clause of the Fourteenth Amendment has been denied, the issue is not whether an infraction of one of the specific provisions of the first eight Amendments is disclosed by the record. The relevant question is whether the criminal proceedings which resulted in conviction deprived the accused of the due process of law to which the United States Constitution entitled him. Judicial review of that guaranty of the Fourteenth Amendment inescapably imposes upon this Court an exercise of judgment upon the whole course of the proceedings in order to ascertain whether they offend those canons of decency and fairness which express the notions of justice of English-speaking peoples even toward [68] those charged with the most heinous offenses. These standards of justice are not authoritatively formulated anywhere as though they were prescriptions in a pharmacopoeia. But neither does the application of the Due Process Clause imply that judges are wholly at large. The judicial judgment in applying the Due Process Clause must move within the limits of accepted notions of justice and is not to be based upon the idiosyncrasies of a merely personal judgment. The fact that judges among themselves may differ whether in a particular case a trial offends accepted notions of justice is not disproof that general rather than idiosyncratic standards are applied. An important safeguard against such merely individual judgment is an alert deference to the judgment of the State Court under review.

Table of Opinions by Mr. Justice Frankfurter

The following table lists all cases in which an opinion by Frankfurter appears. It does not, of course, list those cases where he has concurred or dissented without supporting his action with an opinion, nor those cases in which he has joined in the concurring or dissenting opinions of brethren, nor those in which he was a silent member of the majority. Since it does not, and since it wholly ignores the thousands of memorandum decisions in the *Reports*, there would be no profit whatever in calculating the frequency of dissenting and concurring opinions in relation to each other, or in relation to his opinions for the Court. Preceding each case listed there will be found an abbreviated annotation thus:

> o—Opinion of the Court by Frankfurter
> j—Opinion by Frankfurter representing the Judgment of the Court
> c—Concurring Opinion by Frankfurter
> d—Dissenting Opinion by Frankfurter
> s—All other opinions, including memoranda

A

o	Abel v. United States, 362 U.S. 217, (1960)
o	Achilli v. United States, 353 U.S. 373, (1957)
o	Adams v. United States ex rel McCann, 317 U.S. 269, (1942)
c	Adamson v. California, 332 U.S. 46, (1947)
o	Addison v. Holly Hill Co., 322 U.S. 607, (1944)
d	Adler v. Board of Education, 342 U.S. 485, (1952)
o	Aeronautical District Lodge v. Campbell, 337 U.S. 521, (1949)

s   Agoston v. Pennsylvania, 340 U.S. 844, (1950)

c   Alabama Public Service Commission v. Southern Ry., 341 U.S. 341, (1951)

c   Alabama Public Service Commission v. Southern Ry., 341 U.S. 363, (1951)

o   Algoma Plywood Co. v. Wisconsin Employment Relations Board, 336 U.S. 301, (1949)

o   Alleghany Corp. v. Breswick & Co., 353 U.S. 151, (1957)

s   Altvater v. Freeman, 319 U.S. 359, (1943)

d   Amalgamated Ass'n of Street Employees v. Wisconsin Employment Relations Board, 340 U.S. 383, (1951)

o   Amalgamated Clothing Workers v. Richman Brothers, 348 U.S. 511, (1955)

c   American Communications Association v. Douds, 339 U.S. 382, (1950)

c   A.F.L. v. American Sash Co., 335 U.S. 538, (1949)

o   A.F.L. v. Swing, 312 U.S. 321, (1941)

c   American Power & Light Co. v. S.E.C., 329 U.S. 90, (1946)

d   American Stevedores, Inc. v. Porello, 330 U.S. 446, (1947)

o   American Surety Co. v. Bethlehem Bank, 314 U.S. 314 (1941)

c   American Tobacco Co. v. United States, 328 U.S. 781, (1946)

o   Anderson v. United States, 318 U.S. 350 (1943)

c   Andres v. United States, 333 U.S. 740, (1948)

o   Angel v. Bullington, 330 U.S. 183, (1947)

o   Angelus Milling Co. v. Commissioner, 325 U.S. 293, (1945)

c   Armstrong v. Armstrong, 350 U.S. 568, (1956)

d   Arnold v. Panhandle & S.F. Ry., 353 U.S. 360, (1957)

d   Ashbacker Radio Co. v. F.C.C., 326 U.S. 327, (1945)

c   Associated Press v. United States, 326 U.S. 1, (1945)

j   Association of Employees v. Westinghouse Corp., 348 U.S. 437, (1955)

o   Atlantic Coast Line R.R. v. Phillips, 332 U.S. 168, (1947)

o   Automatic Canteen Co. v. F.T.C., 346 U.S. 61, (1953)

c   Avery v. Georgia, 345 U.S. 559, (1953)

B

d   Baker v. Carr, 369 U.S. 186, (1962)

s   Baker v. Texas & P. Ry., 359 U.S. 227, (1959)

o   Bakery Sales Drivers Union v. Wagshal, 333 U.S. 437, (1948)

s   Ballard v. United States, 329 U.S. 187, (1946)

d   Baltimore & Ohio R. Co. v. Kepner, 314 U.S. 44, (1941)

d   Bankers Life & Casualty Co. v. Holland, 346 U.S. 379, (1953)

o   Bank of America v. Parnell, 352 U.S. 29, (1956)
d   Barr v. United States, 324 U.S. 83, (1945)
d   Barsky v. Board of Regents, 347 U.S. 442, (1954)
o   Bartkus v. Illinois, 359 U.S. 121, (1959)
o   Baumgartner v. United States, 322 U.S. 665, (1944)
o   Bayley v. Commissioner, 331 U.S. 737, (1947)
d   Bay Ridge Operating Co. v. Aaron, 334 U.S. 446, (1948)
o   Beauharnais v. Illinois, 343 U.S. 250, (1959)
c   Beilan v. Board of Education, 357 U.S. 399, (1958)
o   Bell v. United States, 349 U.S. 81, (1955)
c   Bernhardt v. Polygraphic Co., 350 U.S. 198, (1956)
s   Bethlehem Steel Co. v. New York Labor Board, 330 U.S. 767, (1947)
d   Bigelow v. R.K.O. Radio Pictures, 327 U.S. 251, (1946)
s   Billings v. Truesdell, 321 U.S. 542, (1944)
o   Bindczyck v. Finucane, 342 U.S. 76, (1951)
-    Bingham v. Commissioner, see: Trust of Bingham v. Commissioner
d   Bisso v. Inland Waterways Corp., 349 U.S. 85, (1955)
o   Black Diamond S.S. Corp. v. Stewart & Sons, 336 U.S. 386, (1949)
o   Board of Commissioners v. United States 308 U.S. 43, (1939)
o   Board of Trade v. United States, 314 U.S. 534, (1942)
d   Bode v. Barrett, 344 U.S. 583, (1953)
o   Bollenback v. United States, 326 U.S. 607, (1946)
s   Bondholders Inc. v. Powell, 342 U.S. 921, (1952)
c   Boston Metals Co. v. The Winding Gulf, 349 U.S. 122, (1955)
d   Braniff Airways Inc. v. Nebraska State Board, 347 U.S. 590, (1954)
d   Bridges v. California, 314 U.S. 252, (1941)
d   Brillhart v. Excess Insurance Co. 316 U.S. 491, (1942)
c   Brock v. North Carolina, 344 U.S. 424, (1953)
o   Brooks v. N.L.R.B., 348 U.S. 96, (1954)
s   Brown v. Allen, 344 U.S. 443, (1953)
c   Brown v. Gerdes, 321 U.S. 178, (1944)
o   Brown v. United States, 356 U.S. 148, (1958)
d   Brown v. Western R. of Alabama, 338 U.S. 294, (1949)
o   Bruno v. United States, 308 U.S. 287, (1939)
d   Burford v. Sun Oil Co., 319 U.S. 315, (1943)
d   Burns v. Ohio, 360 U.S. 252, (1959)
s   Burns v. Wilson, 346 U.S. 137, (1953)
d   Burns v. Wilson, 346 U.S. 844, (1953)
c   Burstyn v. Wilson, 343 U.S. 495, (1952)
d   Burton v. Wilmington Parking Authority, 365 U.S. 715, (1961)
s   Burton-Sutton Oil Co. v. Commissioner, 328 U.S. 25, (1946)
c   Busby v. Electric Utilities Union, 323 U.S. 72, (1944)
-    Bus Employees v. Wisconsin Board, see: Amalgamated Association of Street Employees v. Wisconsin Employment Relations Board.

d   Coe v. Coe, 334 U.S. 378, (1948)
d   Cold Metal Process Co. v. United Engineering & Foundry, 351 U.S. 445, (1956)
j   Colegrove v. Green, 328 U.S. 549, (1946)
c   Coleman v. Miller, 307 U.S. 433, (1939)
o   Collins v. American Buslines Inc., 350 U.S. 528, (1956)
o   Collins v. Porter, 328 U.S. 46, (1946)
d   Columbia Broadcasting System v. United States, 316 U.S. 407, (1942)
d   Commissioner v. Acker, 361 U.S. 87, (1959)
o   Commissioner v. Bedford, 325 U.S. 283, (1945)
c   Commissioner v. Culbertson, 337 U.S. 733, (1949)
c   Commissioner v. Duberstein, 363 U.S. 278, (1960)
d   Commissioner v. Estate of Church, 355 U.S. 633, (1949)
c   Commissioner v. Lo Bue, 351 U.S. 243, (1956)
d   Commissioner v. Sunnen, 333 U.S. 591, (1948)
o   Commissioner v. Wemyss, 324 U.S. 303, (1945)
d   Commissioner v. Wodehouse, 337 U.S. 369, (1949)
o   Communist Party v. Subversive Activities Control Board, 351 U.S. 115, (1956)
o   Communist Party v. Subversive Activities Control Board, 367 U.S. 1, (1961)
d   Connecticut Life Insurance Co. v. Moore, 333 U.S. 541, (1948)
c   Continental Grain Co. v. The F.B.L. 585, 364 U.S. 19, (1960)
o   Continental Oil Co. v. N.L.R.B., 313 U.S. 212, (1941)
d   Cook v. Cook, 342 U.S. 126, (1951)
c   Cooper v. Aaron, 358 U.S. 1, (1958)
d   Cornell Steamboat Co. v. United States, 321 U.S. 634, (1944)
d   Cory Corp. v. Sauber, 363 U.S. 709, (1960)
s   Covey v. Town of Somers, 351 U.S. 141, (1956)
d   Craig v. Harney, 331 U.S. 367, (1947)
o   Culombe v. Connecticut, 367 U.S. 568, (1961)
c   Czaplicki v. The Hoegh Silvercloud, 351 U.S. 525, (1956)

D

d   Darr v. Burford, 339 U.S. 200, (1950)
c   Davis v. Department of Labor & Industries, 317 U.S. 249 (1942)
d   Davis v. United States, 328 U.S. 582, (1946)
o   De La Rama S.S. Co. v. United States, 344 U.S. 386, (1953)
d   Delli Paoli v. United States, 352 U.S. 232, (1957)
d   Dennis v. United States, 339 U.S. 162, (1950)
s   Dennis v. United States, 340 U.S. 887, (1950)

c Dennis v. United States, 341 U.S. 494, (1951)
d Denver & R.G.W. Ry. v. Union Pacific R.R., 351 U.S. 321, (1956)
d Denver Union Stock Yard Co. v. Producers Livestock Association, 356 U.S. 282, (1958)
c Deputy v. Du Pont, 308 U.S. 488, (1940)
c Dessalernos v. Savoretti, 356 U.S. 269, (1958)
- Detroit v. Murray Corp., see: City of Detroit v. Murray Corp.
j De Veau v. Braisted, 363 U.S. 144, (1960)
o Dibella v. United States, 369 U.S. 121, (1962)
c Dice v. Akron, C. & Y. R.R., 342 U.S. 359, (1952)
d Dick v. New York Life Insurance Co., 359 U.S. 437, (1959)
c D'Oench, Duhme Co. v. F.D.I.C., 315 U.S. 447, (1942)
c Driscoll v. Edison Light & Power Co., 307 U.S. 104, (1939)
o Drummond v. United States, 324 U.S. 316, (1945)
- Dyer v. Sims, see: West Virginia ex rel Dyer v. Sims

E

d Eastern-Central Motor Carriers Association v. United States 321 U.S. 194, (1944)
o East New York Savings Bank v. Hahn, 326 U.S. 230, (1945)
- Eaton v. Price, see; Ohio ex rel Eaton v. Price
o Eccles v. Peoples Bank of Lakewood, 333 U.S. 426, (1948)
s Ecker v. Western Pacific R.R., 318 U.S. 448, (1943)
- Eichenlaub v. Shaughnessy, see: United States ex rel Eichenlaub v. Shaughnessy
d Eisler v. United States, 338 U.S. 189, (1949)
d Electric Power & Light Corp., in re, 337 U.S. 903, (1949)
d Elgin, J. & E. R.R. v. Burley, 325 U.S. 711, (1945)
d Elgin, J. & E. R.R. v. Burley, 327 U.S. 661, (1946)
s Elkins v. United States, 364 U.S. 207, (1960)
d Empresa Siderurgica v. Merced Co., 337 U.S. 154, (1949)
s English v. Cunningham, 361 U.S. 905, (1959)
o Esenwein v. Commonwealth ex rel Esenwein, 325 U.S. 279, (1945)
o Estate of Rogers v. Commissioner, 320 U.S. 410, (1943)
c Estep v. United States, 327 U.S. 114, (1946)
d Estin v. Estin, 334 U.S. 541, (1948)
d Ewing v. Mytinger & Casselberry, 339 U.S. 594, (1950)

F

o Faitoute Iron & Steel Co. v. City of Asbury Park, 316 U.S. 502, (1942)

o   Far East Conference v. United States, 342 U.S. 570, (1952)
c   Farmers Reservoir & Irrigation Co. v. McComb, 337 U.S. 755, (1949)
d   Farmers Union v. WDAY, 360 U.S. 525, (1959)
o   F.C.C. v. Columbia Broadcasting System, 311 U.S. 132, (1940)
d   F.C.C. v. National Broadcasting Co. 319 U.S. 239, (1943)
o   F.C.C. v. Pottsville Broadcasting Co., 309 U.S. 134 (1940)
o   F.C.C. v. R.C.A. Communications Inc., 346 U.S. 86, (1953)
o   Federal Crop Insurance Corp. v. Merrill, 332 U.S. 380, (1947)
d   F.H.A. v. Darlington, Inc., 358 U.S. 84, (1958)
d   Federal Maritime Board v. Isbrandtsen Co., 356 U.S. 481, (1958)
d   F.P.C. v. Hope Natural Gas Co., 320 U.S. 591, (1944)
c   F.P.C. v. Interstate Natural Gas, 336 U.S. 577, (1949)
c   F.P.C. v. Natural Gas Pipeline Co., 315 U.S. 575, (1942)
o   F.P.C. v. Pacific Power & Light Co., 307 U.S. 156, (1939)
o   F.T.C. v. Bunte Brothers, 312 U.S. 349, (1941)
d   F.T.C. v. Motion Picture Advertisting Service Co., 344 U.S. 392, (1953)
o   Feldman v. United States, 322 U.S. 487, (1944)
c   Ferguson v. Georgia, 365 U.S. 570, (1961)
d   Ferguson v. Moore-McCormack, 352 U.S. 521, (1957)
c   Fikes v. Alabama, 352 U.S. 191, (1957)
d   First Iowa Hydro-Electric Coop. v. Commissioner, 328 U.S. 152, (1946)
d   First National Bank of Chicago v. United Air Lines, 342 U.S. 396, (1952)
d   Fisher v. United States, 328 U.S. 463, (1946)
d   Fleming v. Rhodes, 331 U.S. 100, (1947)
d   Florida Lime & Avocado Growers v. Jacobsen, 362 U.S. 73, (1960)
d   Flournoy v. Wiener, 321 U.S. 253, (1944)
o   Fly v. Heitmeyer, 309 U.S. 146, (1940)
c   Foley Brothers v. Filardo, 336 U.S. 281, (1949)
o   Ford Motor Co. v. United States, 335 U.S. 303, (1948)
o   Foster v. Illinois, 332 U.S. 134, (1947)
c   Fowler v. Rhode Island, 345 U.S. 67, (1953)
-   Francis v. Resweber, see: Louisiana ex rel Francis v. Resweber
o   Frank v. Maryland, 359 U.S. 360, (1959)
o   Fred Fisher Music Co. v. M. Witmark & Sons, 318 U.S. 643, (1943)
d   Freeman v. Bee Machine Co., 319 U.S. 448, (1943)
o   Freeman v. Hewit, 329 U.S. 249, (1946)
c   Funk Brothers Seed Co. v. Kalo Co., 333 U.S. 127, (1948)

G

o   Galvan v. Press, 347 U.S. 522, (1954)
s   Garner v. Los Angeles Board of Public Works, 341 U.S. 716 (1951)
c   Garner v. Louisiana, 368 U.S. 157, (1961)
j   Gayes v. New York, 332 U.S. 145, (1947)
c   Gemsco, Inc. v. Walling, 324 U.S. 244, (1945)
c   General Box Co. v. United States, 351 U.S. 159, (1956)
d   General Stores Corp. v. Shlensky, 350 U.S. 462, (1956)
o   General Trading Co. v. State Tax Commission, 322 U.S. 335, (1944)
o   Georgia v. Evans, 316 U.S. 159, (1942)
c   Gibson v. Lockheed Aircraft Service, Inc., 350 U.S. 356, (1956)
d   Gibson v. Phillips Petroleum Co., 352 U.S. 874.
s   Glasser v. United States, 315 U.S. 60, (1942)
o   Goesaert v. Cleary, 335 U.S. 464, (1948)
o   Gomillion v. Lightfoot, 364 U.S. 339, (1960)
o   Gore v. United States, 357 U.S. 386, (1958)
o   Gori v. United States, 367 U.S. 364, (1961)
o   Granville-Smith v. Granville-Smith, 349 U.S. 1, (1955)
c   Graves v. New York ex rel O'Keefe, 306 U.S. 466, (1939)
d   Great Northern Insurance Co. v. Read, 322 U.S. 47, (1944)
d   Green v. United States, 355 U.S. 184, (1957)
c   Green v. United States, 356 U.S. 165, (1958)
j   Green v. United States, 365 U.S. 301, (1961)
c   Greene v. McElroy, 360 U.S. 474, (1959)
c   Greenough v. Tax Assessors, 331 U.S. 486, (1947)
o   Greenwood v. United States, 350 U.S. 366, (1956)
o   Greyhound Lines v. Mealey, 334 U.S. 653, (1948)
d   Griffin v. Griffin, 327 U.S. 220, (1946)
o   Griffin v. Illinois, 351 U.S. 12, (1956)
o   Griffin v. United States, 336 U.S. 704, (1949)
o   Griffiths v. Commissioner, 308 U.S. 355, (1939)
s   Grimes v. Raymond Concrete Pile Co., 356 U.S. 252, (1958)
c   Groban, in re, 352 U.S. 330, (1957)
o   Guaranty Trust Co. v. York, 326 U.S. 99, (1945)
o   Guessefeldt v. McGrath, 342 U.S. 308, (1952)

H

s   Hale v. Bimco Trading Co., 306 U.S. 375, (1939)
s   Haley v. Ohio, 332 U.S. 596, (1948)
c   Haliburton Oil Well Co. v. Walker, 329 U.S. 1, (1946)

c   Halvey v. Halvey, 330 U.S. 610, (1947)
c   Hannah v. Larche, 363 U.S. 420, (1960)
c   Hannegan v. Esquire, Inc., 327 U.S. 146, (1946)
c   Harisiades v. Shaughnessy, 342 U.S. 580, (1950)
d   Harris v. Commissioner, 340 U.S. 106, (1950)
j   Harris v. South Carolina, 338 U.S. 68, (1949)
d   Harris v. United States, 331 U.S. 145, (1947)
s   Hecht Co. v. Bowles, 321 U.S. 321, (1944)
d   Heikkila v. Barber, 345 U.S. 229, (1953)
d   Helvering v. American Dental Co., 318 U.S. 322, (1943)
o   Helvering v. Hallock, 309 U.S. 106, (1940)
d   Henslee v. Union Planters Bank, 335 U.S. 595, (1949)
d   Hill v. Florida ex rel Watson, 325 U.S. 538, (1945)
d   Hoffman v. Blaski, 363 U.S. 335, (1960)
o   Holmberg v. Armbrecht, 327 U.S. 392, (1946)
o   Hotel Employees' Local v. Employment Relations Board, 315 U.S. 437, (1942)
d   H.P. Hood & Sons v. Du Mond, 336 U.S. 525, (1949)
d   Hughes v. Fetter, 341 U.S. 609, (1951)
o   Hughes v. Superior Court, 339 U.S. 460, (1950)
c   Hurd v. Hodge, 334 U.S. 24, (1948)
o   Hysler v. Florida, 315 U.S. 411, (1942)

I

c   Independent Warehouses v. Scheele, 331 U.S. 70, (1947)
-    Indianapolis v. Chase National Bank, see: City of Indianpolis v. Chase National Bank
o   Indian Towing Co. v. United States, 350 U.S. 61, (1955)
o   Inland Waterways Corp. v. Young, 309 U.S. 517, (1940)
c   Inman v. Baltimore & O. R.R., 361 U.S. 138, (1959)
d   Insurance Group v. Denver & R.G.W. Ry., 329 U.S. 607, (1947)
o   International Association of Machinists v. Gonzales, 356 U.S. 617, (1958)
d   International Association of Machinists v. N.L.R.B., 362 U.S. 41, (1960)
d   International Association of Machinists v. Street, 367 U.S. 740, (1961)
d   International Boxing Club v. United States, 358 U.S. 242, (1959)
j   International Brotherhood of Teamsters v. Hanke, 339 U.S. 470, (1950)
o   International Brotherhood of Teamsters v. Vogt, 354 U.S. 284, (1957)

c   Kingsley Pictures Corp. v. Regents, 360 U.S. 684, (1959)
s   Kinsella v. Krueger, 351 U.S. 470, (1956)
o   Kirschbaum Co. v. Walling, 316 U.S. 517, (1942)
d   Klapprott v. United States, 335 U.S. 601, (1949)
o   Knapp v. Schweitzer, 357 U.S. 371, (1958)
-   Knauff v. Shaughnessy, see: United States ex rel Knauff v.
    Shaughnessy
d   Konigsberg v. State Bar of California, 353 U.S. 252, (1957)
c   Korematsu v. United States, 323 U.S. 214, (1944)
d   Kossick v. United States, 365 U.S. 731, (1961)
d   Kovacs v. Brewer, 356 U.S. 604, (1958)
c   Kovacs v. Cooper, 336 U.S. 77, (1949)

L

d   Lambert v. California, 355 U.S. 225, (1958)
s   Land v. Dollar, 341 U.S. 737, (1951)
o   Lane v. Wilson, 307 U.S. 268, (1939)
d   Larson v. Domestic & Foreign Commerce Corp., 337 U.S. 682,
    (1949)
d   Lawler v. National Screen Service Co., 352 U.S. 992, (1957)
o   Leiter Minerals Inc. v. United States, 352 U.S. 220, (1957)
d   Leland v. Oregon, 343 U.S. 790, (1952)
o   Levine v. United States, 362 U.S. 610, (1960)
o   Levinson v. Deupree, 345 U.S. 648, (1953)
s   Leviton v. United States, 343 U.S. 946
d   Lewis v. Benedict Coal Corp., 361 U.S. 459, (1960)

d   Lewis v. United States, 348 U.S. 419, (1955)
d   Lewyt Corp. v. Commissioner, 349 U.S. 237, (1955)
d   Libby, McNeill, & Libby v. United States, 340 U.S. 71, (1950)
c   Louisiana v. N.A.A.C.P., 366 U.S. 293, (1961)
c   Louisiana ex rel Francis v. Resweber, 329 U.S. 459, (1947)
o   Louisiana Power & Light Co. v. City of Thibodaux, 360 U.S. 25,
    (1959)
o   Ludecke v. Watkins, 335 U.S. 160, (1948)
c   Lumberman's Mutual Casualty Co. v. Elbert, 348 U.S. 48, (1954)
d   Lurk v. United States, 366 U.S. 712, (1961)
j   Lustig v. United States, 338 U.S. 74, (1949)
d   Lyon v. Singer, 339 U.S. 841, (1950)

M

d	MacGregor v. Westinghouse Manufacturing Co., 329 U.S. 402, (1947)
s	Mackey v. Mendoza-Martinez, 362 U.S. 384, (1960)
d	Madruga v. Superior Court, 346 U.S. 556, (1954)
d	Magenua v. Aetna Freight Lines, 360 U.S. 273, (1959)
d	Maggio v. Zeitz, 333 U.S. 56, (1948)
-	Mahnomen County v. United States, see: County of Mahnomen v. United States
s	Malinski v. New York, 324 U.S. 401, (1945)
o	Mallory v. United States, 354 U.S. 449, (1957)
d	Marconi Wireless Co. v. United States, 320 U.S. 1, (1943)
-	Marcus v. Hess, see: United States ex rel Marcus v. Hess
c	Marsh v. Alabama, 326 U.S. 501, (1946)
d	Martin v. Struthers, 319 U.S. 141, (1943)
d	Masciale v. United States, 356 U.S. 386, (1958)
d	Mason v. Paradise District, 326 U.S. 536, (1946)
d	Massachusetts Bonding & Insurance Co. v. United States, 352 U.S. 128, (1956)
d	Mastro Plastics Corp. v. N.L.R.B., 350 U.S. 270, (1956)
s	Maryland v. Baltimore Radio Show Inc., 338 U.S. 912, (1950)
j	Maryland Casualty Co. v. Cushing, 347 U.S. 409, (1954)
c	May v. Anderson, 345 U.S. 528, (1953)
d	Maynard v. Durham & Southern R.R., 365 U.S. 160, (1961)
s	Mayo v. Lakeland Highlands Canning Co., 309 U.S. 310, (1940)
s	McAllister v. United States, 348 U.S. 19, (1954)
d	McBride v. Toledo Terminal R.R., 354 U.S. 517, (1957)
s	McCollum v. Board of Education, 333 U.S. 203, (1948)
d	McComb v. Jacksonville Paper Co., 336 U.S. 187, (1949)
s	McDonald v. Commissioner, 323 U.S. 57, (1944)
s	McGowan v. Maryland, 366 U.S. 420, (1961)
o	McKinney v. Missouri, K. & T. Ry., 357 U.S. 265, (1958)
o	McLeod v. Dilworth Co., 322 U.S. 327, (1944)
o	McNabb v. United States, 318 U.S. 332, (1943)
c	Meat Cutters v. N.L.R.B., 352 U.S. 153, (1956)
d	Memphis Natural Gas Co. v. Stone, 335 U.S. 80, (1948)
d	Mercoid Corp. v. Mid-Continent Investment Co., 320 U.S. 661, (1944)
o	Merrill v. Fahs, 324 U.S. 308, (1945)
s	Mesarosh v. United States, 352 U.S. 1, (1956)
s	Mesarosh v. United States, 352 U.S. 808, (1956)
o	Metlakatla Indian Community v. Egan, 363 U.S. 555, (1960)
o	Metlakatla Indian Community v. Egan, 369 U.S. 49, (1962)

P

d Pacific Coast Dairy Inc. v. Department of Agriculture, 318 U.S. 285, (1943)

d Packard Motor Car Co. v. N.L.R.B., 330 U.S. 485, (1947)

o Palermo v. United States, 360 U.S. 343, (1959)

d Palmer v. Connecticut Ry., 311 U.S. 544, (1941)

o Palmer v. Massachusetts, 308 U.S. 79, (1939)

o Pan American Corp. v. Superior Court, 366 U.S. 656, (1961)

d Panhandle Eastern Pipe Line Co. v. Public Service Commission, 341 U.S. 329, (1951)

o Parker v. Los Angeles County, 338 U.S. 327, (1949)

d Parr v. United States, 363 U.S. 370, (1960)

c Paterno v. Lyons, 334 U.S. 314, (1948)

d Pearce v. Commissioner, 315 U.S. 543, (1942)

s Pendergast v. United States, 317 U.S. 412, (1943)

d Penfield Co. v. S.E.C., 330 U.S. 585, (1947)

c Pennekamp v. Florida, 328 U.S. 331, (1946)

o Pennsylvania R.R. v. Day, 360 U.S. 548, (1959)

c Pennsylvania R.R. v. Rychlik, 352 U.S. 480, (1957)

o Perez v. Brownell, 356 U.S. 44, (1958)

- Peru, see: Republic of Peru, ex parte

d Petty v. Tennessee-Missouri Commission, 359 U.S. 275, (1959)

o Phelps Dodge Corp. v. N.L.R.B., 313 U.S. 177, (1941)

o Phillips v. United States, 312 U.S. 246, (1941)

c Phillips Petroleum Co. v. Wisconsin, 347 U.S. 672, (1954)

c Phyle v. Duffy, 334 U.S. 431, (1948)

o Piemonte v. United States, 367 U.S. 556, (1961)

d Pinkerton v. United States, 328 U.S. 640, (1946)

j Poe v. Ullman, 367 U.S. 497, (1961)

d Poff v. Pennsylvania R.R., 327 U.S. 399, (1946)

o Polish National Alliance v. N.L.R.B., 322 U.S. 643, (1944)

d Pope v. Atlantic Coast Line R.R., 345 U.S. 379, (1953)

c Pope & Talbot, Inc. v. Hawn, 346 U.S. 406, (1953)

c Poulos v. New Hampshire, 345 U.S. 395, (1953)

d Powell v. United States Cartridge Co., 339 U.S. 497, (1950)

d Price v. Johnston, 334 U.S. 266, (1948)

d Priebe & Sons v. United States, 332 U.S. 407, (1947)

d Propper v. Clark, 337 U.S. 472, (1949)

o Prudence Realization Corp. v. Ferris, 323 U.S. 650, (1945)

d Public Service Commission v. United States, 356 U.S. 421, (1958)

o Public Utilities Commission v. United Fuel Gas Co., 317 U.S. 456, (1943)

o Puerto Rico v. Rubert Hermanos, Inc., 309 U.S. 543, (1940)

Q

o   Quicksall v. Michigan, 339 U.S. 660, (1950)

R

s   Radio Corp. of America v. United States, 341 U.S. 412, (1951)
c   Radio Officers Union v. N.L.R.B., 347 U.S. 17, (1954)
o   Radio Station WOW v. Johnson, 326 U.S. 120, (1945)
d   Radovich v. National Football League, 352 U.S. 445, (1957)
o   Railroad Commission v. Humble Oil & Refining Co., 311 U.S. 578, (1941)
o   Railroad Commission v. Pullman Co., 312 U.S. 496, (1941)
o   Railroad Commission v. Rowan & Nichols Oil Co., 310 U.S. 573, (1940)
o   Railroad Commission v. Rowan & Nichols Oil Co., 311 U.S. 570, (1941)
o   Railway Employee's Department v. Hanson, 351 U.S. 225, (1956)
d   Railway Labor Executives Association v. United States, 339 U.S. 142, (1950)
c   Railway Mail Association v. Corsi, 326 U.S. 88, (1945)
d   Rathbun v. United States, 355 U.S. 107, (1957)
d   R.F.C. v. Denver & R.G.W. Ry., 328 U.S. 495, (1946)
d   Reed v. Pennsylvania R.R., 351 U.S. 502, (1956)
c   Reid v. Covert, 354 U.S. 1, (1957)
d   Reider v. Thompson, 339 U.S. 113, (1950)
o   Republic Natural Gas Co. v. Oklahoma, 334 U.S. 62, (1948)
d   Republic of Peru, ex parte, 318 U.S. 578, (1943)
c   Reynolds v. Atlantic Coast Line R.R., 336 U.S. 207, (1949)
d   Rice v. Olson, 324 U.S. 786, (1945)
d   Rice v. Sante Fe Elevator Corp., 331 U.S. 218, (1947)
o   Rice v. Sioux City Memorial Park Cemetery, 349 U.S. 70, (1955)
d   Roberts v. United States, 320 U.S. 264, (1943)
o   Rochester Telephone Corp. v. United States, 307 U.S. 125, (1939)
o   Rochin v. California, 342 U.S. 165, (1952)
-    Rogers v. Commissioner, see: Estate of Rogers v. Commissioner
o   Rogers v. Richmond, 365 U.S. 534, (1961)
o   Romero v. International Terminal Co., 358 U.S. 354, (1959)
o   Rorick v. Commissioners, 307 U.S. 208 (1939)
s   Rosenberg v. Denno, 346 U.S. 271, (1953)
s   Rosenberg v. United States, 344 U.S. 889, (1952)
d   Rosenberg v. United States, 346 U.S. 273, (1953)
s   Rosenberg v. United States, 346 U.S. 322, (1953)

o   Rosenberg v. United States, 360 U.S. 367, (1959)
o   Rosenman v. United States, 323 U.S 658, (1945)
o   Rowoldlt v. Perfetto, 355 U.S. 115, (1957)

S

d   Sacher v. United States, 343 U.S. 1, (1952)
o   Safeway Stores v. Oklahoma Grocers, 360 U.S. 334, (1960)
d   Saia v. New York, 334 U.S. 558, (1948)
o   St. Joe Paper Co. v. Atlantic Coast Line R.R., 347 U.S. 298, (1954)
o   San Diego Union v. Garmon, 359 U.S. 236, (1959)
s   Savorgnan v. United States, 338 U.S. 491, (1950)
d   Sawyer, in re, 360 U.S. 622, (1959)
s   Schaffer Transportation Co. v. United States, 355 U.S. 83, (1957)
d   Schulte Co. v. Gangi, 328 U.S. 108, (1946)
d   Schwabacher v. United States, 334 U.S. 182, (1948)
c   Schware v. Board of Bar Examiners, 353 U.S. 232, (1957)
c   Schwartz v. Texas, 344 U.S. 199, (1952)
d   Schwegmann Brothers v. Calvert Corp., 341 U.S. 384, (1951)
d   Scott Paper Co. v. Marcalus Manufacturing Co., 326 U.S. 249, (1945)
o   Scripps-Howard Radio, Inc. v. F.C.C., 316 U.S. 4, (1942)
s   Sears Roebuck & Co. v. Mackey, 351 U.S. 427, (1956)
o   Secretary of Agriculture v. Central Roig Refining Co., 338 U.S. 604, (1950)
o   Secretary of Agriculture v. United States, 347 U.S. 645, (1954)
c   Secretary of Agriculture v. United States, 350 U.S. 162, (1956)
o   S.E.C. v. Chenery Corp., 318 U.S. 80, (1943)
d   S.E.C. v. Chenery Corp., 332 U.S. 194, (1947)
d   S.E.C. v. Drexel & Co., 348 U.S. 340, (1955)
d   S.E.C. v. Howey Co., 328 U.S. 293, (1946)
d   Sentilles v. Inter-Caribbean Shipping Corp., 361 U.S. 107, (1959)
d   Shapiro v. United States, 335 U.S. 1, (1948)
d   Shelton v. Tucker, 364 U.S. 479, (1960)
c   Sherman v. United States, 356 U.S. 369, (1958)
d   Sherrer v. Sherrer, 334 U.S. 343, (1948)
d   Sibbach v. Wilson & Co., 312 U.S. 1, (1941)
d   Simonson v. Granquist, 369 U.S. 38, (1962)
d   Singer v. United States, 323 U.S. 338, (1945)
c   Singer & Sons, v. Union Pacific R.R., 311 U.S. 295, (1940)
o   Sixty-Two Cases of Jam v. United States, 340 U.S. 593, (1951)
o   Skelly Oil Co. v. Phillips Petroleum Co., 339 U.S. 667, (1950)

T

U

d   United States v. California, 332 U.S. 19, (1947)
d   United States v. Carbone, 327 U.S. 633, (1946)
d   United States v. Central Eureka Mining Co., 357 U.S. 155, (1958)
s   United States v. City of Detroit, 355 U.S. 466, (1958)
c   United States v. C.I.O., 335 U.S. 106, (1948)
d   United States v. Cors, 337 U.S. 325 (1949)
d   United States v. Commodities Trading Corp., 339 U.S. 121, (1950)
d   United States v. Contract Steel Carriers, Inc., 350 U.S. 409, (1956)
d   United States v. County of Allegheny, 322 U.S. 174, (1944)
o   United States v. Dege, 364 U.S. 51, (1960)
-    United States v. Detroit, see: United States v. City of Detroit
o   United States v. Dickinson, 331 U.S. 745, (1947)
o   United States v. Dotterweich, 320 U.S. 277, (1943)
c   United States v. Du Pont & Co., 351 U.S. 377, (1956)
d   United States v. Du Pont & Co., 366 U.S. 316, (1961)
d   United States v. F. & M. Schaefer Brewing Co., 356 U.S. 227, (1958)
j   United States v. Felin & Co., 334 U.S. 624, (1948)
c   United States v. Florida, 363 U.S. 121, (1960)
c   United States v. Frankfort Distilleries, 324 U.S. 293, (1945)
o   United States v. Freuhauf, 365 U.S. 146, (1961)
d   United States v. Gilbert Associates, 345 U.S. 361, (1953)
o   United States v. Hood, 343 U.S. 148, (1952)
o   United States v. Hutcheson, 312 U.S. 219, (1941)
d   United States v. International Boxing Club, 348 U.S. 236, (1955)
d   United States v. I.C.C., 337 U.S. 426, (1949)
o   United States v. Johnson, 319 U.S. 503 (1943)
o   United States v. Johnson, 323 U.S. 273,(1944)
d   United States v. Kahriger, 345 U.S. 22, (1959)
c   United States v. Kaiser, 363 U.S. 299, (1960)
d   United States v. Knight, 336 U.S. 505, (1949)
s   United States v. Louisiana, 339 U.S. 699, (1950)
c   United States v. Lovett, 328 U.S. 303, (1946)
d   United States v. Mersky, 361 U.S. 431, (1960)
o   United States v. Minker, 350 U.S. 179, (1956)
o   United States v. Mitchell, 322 U.S. 65, (1944)
d   United States v. Monia, 317 U.S. 424,(1943)
o   United States v. Morgan, 313 U.S. 409, (1941)
d   United States v. National City Lines, 334 U.S. 573, (1948)
d   United States v. Nugent, 346 U.S. 1, (1953)
o   United States v. Nunnally Investment Co., 316 U.S. 258, (1942)
d   United States v. Ogilvie Hardware Co., 330 U.S. 709, (1947)
d   United States v. Paramount Pictures, 334 U.S. 131, (1948)
c   United States v. Petrillo, 332 U.S. 1, (1947)

c United States v. Pink, 315 U.S. 203, (1942)
s United States v. Public Utilities Commission, 345 U.S. 295, (1953)
d United States v. Rabinowitz, 339 U.S. 56, (1950)
c United States v. Raines, 362 U.S. 17, (1960)
s United States v. Republic Steel Corp., 362 U.S. 482, (1960)
o United States v. Rumely, 345 U.S. 41, (1953)
o United States v. Ruzicka, 329 U.S. 287, (1946)
c United States v. Scophony Corp., 333 U.S. 795, (1948)
s United States v. Shannon, 342 U.S. 288, (1952)
o United States v. Shirey, 359 U.S. 255, (1959)
d United States v. South-Eastern Underwriters Association, 322 U.S. 533, (1944)
c United States v. Spelar, 338 U.S. 217, (1949)
d United States v. Storer Broadcasting Co., 351 U.S. 192, (1956)
s United States v. Texas, 339 U.S. 707, (1950)
c United States v. Toronto, H. & B. Navigation Co., 338 U.S. 396, (1949)
d United States v. Tucker Truck Lines, 344 U.S. 33, (1952)
d United States v. Turley, 352 U.S. 407, (1957)
d United States v. Union Pacific R.R., 353 U.S. 112, (1957)
o United States v. United Auto Workers, 352 U.S. 567, (1957)
c United States v. U.M.W., 330 U.S. 258, (1947)
c United States v. United States District Court, 334 U.S. 258, (1948)
c United States v. United States Gypsum Co., 333 U.S. 364, (1948)
o United States v. Universal C.I.T. Credit Corp., 344 U.S. 218, (1952)
o United States v. Westinghouse Co., 339 U.S. 261, (1950)
j United States v. Williams, 341 U.S. 70, (1951)
o United States v. Witkovich, 353 U.S. 194, (1957)
o United States ex rel Chapman v. F.P.C., 345 U.S. 153, (1953)
d United States ex rel Eichenlaub v. Shaughnessy, 338 U.S. 521, (1950)
d United States ex rel Knauff v. Shaughnessy, 338 U.S. 537, (1950)
c United States ex rel Marcus v. Hess, 317 U.S. 537, (1943)
d United States ex rel Smith v. Baldi, 344 U.S. 561, (1953)
c United States ex rel T.V.A. v. Welsh, 327 U.S. 546, (1946)
c United States ex rel Touhy v. Ragen, 340 U.S. 462, (1951)
s United States Bank v. Chase Bank, 331 U.S. 28, (1947)
c United Steelworkers v. United States, 361 U.S. 39, (1959)
o Universal Camera Corp. v. N.L.R.B., 340 U.S. 474, (1951)
o Universal Oil Products Co. v. Root Refining Co., 328 U.S. 575, (1946)
s Uphaus v. Wyman, 5 L Ed. 2d (Not in 364 U.S) (1960)
c Urie v. Thompson, 337 U.S. 163, (1949)

o   Utah Junk Co. v. Porter, 328 U.S. 39, (1946)
d   Uveges v. Pennsylvania, 335 U.S. 437, (1948)

V

d   Vanderbilt v. Vanderbilt, 354 U.S. 416, (1957)
c   Vanston Bondholders Committee v. Green, 319 U.S. 156, (1946)
c   Virginia Electric & Power Co. v. N.L.R.B., 319 U.S. 533, (1943)
s   Vitarelli v. Seaton, 359 U.S. 535, (1959)
s   Von Moltke v. Gillies, 332 U.S. 708, (1948)

W

o   Walden v. United States, 347 U.S. 62, (1954)
d   Walker v. City of Hutchinson, 352 U.S. 112, (1956)
c   Walling v. Harnischfeger Corp., 325 U.S. 427, (1945)
s   Ward v. Atlantic Coast Line R.R. 362 U.S. 396, (1960)
d   Warren v. United States, 340 U.S. 523, (1951)
c   Watkins v. United States, 354 U.S. 179, (1957)
c   Watson v. Employer's Liability Assurance Corp., 348 U.S. 66, (1959)
j   Watts v. Indiana, 338 U.S. 49, (1949)
o   Weber v. Anheuser-Busch Inc., 348 U.S. 468, (1955)
s   Weber v. United States, 344 U.S. 834, (1952)
s   Western Pacific Railroad Case, 345 U.S. 247, (1953)
o   West Virginia ex rel Dyer v. Sims, 341 U.S. 22, (1951)
d   West Virginia State Board of Education v. Barnette, 319 U.S. 624, (1943)
o   Whitehouse v. Illinois Central R.R., 349 U.S. 366, (1955)
-     Whitman v. Wilson, see: New York ex rel Whitman v. Wilson
o   Whitney v. State Tax Commission, 309 U.S. 530, (1940)
c   Wieman v. Updegraff, 344 U.S. 183, (1952)
o   Wiener v. United States, 357 U.S. 349, (1958)
c   Wilburn Boat Co. v. Fireman's Fund Insurance Co., 348 U.S. 310, (1955)
c   Wilkerson v. McCarthy, 336 U.S. 53, (1949)
d   Wilks v. Swan, 346 U.S. 427, (1953)
d   Williams v. Austrian, 331 U.S. 642, (1947)
o   Williams v. Georgia, 349 U.S. 375, (1955)
d   Williams v. Kaiser, 323 U.S. 471, (1945)
c   Williams v. North Carolina, 317 U.S. 287, (1942)
o   Williams v. North Carolina, 325 U.S. 226, (1945)

Bibliography

Bibliographical Note

An acknowledgement is due here to Professor Thomas whose book, *Felix Frankfurter, Scholar on the Bench*, is listed below. Her doctoral dissertation at Johns Hopkins University (1959), of which her book is the published version, contains an excellent bibliography which saved the present author much labor.

The following bibliography does not list every duplication which occurs in the publication of Frankfurter's works. For example, some ninety-six separate items which are collected in *Law and Politics* and *Of Law and Men* (cited in the text as *L and P* and *L and M*, respectively) are not cited to their original sources below, nor are law review articles generally listed below if the article appears as a part of one or another of the listed books. It is suggested that the Table of Opinions by Mr. Justice Frankfurter (Appendix III, *supra*), the following bibliography, the bibliographies in Miss Thomas' and Mr. Gilkey's (see below) dissertations, and the headnotes for the several items in *Law and Politics* and *Of Law and Men* provide a relatively complete bibliography of Frankfurter's published writings.

For the sake of simplicity, the several book reviews of Professor Crosskey's book (see below) listed under "Articles" herein are simply listed as "Book review of Crosskey."

Books

Abraham, H. J. *The Judicial Process*. New York: Oxford University Press, 1962.
Alsop, J., and T. Catledge. *The 168 Days*. Garden City: Doubleday, 1938.
American Bar Association. *Reports*. Vol. LVI. Baltimore: Lord Baltimore Press, 1931.
American Law Institute. *Proceedings*. Vol. IX. Philadelphia: author, 1931.
Anderson, W.C. *A Dictionary of Law*. Chicago: T. H. Flood, 1889.

Aristotle. *Nichomachean Ethics*. Translated by H. Rackham. Cambridge: Harvard University Press, 1939.

_____. *Politics*. Edited by E. Barker. New York: Oxford University Press, 1958.

Benson, G. C. S., M. Diamond, *et al. Essays in Federalism*. Claremont: Institute for Studies in Federalism, 1961.

Berns, Walter. *Freedom, Virtue and the First Amendment*. Baton Rouge: Louisiana State University Press, 1957.

Beth, L.P. *Politics, The Constitution, and the Supreme Court*. Evanston: Row Peterson, 1962.

Blackstone, William. *Commentaries on the Laws of England*. 4th ed. Oxford: Clarendon Press, 1770.

_____. *Commentaries on the Laws of England*. Edited by J. Chitty. 4 vols. London, 1826.

Bouvier, J. *A Law Dictionary*. 2 vols. Philadelphia, 1914.

Bryce, James. *The American Commonwealth*. New York: Macmillan, 1888.

_____. *The American Commonwealth*. Edited and abridged by L. Hacker. New York: Capricorn Books, 1959.

Burke, E. *Political Writings*. Edited by J. Buchan. London: Thos. Nelson, n.d.

Burrill, A. M. *A Law Dictionary and Glossary*. New York: John S. Voorhies, 1859.

Cardozo, B. *The Nature of the Judicial Process*. New Haven: Yale University Press, 1960.

Chitty, J. *A Practical Treatise on the Criminal Law*. London: A. J. Valpy, 1816.

Coke, Sir Edward. *The Second Part of the Institutes of the Laws of England*. London: W. Clarke & Sons, 1809.

Corpus Juris Secundum. Brooklyn: American Law Book Co., 1956.

Cox, Richard. *Locke on War and Peace*. Oxford: Clarendon Press, 1960.

Crosskey, William Winslow. *Politics and the Constitution in the History of the United States*. 2 vols. Chicago: University of Chicago Press, 1953.

Curtis, Charles P. *Lions under the Throne*. Boston: Houghton-Mifflin, 1947.

Devlin, Sir Patrick. *The Enforcement of Morals*. London: Oxford University Press, 1959.

Edgeworth, P. "Mr. Justice Frankfurter and the Administration of Criminal Justice." Unpublished Master's thesis, University of Chicago, 1955.

Fellman, David. *The Defendant's Rights*. New York: Rinehart, 1958.

Finer, Herman. *Theory and Practice of Modern Government*. 2 vols. New York: Holt, 1949.

Flack, Horace Edgar. *The Adoption of the Fourteenth Amendment*. Baltimore: Johns Hopkins Unversity Press, 1908.

Frankfurter, F., with J. M. Landis. *The Business of the Supreme Court*. New York: Macmillan, 1928.

Frankfurter, F., with J. F. Davison. *Cases and Materials on Administrative Law*. Chicago: Foundation Press, 1935.

Frankfurter, F., with H. Shulman. *Cases on Federal Jurisdiction and Procedure*. Revised edition. Chicago: Callaghan & Co., 1937.

Frankfurter, F., with N. Greene. *The Labor Injunction*. New York: Macmillan, 1930.

Frankfurter, F. *The Commerce Clause Under Marshall, Taney and Waite*. Chapel Hill: University of North Carolina Press, 1937.

_____. *Felix Frankfurter Reminisces*. Edited by H. B. Phillips. New York: Reynal, 1960.

_____. *Law and Politics: Occasional Papers of Felix Frankfurter 1913-1938*. Edited by Archibald MacLeish and E. F. Prichard. New York: Harcourt Brace, 1939.

_____. *Mr. Justice Holmes and the Supreme Court*. Cambridge: Harvard University Press, 1938.

_____. *Mr. Justice Holmes and the Supreme Court*. Cambridge: Harvard University Press, 1961.

_____. *Of Law and Men: Papers and Addresses of Felix Frankfurter, 1939-1956*. Edited by P. Elman. New York: Harcourt-Brace, 1956.

_____. *The Public and Its Government*. New Haven: Yale University Press, 1930.

_____. *A Selection of Cases under the Interstate Commerce Act*. Cambridge: Harvard University Press, 1922.

Freund, P. *The Supreme Court of the United States*. Cleveland: Meridian Books, 1961.

Gilkey, Royal C. "Mr. Justice Frankfurter and Civil Liberties as Manifested in and Suggested by the Compulsory Flag Salute Controversy." Unpublished Ph.D. Dissertation, University of Minnesota, 1957.

Griswold, Erwin. *The Fifth Amendment Today*. Cambridge: Harvard University Press, 1955.

Grotius, H. *Prolegomena to the Law of War and Peace*. Translated by F. W. Kelsey. New York: Liberal Arts Press, 1957.

Hamilton, Alexander, James Madison and John Jay. *The Federalist*. Edited by J. E. Cooke. Cleveland: Meridian Books, 1961.

Hamilton, A. *Works*. Edited by H. C. Lodge. New York: Federal Edition, Putnam, 1904.

Hand, Learned. *The Bill of Rights*. Cambridge: Harvard University Press, 1958.

Hobbes, T. *Leviathan*. Oxford: Blackwell, 1955.

Jackson, R. H. *The Struggle for Judicial Supremacy*. New York: Vintage, 1962.

Jacob, G. *A New Law Dictionary*. London, 1772 and 1797.

Jacobs, Clyde. *Justice Frankfurter and Civil Liberties*. ("University of California Publications in Political Science," Vol. XII.) Berkeley and Los Angeles: University of California Press, 1961.

James, Joseph B. *The Framing of the Fourteenth Amendment*. Urbana: University of Illinois Press, 1956.

Jaffa, Harry V. *The Crisis of the House Divided*. New York: Doubleday, 1959.

Jeudwine, J. W. *The Manufacture of Historical Material*. London, 1905.

Kent, J. *Commentaries on American Law*. Edited by O. W. Holmes, Jr. 12th ed. Boston: Little Brown, 1873.

Konefsky, Samuel J. (ed.) *The Constitutional World of Mr. Justice Frankfurter—Some Representative Opinions*. New York: Macmillan, 1949.

_____. *The Legacy of Holmes and Brandeis; A Study in the Influence of Ideas*. New York: Macmillan, 1956.

Locke, John. *Two Treatises of Government*. Edited by P. Laslett. Cambridge: Cambridge University Press, 1960.

Marx, K. and F. Engels. *Basic Writings on Politics and Philosophy*. New York: Anchor Books, 1959.

McCloskey, Robert G. *Essays in Constitutional Law*. New York: Knopf, 1957.

McKechnie, W. S. *Magna Carta*. 2d ed. Glasgow: J. Maclehose, 1914.

Mendelson, W. *Capitalism, Democracy and the Supreme Court*. New York: Appleton-Century-Crofts, 1960.

_____. *Justices Black and Frankfurter: Conflict in the Court*. Chicago: University of Chicago Press, 1961.

Montesquieu, C. S., B. de. *De L'Esprit Des Lois*. Paris: Editions Garnier Freres, n.d.

National Popular Government League. *To the American People, Report upon the Illegal Practices of the United States Department of Justice*. Washington: author, 1920.

Pollock, Sir Frederick. *Principles of Contract at Law and in Equity*. 2d ed. London: Stevens, 1878.

Pound, Roscoe. *An Introduction to the Philosophy of Law*. New Haven: Yale University Press, 1959.

_____. *Law Finding Through Experience and Reason*. Athens, Georgia: University of Georgia Press, 1960.

Pritchett, C. Herman. *The American Constitution*. New York: McGraw-Hill, 1959.

_____. *Civil Liberties and the Vinson Court*. Chicago: University of Chicago Press, 1954.

_____. *The Political Offender and the Warren Court*. Boston: Boston University Press, 1958.

_____. *The Roosevelt Court: A Study in Judicial Politics and Values 1937-1947*. New York: Macmillan, 1948.

Proceedings in Honor of Mr. Justice Frankfurter and Distinguished Alumni. Harvard Law School Occasional Pamphlet No. 3. Cambridge: Harvard Law School, 1960.

Rodell, Fred. *Nine Men: A Political History of the Supreme Court from 1790 to 1955*. New York: Random House, 1955.

Schmidhauser, J. R. *The Supreme Court: Its Politics, Personalities and Procedures*. New York: Holt, Rinehart & Winston, 1960.

Smith, J. M. and P. L. Murphy. *Liberty and Justice*. New York: Knopf, 1958.

Spicer, G. W. *The Supreme Court and Fundmental Freedoms*. New York: Appleton-Century-Crofts, 1959.

Sutherland, A. E. *The Law and One Man Among Many*. Madison: University of Wisconsin Press, 1956.

Tayler, T. *The Law Glossary*. 7th ed. New York: Lewin and Blood, 1861.

Thagard, T. W. "Justice Felix Frankfurter's Doctrine of Judicial Self-Restraint." Unpublished Master's thesis, Emory University, 1957.

Thomas, H. Shirley. *Felix Frankfurter, Scholar on the Bench*. Baltimore: Johns Hopkins University Press, 1960.

Tocqueville, A. de. *Democracy in America*. 2 vols. New York: Vintage, 1959.

"Traver, Robert" (Voelker, J. D.). *Anatomy of a Murder*. New York: St. Martins, 1958.

Voelker, J. D. *See* "Robert Traver."

Westin, A. F. (ed.) *The Supreme Court: Views from the Inside*. New York: Norton, 1961.

Wigmore, J. H. *A Treatise on the Anglo-American System of Evidence*. 3d ed., 10 vols. Boston: Little Brown, 1940.

Winfield, C. H. *Adjudged Words and Phrases*. Jersey City, 1882.

Winfield, Percy H. *The Chief Sources of English Legal History*. Cambridge: Harvard University Press, 1925.

Words & Phrases. St. Paul: West Publishing Co., 1951.

Wright, B. F. *The Growth of American Constitutional Law*. New York: Holt, 1942.

Public Documents

Annotated California Codes. St. Paul: West Publishing Co., 1955.

Connecticut General Statutes Revised. Bristol, Conn.: Hildreth Press, 1958.

Corwin, Edward S. *Constitution of the United States of America, Revised and Annotated 1952*. Washington: U.S. Government Printing Office, 1953.

Richardson, J. D. *Messages and Papers of the Presidents.* Washington: U.S. Government Printing Office, 1898.

United States Code. Washington: U.S. Government Printing Office, 1946, 1952, 1958.

United States Congress. *Statutes at Large.* Washington: U.S. Government Printing Office.

_____. *Congressional Globe 39th Congress, 1st Session.* Washington: Congressional Globe, 1866.

_____. 76th Congress, First Session, Senate, Subcommittee of the Committee on the Judiciary. *Hearings on the Nomination of Felix Frankfurter to be an Associate Justice of the Supreme Court.* Washington: U.S. Government Printing Office, 1939.

United States Supreme Court Reports, Vol. CCCXXXII, *Records and Briefs*, Part I, 1947.

Articles

Angell, J. K. "Restrictions upon State Power in Relation to Private Property," *United States Law Intelligencer and Review*, Vol. I (1829), *passim*.

Arnold, T. "Professor Hart's Theology," *Harvard Law Review*, LXXIII (May, 1960), 1298.

Bickel, A. M. "Justice Frankfurter at Seventy-Five," *New Republic*, November 18, 1957, p. 7.

Braden, G. D. Book review of Crosskey, *Yale Law Journal*, LXII (June, 1953), 1145.

Brant, I. Book review of Crosskey, *Columbia Law Review*, LIV (March, 1954), 443.

Brown, E. J. Book review of Crosskey, *Harvard Law Review*, LXVII (June, 1954), 1439.

_____. "The Open Economy: Justice Frankfurter and the Position of the Judiciary," *Yale Law Journal*, LXVII (December, 1957), 219.

Bundy, McG. Book review of L. Hand, *The Bill of Rights.* Cambridge: Harvard University Press, 1958; W. Berns, *Freedom, Virtue and the First Amendment.* Baton Rouge: Louisiana State University Press, 1957; and M. R. Konvitz, *Fundamental Liberties of a Free People.* Ithaca: Cornell University Press, 1957, in *Yale Law Journal*, LXVII, No. 5 (April, 1958), 944.

Clark, C. E. "Professor Crosskey and the Brooding Omnipresence of Erie-Tompkins," *University of Chicago Law Review*, XXI (Autumn, 1953), 24.

Cohen, M. R. "The Place of Logic in the Law," *Harvard Law Review*, XXIX (April, 1916), 622.

Corbin, A. L. Book review of Crosskey, *Yale Law Journal*, LXII (June, 1953), 1137.

Corwin, E. S. "The Doctrine of Due Process of Law Before the Civil War," *Harvard Law Review*, XXIV (March and April, 1911), 366, 460.

Cropsey, J. "The Relation Between Political Science and Economics," *American Political Science Review*, LIV (1960), 3.

Crosskey, W. W. "Charles Fairman, 'Legislative History,' and the Congressional Limitations on State Authority," *University of Chicago Law Review*, XXII (Autumn, 1954), 1.

Duffus, R. L. "Felix Frankfurter: The Man Behind the Legend," *New York Times*, January 15, 1939, Sec. VII, p. 3.

Durham, J. A. "Crosskey on the Constitution: An Essay-Review," *California Law Review*, XLIX (Summer, 1953), 209.

Editorial on Frankfurter's declination of appointment to Supreme Judicial Court of Massachusetts, *Nation*, July 27, 1932, p. 67.

Edson, A. "Frankfurter—Man and Judge," Baltimore *Sun*, July 22, 1962, Sec. A, p. 3.

Ernst, Morris L. and others. "The Legal Profession: A Fifty-Year Stocktaking," *Journal of Public Law*, V (Fall, 1956), 283.

Fairman, Charles A. "Does the Fourteenth Amendment Incorporate the Bill of Rights?—The Original Understanding," *Stanford Law Review*, II (December, 1949), 5.

_____. "A Reply to Professor Crosskey," *University of Chicago Law Review*, XXII (Autumn, 1954), 144.

_____. "The Supreme Court and the Constitutional Limitations on State Governmental Authority," *University of Chicago Law Review*, XXI (Autumn, 1953), 40.

"Felix Frankfurter's Tribute to Learned Hand," *Reporter*, April 30, 1959, p. 4.

Field, O. P. Book review of Crosskey, *New York University Law Review*, XXVIII (October, 1953), 1197.

Frank, J. P. Book review of Crosskey, *Northwestern University Law Review*, XLIX (March-April, 1954), 132.

Frankfurter, Felix, with J. M. Landis. "The Compact Clause of the Constitution—A Study in Interstate Adjustments," *Yale Law Journal*, XXXIV (May, 1925), 685.

Frankfurter, Felix, with N. Greene. "Congressional Power over the Labor Injunction," *Columbia Law Review*, XXXI (March, 1931), 385.

Frankfurter, Felix, with T. G. Corcoran. "Petty Federal Offenses and the Constitutional Guaranty of Trial by Jury," *Harvard Law Review*, XXXIX (June, 1926), 917.

Frankfurter, Felix, and James M. Landis. "Power of Congress over Procedure in Criminal Contempts in 'Inferior' Federal Courts—A Study in Separation of Powers," *Harvard Law Review*, XXXVII (June, 1924), 1010.

Frankfurter, Felix, with W. J. Haley. "The Real Mhicneachdain," *Law Quarterly Review*, LXXIV (July, 1958), 321.

Frankfurter, Felix, with James M. Landis. "The Supreme Court under the Judiciary Act of 1925, *Harvard Law Review*, XLII (November, 1928), 1.

Frankfurter, Felix, with N. Greene. "The Use of the Injunction in American Labor Controversies," *Law Quarterly Review*, XLIV (April, 1928), 164 and XLV (January, 1929), 19.

Frankfurter, Felix. *Address by Associate Justice Felix Frankfurter at the Inauguration of Dr. Harry N. Wright, Sixth President of the City College of the College of the City of New York on Wednesday, September 30, 1942*. New York: C.C.N.Y., 1942.

_____. Address to the Harvard Law Society of Illinois, Chicago, April 28, 1955. Harvard Law Society.

_____. Book review of A. A. Bruce, *The American Judge*. New York: Macmillan, 1924. *New Republic*, April 23, 1924, p. 236.

_____. Book review of W. W. Dewhurst, *The Rules of Practice in the United States Courts, Annotated*. New York: Banks Law Publishing Co., 1907. *Harvard Law Review*, XXI (February, 1908), 300-01.

_____. Book review of C. S. Hamlin, *The Act to Regulate Commerce*. Boston: Little Brown, 1907. *Harvard Law Review*, XX (April, 1907), 508-9.

_____. Book review of A. W. Machen, Jr., *A Treatise of the Modern Law of Corporations*. Boston: Little Brown, 1908. *Harvard Law Review*, XXII (June, 1909), 618-19.

_____. Book review of *The Federal Penal Code*, Annotated by G. F. Tucker, and C. W. Blood. Boston: Little Brown, 1910. *Harvard Law Review*, XXIV (May, 1911), 590.

_____. "Calvert Magruder," *Harvard Law Review*, LXXII (May, 1959), 1201.

_____. "The Conservation of the New Federal Standards," *The Survey*, December 7, 1918, p. 291.

_____. "The Constitutional Opinions of Mr. Justice Holmes," *Harvard Law Review*, XXIX (April, 1916), 683.

_____. "Democracy and the Expert," *Atlantic Monthly*, CXLVI (November, 1930), 649.

_____. "A Distinctive American Constitution," *American Labor Legislation Review*, XXIII (December, 1933), 169.

_____. "Distribution of Judicial Power Between United States and State Courts," *Cornell Law Quarterly*, XIII (June, 1928), 499.

_____. "The Enforcement of Prohibition," *New Republic*, January 3, 1923, p. 149.

_____. "The Federal Courts," *New Republic*, April 24, 1929, p. 273.

_____. "The Federal Securities Act," *Fortune*, X, No. 2 (August, 1933), 50.

_____. Foreword to "A Symposium on Statutory Construction," *Vanderbilt Law Review*, III (April, 1950), 365.

_____. Foreword to "Courts and Administrative Law—The Experience of English Housing Legislation," *Harvard Law Review*, XLIX (January, 1936), 426.

_____. Foreword to J. Story, "American Law," *American Journal of Comparative Law*, III (1954), 1.

_____. Foreword to the *Columbia Law Review* for April, 1941, devoted to the Final Report of the Attorney General's Committee on Administrative Procedure, *Columbia Law Review*, XLI (April, 1941), 585.

_____. Foreword to the *Yale Law Journal* for February, 1938, devoted to Administrative Law, *Yale Law Journal*, XLVII (February, 1938), 515.

_____. "Government Lawyer," *Federal Bar Journal*, XVIII (January-March, 1958), 24.

_____. "Hands off the Investigations," *New Republic*, May 21, 1929, p. 329.

_____. "The Health of the Society," *Journal of Society of Public Teachers of Law*, I (N.S.), 363 (1950).

_____. "Hours of Labor and Realism in Constitutional Law," *Harvard Law Review*, XXIX (February, 1916), 353.

_____. "Immigrant in the United States," *Survey Graphic*, XXVIII, No. 2 (February, 1939), 148.

_____. "In Answer to Mr. Beck," *New Republic*, January 18, 1922, p. 315.

_____. Introduction to "A Symposium on Administrative Law Based upon Legal Writings 1931-33," *Iowa Law Review*, XVIII (January, 1933), 129.

_____. "Jerome N. Frank," *University of Chicago Law Review*, XXIV (Summer, 1957), 625.

_____. "Job of a Supreme Court Justice," *New York Times*, November 28, 1954, Sec. 6, p. 14.

_____. "Joining the League," *Nation*, May 16, 1923, p. 571.

_____. "The Law and the Law Schools," *American Bar Association Journal*, I, No. 4 (October, 1915), 532.

_____. "A Lawyer's Dicta on Doctors," *Harvard Medical Alumni Bulletin*, July, 1958.

_____. *"Mr. Justice Holmes and the Constitution,"* Harvard Law Review, XLI (December, 1927), 121.

_____. "Moral Grandeur of Justice Brandeis," *New York Times*, November 11, 1956, Sec. 6, p. 26.

_____. "A National Policy for the Enforcement of Prohibition," *Annals of the American Academy of Political and Social Science*, CIX, No. 198 (September, 1923), 193.

_____. "A Note on Advisory Opinions," *Harvard Law Review*, XXXVII (June, 1924), 1002.

_____. "A Note on Diversity Jurisdiction—In Reply to Professor Yntema," *University of Pennsylvania Law Review*, LXXIX (June, 1931), 1097.

_____. "The Palestine Situation Restated," *Foreign Affairs*, IX (April, 1931), 409.

_____. "Personal Ambitions of Judges: Should a Judge Think Beyond the Judicial?," *American Bar Association Journal*, XXXIV (August, 1948), 656, 747.

_____. Note: "The Present Approach to Constitutional Decisions on the Bill of Rights," *Harvard Law Review*, XXVIII (June, 1915), 790.

_____. Progress Report of Harvard Survey of Crime and Law in Boston. Cambridge: Harvard Law School, June 14, 1927.

_____. "Reconstruction and the Laws," *Proceedings of the Bar Association of the State of New Hampshire, 1923-33*. Rochester, N.H.: Record Press, 1933, p. 73.

_____. "Rigid Outlook in a Dynamic World," *Survey Graphic*, XXVII, No. 1 (January, 1938), 5.

_____. "Summation of the Conference," *American Bar Association Journal*, XXIV (April, 1938), 282.

_____. "Supreme Court and the Public," *Forum*, LXXXIII, No. 6 (June, 1930), 329.

_____. "The Supreme Court in the Mirror of Justices," *University of Pennsylvania Law Review*, CV (April, 1957), 781; *American Bar Association Journal*, XLI (August, 1958), 723.

_____. "The Supreme Court's Traditions of Dissent," *American Bar Association Journal*, IX (August, 1923), 536.

_____. "Taney and the Commerce Clause," *Harvard Law Review*, XLIX (June, 1936), 1286.

_____. "There is No Middle Way," *Saturday Review of Literature*, October 26, 1946, p. 21.

_____. "Twenty Years of Mr. Justice Holmes' Constitutional Opinions," *Harvard Law Review*, XXXVI (June, 1923), 909.

_____. "United States Supreme Court Molding the Constitution," *Current History*, XXXII, No. 2 (May, 1930), 235.

_____. "What Has Prohibition Done to America?", *New Republic*, November 15, 1922, p. 305.

_____. "What the President Wanted," *Atlantic Monthly*, CCVII, No. 3 (March, 1961), 39.

_____. "Worth of our Past," *Vital Speeches*, July 15, 1941, p. 601.

"Frankfurter v. Stone," *New Republic*, June 24, 1940, p. 843.

Freund, P. A. Book review of F. Frankfurter, *Of Law and Men*. New York: Harcourt-Brace, 1956. *Harvard Law Review*, LXX (January, 1957), 568.

_____. "Mr. Justice Frankfurter," *University of Chicago Law Review*, XXVI, No. 2 (Winter, 1959), 205.

_____. "The Rule of Law," *Washington University Law Quarterly*, (June, 1956), p. 314.

Frisch, M. J. An article on Roosevelt's 1937 judiciary bill, to be published early 1963 in the *Journal of Politics*.

Gilkey, R. C. Mr. Justice Frankfurter's Interpretation of the Constitutional Rights of Labor in a Statutory Context with Special Attention to Picketing and Associated Union Activity, *University of Kansas City Law Review*, XVIII (December-February, 1950), and XVIII (April-June, 1950), 133.

Goebel, J., Jr. Book review of Crosskey, *Columbia Law Review*, LIV (March, 1954), 450.

Gooch, R. K. Book review of Crosskey, *American Bar Association Journal*, XL (1954), 313.

Hamilton, W. H. Book review of C. P. Curtis, *Lions under the Throne*. Boston: Houghton-Mifflin, 1947, and W. McCune, *The Nine Young Men*. New York: Harper, 1947. *Yale Law Journal*, LVI (June, 1947), 1458.

_____. "The Constitution—Apropos of Crosskey," *University of Chicago Law Review*, XXI (Autumn, 1953), 79.

_____. "Preview of a Justice," *Yale Law Journal*, XLVIII (March, 1939), 819.

Hand, Augustus N. "Mr. Justice Frankfurter," *Harvard Law Review*, LXII (January, 1949), 353.

Hand, L. "The Speech of Justice," *Harvard Law Review*, XXIX (April, 1916), 617.

Hart, H. M., Jr. Book review of Crosskey, *Harvard Law Review*, LXVII (June, 1954), 1456.

_____. "The Time Chart of the Justices," Foreword to "The Supreme Court,1958 Term," *Harvard Law Review*, LXXIII (November, 1959), 84.

Hurd, Charles W. *"New Appointees in Limelight,"* *New York Times*, January 15, 1939, Sec. 4, p. 6.

Jaffee, L.L. "The Court Debated—Another View," *New York Times*, June 5, 1960, Sec. 7, p. 36.

_____. "The Judicial Universe of Mr. Justice Frankfurter," *Harvard Law Review*, LXII (January, 1949), 357.

Josephson, M. "Profiles: Jurist," *New Yorker*, November 30, 1940, p. 24; December 7, 1940, p. 36; and December 14, 1940, p. 32.

"Justice Frankfurter," *Nation*, January 24, 1939, p. 52.

Krash, A. "A More Perfect Union: The Constitutional World of William Winslow Crosskey," *University of Chicago Law Review*, XXI (Autumn, 1953), 1.

Kurland, Philip B. "Mr. Justice Frankfurter," *University of Chicago Law Review*, XXVI, No. 1 (Autumn, 1958), 1.

_____. "Mr. Justice Frankfurter, the Supreme Court and the Erie Doctrine in Diversity Cases," *Yale Law Journal*, LXVII (December, 1957), 187.

Lerner, M. "Holmes and Frankfurter," *Nation*, November 19, 1938, p. 537.

Lewis, Anthony. "Appreciation of Justice Frankfurter," *New York Times*, November 10, 1957, Sec. 6, p. 25.

_____. "Portraits of Nine Men Under Attack," *New York Times*, May 18, 1958, Sec. 7, p. 14.

_____. "Professor Among the Presidents," *New York Times*, May 29, 1960, Sec. 7, p. 1.

MacLeish, A. "The Significance of Mr. Justice Frankfurter," *Reader's Digest*, XXXVI, No. 216 (April, 1940), 33.

McCloskey, Robert G. "The Supreme Court Finds a Role: Civil Liberties in the 1955 Term," *Virginia Law Review*, XLII (October, 1956), 735.

McGovney, D. O. "Privileges or Immunities Clause, Fourteenth Amendment," *Iowa Law Bulletin*, IV (November, 1918), 219.

Mendelson, W. "Foreign Reactions to American Experience with 'Due Process of Law,'" *Virginia Law Review*, XLI (May, 1955) 493.

_____. "Justices Black and Frankfurter: Supreme Court Majority and Minority Trends," *Journal of Politics*, XII (February, 1950), 66.

_____. "Mr. Justice Frankfurter and the Process of Judicial Review," *University of Pennsylvania Law Review*, CIII (December, 1954), 295.

_____. "Mr. Justice Frankfurter—Law and Choice," *Vanderbilt Law Review*, X (February, 1957), 333.

_____. "Mr. Justice Frankfurter on Administrative Law," *Journal of Politics*, XIX (August, 1957), 441.

_____. "Mr. Justice Frankfurter on the Construction of Statutes," *California Law Review*, XLIII (October, 1955), 652.

_____. "Mr. Justice Frankfurter on the Distribution of Judicial Power in the United States," *Midwest Journal of Political Science*, II, No. 1 (February, 1958), 40.

Merrill, Maurice H. Book review of H. S. Thomas, *Felix Frankfurter: Scholar on the Bench*. Baltimore: Johns Hopkins University Press, 1960. *Oklahoma Law Review*, XIII (November, 1960), 476.

"Mr. Justice Frankfurter," *U.S. Law Review*, LXXIII (January, 1939), 14.

"Mr. Justice Frankfurter," *New Republic*, January 18, 1939, p. 297.

Morrison, S. "Does the Fourteenth Amendment Incorporate the Bill of Rights?—The Judicial Interpretation," *Stanford Law Review*, II (December, 1949), 140.

Nathanson, Nathaniel L. Book review of Crosskey, *Northwestern University Law Review*, XLIX (March-April, 1954), 118.

_____. "Mr. Justice Frankfurter and Administrative Law," *Yale Law Journal*, LXVII (December, 1957), 240.

Note on "Priority of Subsequent Creditors over a Mortgage," *Harvard Law Review*, XVIII (June, 1905), 605-6.

Note on "Liability of Stockholders as Partners when Incorporation is Defective," *Harvard Law Review*, XIX (March, 1906), 389-91.

Note on "The Appointment of Professor Frankfurter," *Harvard Law Review*, XXVIII (November, 1914), 82-83.

"Notes From the Capital: Felix Frankfurter," *Nation*, March 15, 1917, p. 320

Patterson, C. P. Book review of Crosskey, *Texas Law Review*, XXXII (December, 1953), 251.

Petro, S. Book review of Crosskey, *Michigan Law Review*, LIII (December, 1954), 312.

Pittman, R. C. Book review of Crosskey, *American Bar Association Journal*, XL (1954), 389.

Pollak, Louis H. "Mr. Justice Frankfurter: Judgment and the Fourteenth Amendment," *Yale Law Journal*, LXVII (December, 1957), 304.

Pound, Roscoe. "The Etiquette of Justice," *Proceedings of the Nebraska State Bar Association*, III (1909), 231.

Prosser, W. L. "Obituary," *Journal of Legal Education*, XII (Summer, 1960), 559.

Quinn, T. B. "Theodore Roosevelt Foresaw Felix Frankfurter," *American Mercury*, LXXXVI, No. 409 (February, 1958), 115.

Ribble, F. D. G. Book review of Crosskey, *Virginia Law Review*, XXXIX (October, 1953), 863.

Rodell, F. "Academic Adjudicator," *Saturday Review of Literature*, September 1, 1956, p. 15.

_____. "Crux of the Court Hullabaloo," *New York Times*, May 29, 1960, Sec. 7, p. 13.

_____. "Felix Frankfurter, Conservative," *Harper's*, CLXXXIII (October, 1941), 449.

Sacks, Albert M. "Mr. Justice Frankfurter," *University of Chicago Law Review*, XXVI, No. 2 (Winter, 1959), 217.

Schwartz, Bernard. "The Administrative World of Mr. Justice Frankfurter," *Yale Law Review*, LVIII (June, 1950), 1228.

Sharp, M. Book review of Crosskey, *Columbia Law Review*, LIV (March, 1954), 439.

Stern, R. L. Book review of Crosskey, *Northwestern University Law Review*, XLIX (March-April, 1954), 107.

Stevens, R. G. Book review of W. Mendelson, *Justices Black and Frankfurter: Conflict in the Court*. Chicago: University of Chicago Press, 1961. *William and Mary Law Review*, III (1961), 206.

Stone, H. F. "The Common Law in the United States," *Harvard Law Reveiw*, L (November, 1936), 4.

Stone, I. F. "Frankfurter Injunction," *Nation*, February 22, 1941, p. 203.

Summers, Clyde W. "Frankfurter, Labor Law and the Judge's Function," *Yale Law Journal*, LXVII (December, 1957), 266.

Sutherland, A. E. Book review of Crosskey, *Cornell Law Quarterly*, XXXIX (Fall, 1953), 160.

Suthon, W. J., Jr. "The Dubious Origin of the Fourteenth Amendment," *Tulane Law Review*, XXVIII (December, 1953), 22.

Varney, H. L. "Frankfurter: Man Behind the Scenes," *American Mercury*, LXXXIV, No. 400 (May, 1957), 113.

Warren, C. "The New Liberty under the Fourteenth Amendment," *Harvard Law Review*, XXXIX (February, 1926), 431.

Wechsler, H. "Toward Neutral Principles of Constitutional Law," *Harvard Law Review*, LXXIII (November, 1959), 1.

Westin, A. F. "Also on the Bench: 'Dominant Opinion,'" *New York Times*, October 21, 1962, Sec. 7, p. 30.

Yntema, H. E. Book review of Crosskey, *American Journal of Comparative Law*, II (1953), 582.

A Selected Bibliography of Related Works Published Since 1963

Baker, Liva. *Felix Frankfurter.* New York: Coward-McCann, 1969.

Baker, Leonard. *Brandeis and Frankfurter.* New York: Harper and Row, 1984.

Canavan, Francis, "A New Fourteenth Amendment," *Human Life Review,* 12 (Winter, 1986), 30-48.

Deutsch, Jan G., and Michael H. Hoeflich. "Legal Duty Judicial Style: The Meaning of Precedent," *St. Louis University Law Journal,* 25 (March 1981), 87-95.

Frankfurter, Felix. *Of Law and Life and Other Things That Matter,* ed. Philip B. Kurland. Cambridge: Belknap Press, 1965.

Freedman, Max. *Roosevelt and Frankfurter: Their Correspondence 1928-1945.* Boston: Little Brown, 1967.

Grossman, James A. "A Note on Felix Frankfurter," *Commentary,* 41 (March 1966), 59-64.

Hirsch, H.N. *The Enigma of Felix Frankfurter.* New York: Basic Books, 1981.

Jacobs, Clyde Edward. *Justice Frankfurter and Civil Liberties.* New York: DaCapo Press, 1974.

James, Joseph B. *The Ratification of the Fourteenth Amendment.* Macon, GA: Mercer University Press, 1984.

Konefsky, Alfred. "Men of Great and Little Faith: Generations of Constitutional Scholars," *Buffalo Law Review,* 30 (Spring 1981), 365-384.

Konefsky, Samuel J., ed. *The Constitutional World of Mr. Justice Frankfurter.* New York: Hafner Co., 1971.

Kurland, Philp B. *Felix Frankfurter on the Supreme Court.* Cambridge: Belknap Press, 1970.

Kurland, Philip B. *Mr. Justice Frankfurter and the Constitution.* Chicago: University of Chicago Press, 1971.

Lash, Joseph P. *From the Diaries of Felix Frankfurter.* lst ed. New York: Norton, 1975.

McWilliams, Wilson C. "The Constitutional Doctrine of Mr. Justice Frankfurter," *Political Science,* 15 (January 1963), 34-44.

Mendelson, Wallace, ed. *Felix Frankfurter: A Tribute.* New York: Reynal, 1964.

Mendelson, Wallace, ed. *Felix Frankfurter: The Judge.* New York: Reynal, 1964.

Meyer, Hermine Herta. *The History and Meaning of the 14th Amendment: Judicial Erosion of the Constitution Through the Misuse of the 14th Amendment.* New York: Vantage Press, 1977.

Murphy, Bruce Allen. *The Brandeis/Frankfurter Connection: The Secret Political Activities of Two Supreme Court Justices.* New York: Oxford University Press, 1982.

Mykkeltvedt, Ronald Y. *The Nationalization of the Bill of Rights: 14th Amendment, Due Process and Procedural Rights.* Port Washington, NY: Associated Faculty Press, 1983.

Parrish, Michael E. *Felix Frankfurter and His Times.* New York: Free Press; London: Collier-Macmillan, 1982.

Silverstein, Mark. *Constitutional Faiths: Felix Frankfurter, Hugo Black and Constitutional Decision-Making.* Ithaca: Cornell University Press, 1982.

Silverstein, Mark. *Liberalism, Democracy and the Court: Felix Frankfurter, Hugo Black and Constitutional Decision-Making.* Ithaca: Cornell University Press, 1982.

Walsh, James Augustine. "The Political Ideas of Felix Frankfurter: 1911-1939." Diss. American University, 1976.

Table of Cases Cited

General Index

Adamson, Admiral Dewey, 1, 3-5, 7, 9, 122, 153, 187, 195, 202
Alsop, Joseph, 147
Angell, Joseph K., xxxviii, 78
Aristotle, xxxiv, 21, 44, 123, 142, 197, 206
Arthur, C.J., xxvii
Bagehot, Walter, xiv
Bate, W.J., 182
Bateman, Charles, 136-138, 150
Benson, George C.S., 103, 205
Berns, Walter F., 102, 104-105, 107, 117, 148
Bingham, John Armour, Congressman, 16-18, 20, 22-28, 32-25, 37-40, 43-45
Black, Hugo L., Justice, xx, xl, 1-2, 11, 15-20, 22-25, 27-28, 43-46, 77, 79, 83, 87-92, 96-97, 102, 122, 137-138, 140, 153, 168-169, 173-174, 176, 191-193
Black's Law Dictionary, 69
Blackstone, William, Sir, 79, 81, 95, 109-110, 134, 144, 150
Bloom, Allan, xxx
Boutwell, George Sewall, Congressman, 31, 46
Bouvier's Law Dictionary, 67-69, 80-81, 94-95, 103
Braden, George D., 78
Brandeis, Louis D., Justice, 93, 96, 104
Brant, Irving, 79
Brennan, William, Justice, 11, 174, 186, 198
Brown, Ernest J., 51-52, 79, 139
Browning, James R., Judge, 103
Bryce, James, Lord, 107-109, 111, 113, 147, 159, 205

Buchan, J., 181
Bundy, McGeorge, 206
Burke, Edmund, xl, 110, 177, 181-182
Burrill's Law Dictionary, 67, 80
Burton, Harold H., Justice, 1, 174, 183
Buxton, C. Lee, Dr., 187
Canavan, Francis, 44
Cardozo, Benjamin, Justice, xx, 121, 127, 149
Carter, J., 12
Catledge, Turner, 147
Chanler, John Winthrop, Congressman, 18
Clark, Charles E., Judge, 52
Clark, Tom C., Justice, 11, 183, 186, 198
Coke, Edward, Sir, 73, 81, 162
Colledge, Stephen, 136
Conkling, Roscoe, Congressman, 16
Coolidge, Calvin, President, 120
Corbin, Arthur L., 78
Corwin, Edward S., 11, 13, 46, 81
Cox, Richard, 205
Cropsey, Joseph, 81
Crosskey, William Winslow, xxxii-xxxiii, xxxviii, 46-57, 59-60, 63-83, 100, 105, 122
Curtis, Benjamin R., Justice, xxxiv-xxxv, 74-75, 80, 83, 85, 88
Davis, John W., 120
DeMille, Cecil B., 78
Diamond, Martin, xvi, xxx, xxviii, 103, 205
Dicey, Albert Venn, xiv-xv, xxxviii
Dickinson, Judge, 104
Douglas, William O., Justice, xx, 1, 11, 92, 103, 174